Florence & Tuscany
day BY day™

2nd Edition

by Donald Strachan

WILEY

Wiley Publishing, Inc.

Contents

Published by:

Wiley Publishing, Inc.

111 River St.
Hoboken, NJ 07030-5774

ISBN 978-0-470-42209-0
Editor: Cate Latting
Production Editor: M. Faunette Johnston
Photo Editor: Richard Fox
Cartographer: Andrew Murphy
Production by Wiley Indianapolis Composition Services

For information on our other products and services or to obtain technical support, please contact our Customer Care Department within the U.S. at 800/762-2974, outside the U.S. at 317/572-3993 or fax 317/572-4002.

Wiley also publishes its books in a variety of electronic formats. Some content that appears in print may not be available in electronic formats.

Manufactured in China

5   4   3   2

A Note from the Editorial Director

Organizing your time. That's what this guide is all about.

Other guides give you long lists of things to see and do and then expect you to fit the pieces together. The Day by Day guides are different. These guides tell you the best of everything, and then they show you how to see it *in the smartest, most time-efficient way*. Our authors have designed detailed itineraries organized by time, neighborhood, or special interest. And each tour comes with a bulleted map that takes you from stop to stop.

Hoping to relive the glory days of the Florentine Renaissance, or to tour the highlights of Siena? Planning a drive through Chianti Country, or a tour of Tuscany's most charming small towns? Whatever your interest or schedule, the Day by Days give you the smartest routes to follow. Not only do we take you to the top attractions, hotels, and restaurants, but we also help you access those special moments that locals get to experience—those "finds" that turn tourists into travelers.

The Day by Days are also your top choice if you're looking for one complete guide for all your travel needs. The best hotels and restaurants for every budget, the greatest shopping values, the wildest nightlife—it's all here.

Why should you trust our judgment? Because our authors personally visit each place they write about. They're an independent lot who say what they think and would never include places they wouldn't recommend to their best friends. They're also open to suggestions from readers. If you'd like to contact them, please send your comments our way at feedback@frommers.com, and we'll pass them on.

Enjoy your Day by Day guide—the most helpful travel companion you can buy. And have the trip of a lifetime.

Warm regards,

Kelly Regan

Kelly Regan, Editorial Director
Frommer's Travel Guides

About the Author

Donald Strachan is a London- and Italy-based writer, editor, and journalist. He has written about Italian travel for publications worldwide, including *The Times*, *Sunday Telegraph*, and *Sydney Morning Herald*, among others. His recent *Frommer's Tuscany & Umbria with Your Family* was judged Best Guidebook at the 2008 ENIT Travel Writing Awards. He is also co-author of *Frommer's The Balearics with Your Family* (2007).

Acknowledgments

My first and greatest debt is to my girls, Lucia, Lili, and Ruby, without whom this book would never have been written. Among some great *turismo* professionals too numerous to list, I'm especially grateful to: Adriana Vacca at ENIT in London; Fabrizio Quochi in Pisa; Claudia Bolognesi and everyone at Volterratur (again!); Massimo Giovanetti and Tania Pasquinelli in Montecatini Terme; Francesco Colucci and his staff, as well as Renzo Baldaccini, in Lucca; and, in Florence, Roberta Romoli at APT Firenze, Cristina Acidini at the Soprintendenza, Elena Montali at IMSS and Alba Scarpellini at the MSN.

Thanks, too, to everyone else who helped with my research, often at horribly short notice—there were a lot of you, and I really appreciate it. Finally, I'd like to thank Cate Latting, my editor, and everyone Frommer's, who have been a joy to work with again. I can't finish without dedicating this book to my friend Mario Lanza, who died way too soon in 2008. If I've ever written anything about Italy worth reading, it's in part thanks to Mario. I miss him—and hope I've written a guidebook he'd be proud of.

An Additional Note

Please be advised that travel information is subject to change at any time—and this is especially true of prices. We therefore suggest that you write or call ahead for confirmation when making your travel plans. The authors, editors, and publisher cannot be held responsible for the experiences of readers while traveling. Your safety is important to us, however, so we encourage you to stay alert and be aware of your surroundings.

Star Ratings, Icons & Abbreviations

Every hotel, restaurant, and attraction listing in this guide has been ranked for quality, value, service, amenities, and special features using a **star-rating system.** Hotels, restaurants, attractions, shopping, and nightlife are rated on a scale of zero stars (recommended) to three stars (exceptional). In addition to the star-rating system, we also use a **kids icon** to point out the best bets for families. Within each tour, we recommend cafes, bars, or restaurants where you can take a break. Each of these stops appears in a shaded box marked with a coffee-cup-shaped bullet.

The following **abbreviations** are used for credit cards:

AE	American Express	DISC	Discover	V	Visa
DC	Diners Club	MC	MasterCard		

Frommers.com

Now that you have this guidebook to help you plan a great trip, visit our website at **www.frommers.com** for additional travel information on more than 4,000 destinations. We update features regularly to give you instant access to the most current trip-planning information available. At Frommers. com, you'll find scoops on the best airfares, lodging rates, and car rental bargains. You can even book your travel online through our reliable travel booking partners. Other popular features include:

- Online updates of our most popular guidebooks
- Vacation sweepstakes and contest giveaways
- Newsletters highlighting the hottest travel trends
- Podcasts, interactive maps, and up-to-the-minute events listings
- Opinionated blog entries by Arthur Frommer himself
- Online travel message boards with featured travel discussions

A Note on Prices

In the "Take a Break" and "Best Bets" sections of this book, we have used a system of dollar signs to show a range of costs for 1 night in a hotel (the price of a double-occupancy room) or the cost of an entree at a restaurant. Use the following table to decipher the dollar signs:

Cost	Hotels	Restaurants
$	under $100	under $10
$$	$100–$200	$10–$20
$$$	$200–$300	$20–$30
$$$$	$300–$400	$30–$40
$$$$$	over $400	over $40

An Invitation to the Reader

In researching this book, we discovered many wonderful places—hotels, restaurants, shops, and more. We're sure you'll find others. Please tell us about them, so we can share the information with your fellow travelers in upcoming editions. If you were disappointed with a recommendation, we'd love to know that, too. Please write to:

Frommer's Florence & Tuscany, Day by Day, 2nd Edition
Wiley Publishing, Inc. • 111 River St. • Hoboken, NJ 07030-5774

17 Favorite **Moments**

17 Favorite **Moments**

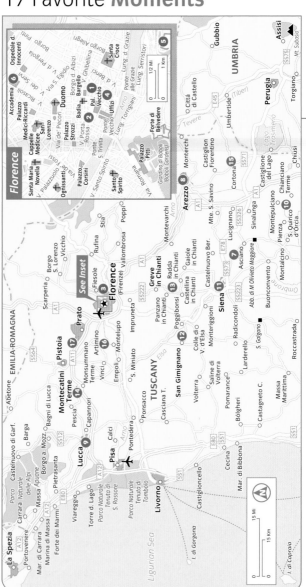

Previous page: Torre Grossa and the rooftops of San Gimignano.

The treasures of the Uffizi and Michelangelo's *David* are just the start of an awe-inspiring journey into Tuscany: There is so much more to the region than the magnificence of Florence. Beyond the city that cradled the Renaissance lie snow-capped mountains, stately cypresses, Tyrrhenian Sea coastline, and silver-green olive groves. With Chianti's vineyards, Pisa's Tower, San Gimignano's medieval "skyscrapers," and a wealth of Florentine and Sienese art and architecture, it's difficult to single out 17 highlights, but this list is our best attempt to do just that.

❶ Eating the world's best *gelato*. At Florence's **Vivoli**, San Gimignano's **"di Piazza"** or Siena's **Brivido**, the ice cream is most definitely not just for kids. You name the flavor, you'll probably find it. Vespa-riding punks and contessas alike come for their daily fix. *See p 26, 158, and 167.*

❷ Sitting in a cafe on Florence's Piazza della Signoria. Sip espresso on Tuscany's grandest square—the site of Savonarola's infamous "Bonfire of the Vanities." From your comfortable perch, you'll take in Benvenuto Cellini's *Perseus* with the head of Medusa, a replica (to scale) of Michelangelo's *David,* the Uffizi,

Cafe tables on Piazza della Signoria in Florence.

Neptune, one of Piazza della Signoria's many marble deities.

and the Palazzo Vecchio. Coffee never tasted so good. *See p 13.*

❸ Walking the road of the ancients from Fiesole to Florence. At twilight, start at Fiesole's Piazza Mino and follow the road through San Domenico, that links this hilltown with Florence, below. Untamed vegetation pours over the high walls that line the way past gnarled olive groves, private gardens, and 18th-century villas—and a panoramic vista of the city that opens suddenly. *See p 22.*

❹ Catching a glimpse of where Tuscan art was born. In Room 2 of the Uffizi the great *Madonnas* of Cimabue, Duccio, and

Giotto are displayed side-by-side. Between them, these three painters shaped Florentine and Sienese art for generations. *See p 37.*

⑤ Basking in the lights of the Renaissance, at twilight, from Piazzale Michelangelo. The bronze *David* here may be faux, and tourists abound, but the view of the city twinkling from this balustraded terrace will rank among the greatest you've seen. *See p 13.*

⑥ Standing in awe at the foot of Michelangelo's *David*. Even if you've seen the *Venus de Milo,* the massive genius of Michelangelo's masterpiece, at the Accademia, may bowl you over—even from behind its Plexiglas barrier. Even after five centuries, it is still miraculously alive, embodying the ideals of the Tuscan High Renaissance. *See p 14.*

⑦ Seeing Siena for the first time—from the hills of Le Crete. The S438 from Asciano to Siena traverses Tuscany's most photogenic landscape. And that first, unmistakable sight of the 102m (335 ft.) Torre del Mangia in the distance is one you won't forget. *See p 107.*

⑧ Following the Piero della Francesca trail. His iconic work is Tuscany's best fresco cycle, *The Legend of the True Cross* at San

The real thing: Michelangelo's David *at the Accademia.*

Francesco in Arezzo, But his trail continues to Monterchi's museum for a rarity in Italian art, a pregnant *Madonna*. His hometown of Sanselpolcro still holds the painting Aldous Huxley claimed was the greatest ever painted, Piero's 1463 *Resurrection of Christ*. *See p 124 and 89.*

⑨ Biking the walls of Lucca. Kids and octogenarians alike peddle Tuscany's greatest cycle track, 5km (2¾ miles) in length, on 16th-century ramparts so thick they now function as a tree-lined promenade. The

Florence at night from Piazzale Michelangelo.

The lush Tuscan countryside viewed from a San Gimignano "skyscraper."

chestnut and ilex trees are compliments of Marie-Louise of Bourbon, from the 1800s. *See p 135.*

🔟 **Dining *al fresco* in autumn.** What could be finer than a *bistecca alla fiorentina* dripping with olive oil and fresh herbs, grilled over a chestnut-wood fire? One served outdoors, of course, in Tuscany in autumn. When the leaves are turning red and gold, regional staples—black truffles, grilled pheasant, porcini mushrooms—taste their best. Try La Porta, in Monticchiello close to Pienza and Montepulciano. *See p 149.*

⓫ **Attending the Palio, Italy's grandest medieval spectacle.** This breakneck, bareback horse race around Siena's dirt-packed Piazza del Campo takes place twice a year, in July and August, in honor of the Virgin Mary. Beyond the race, it's bacchanalia—with days of pageantry and serious partying. *See p 166.*

⓬ **Wandering San Gimignano's historic center at dusk.** Its unique skyline pierced by 14 towers (locals call them "skyscrapers") secures the #1 spot on the hilltown trail. When the tour buses have left, the quiet streets exude a haunted, medieval air quite unlike anywhere else in Tuscany. *See p 73.*

⓭ **Tasting the wine in Chianti Country.** The green vineyard-studded hills between Florence and Siena nurture Italy's most famous product. Against a backdrop of ancient villages and crenelled castles from the Middle Ages, you can sample the vino from cantinas around Castellina, Greve, and Radda. *See p 93.*

Pomp and circumstance overtake Siena during the Palio festival.

A Tuscan vintner in the fertile Chianti region south of Florence.

⑭ Taking the waters at Montecatini. In the "Valley of Mists" lies Montecatini Terme, grande dame of all Italian spas. Giuseppe Verdi composed *Othello* while taking the waters here, but you can just relax, in mudpacks, drinking mineral-rich waters as radioactive vapors are steamed in your face. *See p 112.*

Da Delfina, outside Florence.

⑮ Discovering your favorite Tuscan hilltown. Our vote goes to Cortona, one of the great cities of the Etruscans, with a magical art museum, and surrounded by the olive groves and rich plains of the Valdichiana. To huff and puff up and down its narrow, steep, cobbled streets is to wander back into the Middle Ages. *See p 128.*

⑯ Dining Tuscan-style in the country at Artimino. A 15-minute train ride outside Florence in the medieval walled village of Artimino, Da Delfina is an earthy and authentic dining experience. Follow the aroma of freshly caught fish grilling over a wood-burning fireplace, served with produce from the nearby fields. *See p 51.*

⑰ Riding the train from town to town. There's no better way to fit right in than arriving like a local on Italy's cheap and easy rail network. Prato and Pistoia are perfect destinations for your day on the train. *See p 100.* ●

1 Strategies for Seeing **Tuscany**

Strategies for Seeing **Tuscany**

Tuscany isn't Tokyo or New York; racing around the region try-ing to "see" everything runs against the grain and the pace of the place, and might prevent you from really *experiencing* it. It's tempt-ing to want to make tracks, given that there is so much to see within a relatively small region easily traversed by car. But structuring a relaxed itinerary makes for a memorable trip. In this chapter I pro-vide some suggestions for maximizing your time in Tuscany.

Rule #1: Keep your expecta-tions reasonable.

Consider the experience of two cou-ples I know who recently visited the region. One fashioned an aggressive itinerary that encompassed most of the major towns I cover in chapter 6. And while they were able to say they saw town after town, church after church, and artwork after

Previous page: Vineyards in the Chianti region.

artwork, they spent 2 or 3 hours a day stuck in the car, fighting traffic, the heat, and crazy truck drivers. The other couple decided to take on less turf and, naturally, didn't see as much; they even missed Cortona and some of our other favorite towns. Instead, they spent an entire afternoon in a Montepulciano cafe, splitting a chilled bottle of Orvieto Classico, staring over a wrought-iron balcony at a church in the distance.

The countryside near Panzano, in Chianti Country.

In hindsight, they considered that stop the pinnacle of their trip, writing, "We wouldn't have traded that lazy Tuscan afternoon for the world."

Rule #2: Remember, distances between towns are short.

Visiting Tuscany is as easy as traveling around a small U.S. state or mid-sized Mediterranean island. You can drive from Florence to San Gimignano, Lucca, or Siena in less than an hour. The entire Chianti wine country is only 48km (30 miles) from north to south, and 32km (20 miles) at its widest point. What's more, it begins only 4km (2½ miles) south of Florence. You can even drive from Florence west to Pisa in an hour. Once you veer off the autostrada, the roads become slower, but unless you're going to the most remote hamlet in Tuscany, they're generally well maintained and signposted (if sometimes erratically). The only problem in summer will be occasional heavy traffic caused by thousands of other visitors aiming for the same hilltowns as you.

Rule #3: Decide whether to hotel hop or stay in one place.

Checking in and out of hotels is often a tedious hassle—involving luggage transfers, packing and unpacking, registering and checking out, and other technicalities that can drain pleasure from a vacation. Because most Tuscan towns are within easy reach of one another, you can set up camp in the same

Passing the time in a Tuscan outdoor cafe.

Pick Your Point of Entry

The logical start to your Tuscan adventure is Galileo Galilei airport in Pisa. Keenly priced flights connect it with most of Europe—and there's a direct flight to New York's JFK 5 days a week. However, if you're already touring near Milan, Venice, or Rome, there's no need to think about connecting to Pisa by air. All are well linked to Tuscany by rail or autostrada. Rome and Milan are alternative, hassle-free intercontinental air gateways—both about 3 hours from Florence by train. From Rome, a 277km (172 mile) drive north to Florence on the fast-moving A1 takes you right past some of the highlights of southern and eastern Tuscany: Break your trip in Montepulciano, Cortona, or Arezzo. Milan is slightly farther—298km (183 miles) northwest of Florence—but worth the minimal extra distance if you find a cheaper flight there. A drive down to Florence can easily be broken in Pisa or Lucca. For more about reaching Tuscany by plane, and the options for getting between airports and your final destination, see the "By Plane" section in "Getting There/Getting Around," in Savvy Traveler (p 187).

hotel for 3 nights—in Siena, for example—and venture to smaller towns nearby on day trips. From Siena, you can easily visit San Gimignano, Pienza, Montepulciano, or even the Chianti wine country without wasting too much time in the car. You'll save a lot of wear and tear on your soul with this tack, reserving your energy for hotel changes required by longer hauls.

Rule #4: Plan your excursions around lunch.

If you're driving from town to town, plan to reach your destination by noon. Restaurants usually serve lunch until 2 or 2:30pm, but you'll need time to park (which is often tricky) and to locate the address of your restaurant (ditto). If you don't want to follow a schedule, pack a lunch before setting out and follow your bliss to the ideal picnic spot somewhere under the Tuscan sun. There's no shortage of them.

Rule #5: Every now and then, let the train take the strain.

It's cheaper, greener, and hassle free arriving in your Tuscan town for the day by train. The Italian network is inexpensive, accessible, and easy to use—even for beginners. Not every town is handily reached by rail, but the highlights of the region's northwest like Lucca, Pisa, or Prato are all made for seeing by train.

Rule #6: Don't follow these ideas to the letter; use them as building blocks for your trip.

This guide was designed to help you piece together your own dream getaway. You can plan your time in Florence using one section and then hop about Tuscany, in the next few days, using another. It's like an a la carte menu—select one item from column A and another from column B, according to your own tastes and interests, to make the most of our advice. ●

Florence in One Day

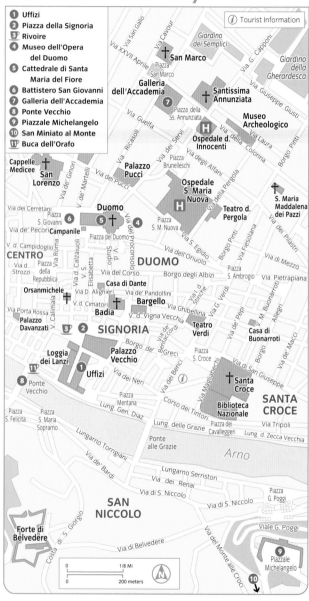

1. Uffizi
2. Piazza della Signoria
3. Rivoire
4. Museo dell'Opera del Duomo
5. Cattedrale di Santa Maria del Fiore
6. Battistero San Giovanni
7. Galleria dell'Accademia
8. Ponte Vecchio
9. Piazzale Michelangelo
10. San Miniato al Monte
11. Buca dell'Orafo

ⓘ Tourist Information

Previous page: Florence's spectacular Duomo.

Florence in 1 day? *"Impossibile,"* a Florentine might tell you before throwing up his hands in despair and walking away, convinced you are mad. But 1 day in Florence is better than none—provided you rise with the roosters and move with steely discipline and stamina, to make the most of it. This "greatest hits" itinerary begins with the highlights of the Uffizi, the most rewarding and time consuming stop. After lunch in Piazza della Signoria, you'll take in the city's majestic ecclesiastical complex: the Duomo, the Baptistery, and Giotto's Bell Tower. Then you'll round out the day with a trek to see Michelangelo's *David* at the Accademia—a mandatory stop—followed by a stroll across the Ponte Vecchio and a Tuscan meal in an authentic *buca* (cellar). START: **Take bus B or 23 to the Uffizi.**

① ★★★ **Uffizi.** This is one of the world's great museums, and its single best repository of Renaissance art. In room after room, you'll confront masterpiece after masterpiece—including Leonardo da Vinci's *Annunciation* (with an angel that could be Mona Lisa's brother), Michelangelo's *Holy Family,* Sandro Botticelli's *Birth of Venus,* Giotto's *Ognissanti Madonna,* and more. In Italian, *uffizi* means offices, and that's what Vasari deigned this building to be in 1550. But it's come a long way, *bambino.* These Uffizi will dazzle you. (Serious art devotees may want to spend the entire day here.) ⏲ *3 hr. See p 36.*

② ★★ **Piazza della Signoria.** The monumental heart of Florence (and Tuscany's most famous square) is an open-air museum of sculpture, dominated by Michelangelo's *David* (a copy of the original, which used to stand here). The powerful mass of the Palazzo Vecchio dominates one side of the square; another is defined by the 14th-century **Loggia dei Lanzi,** filled with ancient and Renaissance statues (the most celebrated being Bevenuto Cellini's *Perseus* holding aloft the severed head of Medusa). Also check out Giambologna's *Rape of the Sabines,* which marks the point (1584) when Tuscan tastes abandoned drama in favor of melodrama. ⏲ *30 min.*

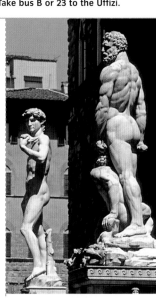

Hercules, David, *and other superheroes loom over Piazza della Signoria.*

③ ★ **Rivoire.** Regrettably filled with tourists and overpriced, Rivoire still occupies one of the greatest pieces of real estate in the world. Smartly clad waiters hustle to deliver lunch platters and elegant sandwiches—as though anyone's paying attention to anything but the view. *Piazza della Signoria.* ☎ *055-212412. $–$$$.*

A rear view of the Duomo (Cattedrale di Santa Maria del Fiore).

④ ★ **Museo dell'Opera del Duomo.** For connoisseurs of Renaissance sculpture, this museum across from the Duomo is a shrine, hosting everything from an unfinished, heart-wrenching Michelangelo *Pietà* to its premier attraction—the restored panels of Lorenzo Ghiberti's *Gates of Paradise*. The works here were deemed too precious to be left to the elements, and so were moved inside. ⏱ 1 hr. See p 41, ④.

⑤ ★★ kids **Cattedrale di Santa Maria del Fiore (Duomo).** Consecrated in 1436, one of Europe's most majestic cathedrals rests under Filippo Brunelleschi's revolutionary dome, a triumph of engineering over

gravity. As the symbol of Florence itself, it's a tourist stamping ground of horrendous proportions—but justifiably so. It's part church, part candy cane, part zebra—in stripes of marble-white, bottle-green, and pink. The interior, by contrast, is spartan but has one of Europe's classic views from the top of the cupola. ⏱ 45 min. See p 27, ⑧.

⑥ ★★★ **Battistero San Giovanni.** On a hurried first-day tour of Florence, you need invade the inner precincts of the Baptistery only to take in the magnificent 13th-century mosaics lining the inner dome. The excitement is outside, on the world-famous bronze doors. Sure, they're replicas (the original work is in the Museo dell'Opera del Duomo; see ④, above); but even the copies are masterpieces. Ghiberti's north doors—a commission he won in 1401 in a public competition against Brunelleschi, Donatello, and Jacopo Della Quercia—are said to mark the start of the Renaissance. ⏱ 30 min. See p 28, ⑩.

⑦ ★★ **Galleria dell'Accademia.** You've seen the mock of Michelangelo's *David* all over the world. This gallery has the real thing (1501–04)—a monumental icon of youthful male beauty and a stellar example of

A panel from Ghiberti's doors at the Battistero San Giovanni.

Titian's Venus of Urbino *is a hallmark of the Uffizi collection.*

Michelangelo's humanism. His four unfinished *Slaves* are equally expressive. It can require an hour-long wait, unless you reserve space. ⏱ *30 min., without wait. Via Ricasoli 60.* ☎ *050-294883 to reserve tickets (in English). www.firenzemusei.it. Admission 6.50€–10€ (higher prices are for special exhibitions). Tues–Sun 8:15am–6:50pm. Bus: A, C, 1, 6, 7, 10, 11, 17, 20, 25, 31, 32, 33, 57.*

⑧ ★★ **kids Ponte Vecchio.** The Ponte Vecchio, as its name suggests, is the city's oldest bridge; its latest incarnation dates to 1345, but the shops along it have been taking advantage of the foot traffic since at least the 12th century. Originally occupied by blacksmiths, butchers, and tanners, the shops that flank the bridge have mostly sold gold and silver since the reign of the Medici. Sunset is the ideal time to cross. ⏱ *15 min. See p 24,* ❶.

⑨ ★ **kids Piazzale Michelangelo.** For a final *arrivederci* to Florence, head for its panoramic piazza, laid out in 1885. From this balustraded terrace, the city of the Renaissance unfurls before you. In the center of the square is yet another *David.* ⏱ *15 min. Bus: 12, 13.*

⑩ ★★★ **San Miniato al Monte.** As the city's lights start to twinkle, there's no better spot to drink in the views, and the silence, than this ancient Romanesque church surrounded by its monumental graveyard. Time it right and you'll catch the Benedictine monks who still inhabit the complex celebrating Vespers with Gregorian chant. ⏱ *30 min. See p 35,* ⑪.

⑫ ★ **Buca dell'Orafo.** For your farewell meal, head to this famous cellar restaurant, in the former workshop of a Renaissance goldsmith, for Tuscan cuisine served at communal tables. It's on an arched alleyway near the Ponte Vecchio. (If you want to dine with locals, book a late table.) *See p 51.*

An evening stroll along the Ponte Vecchhio.

Florence in Two Days

- ① Palazzo Pitti
- ② Giardino di Boboli
- ③ Mamma Gina
- ④ Santa Trinita
- ⑤ Cappelle Medicee
- ⑥ Museo di San Marco
- ⑦ Palazzo Vecchio
- ⑧ Santo Spirito

ⓘ Tourist Information

On your second day in Florence, spend the morning wandering Oltrarno, the district on the left bank of the Arno. The set-piece attraction here is the Palazzo Pitti and adjacent Giardino di Boboli. Even if you take all morning, you will see only a part of the Pitti Palace's great collection of art, which encompasses not only Renaissance works, but painting and sculpture by later European masters. Stroll through the Boboli Garden before a typical Oltrarno lunch in a local trattoria, then head back to the Centro Storico for the Medici Chapels (with Michelangelo's sculptures), the artistic delights of Fra' Angelico at San Marco, and Florence's Gothic town hall, the Palazzo Vecchio. START: Take bus D, 11, 36, or 37 to Piazza de' Pitti.

1 ★★ **Palazzo Pitti.** This 15th-century Medici palace on the south side of the Arno is second only to the Uffizi in its wealth of artwork. The **Galleria Palatina** on the second floor is reason enough to come to Florence; visit for the Raphaels alone. And the Palatina only primes you for what's to come: the city's most extensive coterie of museums—including exhibitions of costume, modern art, and even the Medici's private digs. 🕐 *2 hr. See p 32,* **5**.

Medici Skywalk. After Cosimo I moved to the Pitti Palace, he commissioned Giorgio Vasari to build a private, aboveground tunnel to the Uffizi and Palazzo Vecchio. The **Corridoio Vasariano,** built in just 5 months in 1565, runs from the Pitti Palace past the Boboli and above Santa Felicità to the Ponte Vecchio, crosses the river above the bridge's shops, then continues on to the museum that once served as the Medici offices. Lined with paintings and windows, it's usually open to group visits only, but this status changes regularly, so call ahead. 🕐 *1 hr. Reservations (required) and information* ☎ *055-2654321.*

2 ★ kids **Giardino di Boboli.** Laid out between 1549 and 1656, this is the grand Renaissance garden of Europe. After a stroll

The Palazzo Pitti was Europe's grandest residence when it was home to the Medicis.

The Boboli Garden.

through the garden, climb to the top of the **Fortezza di Belvedere** for a panoramic view of the city and its spires. Before departing, stroll down the Viottolone, a stunning avenue of pines and cypresses. ⏱ *30 min. See p 33,* ⑥.

3 **Mamma Gina.** This is the most famous—and one of the best—*trattorie* on the Left Bank of the

The Museo di San Marco honors Florentine painter Fra' Angelico.

Arno, ideal for a luncheon stopover after the Pitti and the Boboli Garden. One of the succulent pasta dishes along with a garden salad makes for an ideal repast before you venture into the sun again. After lunch, head across the Ponte Santa Trinita back to the Centro Storico. *See p 52.*

4 ★★ **Santa Trinita.** There aren't many corners of Florence where you can admire the finest works of the *Quattrocento* (1400s) in peace, but the historic church of Santa Trinita is one of them. The frescoed chapels are by Lorenzo Monaco (1370–1425) and Domenico Ghirlandaio (1449–94), Michelangelo's first teacher. The marble tomb of Benozzo Federighi was sculpted in 1454 by Luca Della Robbia. ⏱ *30 min. See p 47,* ⑦.

5 ★★ **Cappelle Medicee.** The big deal here are the two celebrated Medici tombs by Michelangelo. Regrettably, two of his grandest creations honored scurrilous members of the clan. Nevertheless, the great artist portrayed them as idealized princes of the Renaissance. Allegorical figures representing *Night* and *Day,* and *Dawn* and *Dusk,* face each other across the perfectly proportioned Renaissance sacristy. ⏱ *30 min. See p 45,* ②.

6 ★★ kids **Museo di San Marco.** This Dominican convent has been converted to a unique museum honoring Florence's gentlest painter of the "international Gothic" style, Fra' Angelico (1395–1455). Angelico's art is touched with a pacifying power, especially his iconic *Annunciation,* as are the walls of the 44 friars' cells upstairs, which he frescoed with scenes (and plenty of Dominican saints) to foster meditation. Don't leave without stopping in at the Pilgrim's Hospice, now a mini-museum to Angelico, centered on his beatific,

Florence's town hall, the Palazzo Vecchio, on Piazza della Signoria.

weightless *Deposition*. 🕐 *1hr. Piazza San Marco 3.* ☎ *055-2388608. Admission 4€. Mon–Fri 8:15am–1:20pm; Sat–Sun 8:15am–6:20pm; closed 1st,* 3rd, and 5th Sun and 2nd and 4th Mon of month. Bus: A, C, 1, 6, 7, 10, 11, 17, 20, 25, 31, 32, 33, 57.

7 ★★ kids **Palazzo Vecchio.** In the heart of Florence, this crenellated 13th-century palace is still the city hall, putting to shame others around the world. The highlight is the **Salone dei Cinquecento,** or "Hall of the 500," where the great council met. It's decorated with gaudy Vasari frescoes, but houses Michelangelo's *Genius of Victory*, originally intended for the tomb of Pope Julius II. 🕐 *1 hr. See p 25,* **3**.

8 ★★ **Santo Spirito.** Dine on the piazza at this trattoria that's a notch above the Florentine average. You can plot a seafood or terrestrial route through the menu, before hitting the bars of Oltrarno with a full stomach. *See p 53.*

Docents in Renaissance garb run guided tours through Palazzo Vecchio.

Florence **in Three Days**

1 Basilica di Santa Croce
2 Museo Nazionale del Bargello
3 Festival del Gelato
4 Orsanmichele
5 Campanile di Giotto
6 Da Mario
7 Santa Maria Novella
8 Fiesole
9 Cave di Maiano

(i) Tourist Information

A third day in Florence will yield another glimpse of the city's treasures. The Museo Nazionale del Bargello is a worthy stop, as the world's greatest museum of Renaissance sculpture. Few dare to sneak out of Florence without paying a visit to the city headquarters of the Dominicans and Franciscans, the Basilica di Santa Maria Novella and the Basilica di Santa Croce, respectively. Michelangelo and Galileo, among others, are buried in the latter. As dusk approaches, head for the hills for a stroll and a romantic dinner in the Etruscan hilltown of Fiesole. START: **Bus C or 23 to Piazza Santa Croce.**

1 ★★ kids **Basilica di Santa Croce.** Victorian critic John Ruskin had the right idea: "Wait then for an entirely light morning: rise with the sun and go to Santa Croce, with a good opera glass in your pocket." Locals call it "the Westminster Abbey of Tuscany," because this 14th-century church contains the tombs of the Renaissance's brightest lights—notably Michelangelo and Galileo. The great Giotto di Bondone (ca 1267–1337) frescoed two tiny, timeworn chapels in the right transept, but is overshadowed by

better preserved works by his own student, Taddeo Gaddi, who frescoed *Scenes from the Life of the Virgin* between 1332 and 1338, including the first night scene ever painted. ⏱ *1 hr. See p 26,* **5**.

2 ★★ **Museo Nazionale del Bargello.** This Gothic fortress is now a vast repository holding some of the finest sculpture created during the Renaissance and later, including Donatello's *John the Baptist* and his own bronze *David.* The Bargello also houses, along with countless

Michaelangelo's tomb, one of many in Santa Croce.

other works, another Michelangelo *David*—created 3 decades after the version in the Accademia. ⏱ 1½ hr. See p 27, ⑦.

③★ Festival del Gelato.
You better have your decisive hat on if you stop for an ice cream here. I lost count of the fantastical flavors at 70. *Via del Corso 75R. No phone. $. Bus: A.*

④ ★★ Orsan-michele.
Though the museum is now closed indefinitely, a circuit round the outside of this grain warehouse turned church is the perfect accompaniment to your *gelato*. Each of the sculpted niches was commissioned by one of Florence's great trades guilds, including the powerful Arte della Lana (wool manufacturers). ⏱ 15 min. See p 46, ⑥.

The Bargello claims one of the world's finest troves of Renaissance sculpture.

⑤ ★★ kids Campanile di Giotto.
An ideal counterpoint to Brunelleschi's dome, this Gothic bell

Festival del Gelato is a perfect stop in a day of sightseeing.

tower was completed at the end of the 14th century, long after Giotto, its designer, had died. Walk 414 steps to the top of the campanile for a panoramic view of the dome and all central Florence. Queues here are usually much shorter than those for the Duomo. ⏱ 30 min. See p 28, ⑨.

⑥★ Da Mario.
A tiny trattoria that has become a lunchtime institution: expect uncompromising Florentine food, communal tables, keen prices and a smiling crush of local workers, tourists, and market traders. *Via Rosina 2R (at Piazza del Mercato Centrale).* ☎ 055-218550. *www.trattoriamario. com. $–$$. Bus: 12, 25, 33, 80.*

⑦ ★★ Basilica di Santa Maria Novella.
Built from 1246 by the Dominicans, this church is filled with some of Tuscany's most important frescoes, notably the *Scenes from the Lives of the Virgin Mary and St. John the Baptist* (1485–90) in the apse by Michelangelo's teacher, Domenico Ghirlandaio. Twelve years later, Filippino Lippi, illegitimate son of Filippo and nun Lucrezia Buti, decorated the **Capella Filippo Strozzi** with scenes from the life of his patron's name-saint, St. Philip. Other treasures include a carved *Crucifix* by Filippo Brunelleschi. ⏱ 45 min. See p 44, ①.

⑧ ★ kids Fiesole.
Despite some overpriced and underwhelming

neighbor down in the valley: It was already an important Etruscan settlement in the 8th century B.C. The best thing to do is stroll: a route along Via Marini, Via delle Mura Etrusche, then uphill on Via Giovanni and Via del Cimitero, skirts the Roman ruins, takes in the splendid little Franciscan convent, and ends up at the most spectacular balcony above Florence. 🕐 1½ hr. Bus: 7 (20 min. from Santa Maria Novella).

🖐 ★ **Cave di Maiano.** For a final goodbye to the city, take the short ride to this converted farmhouse where Florentines escape the heat on summer nights. The hearty regional cuisine—such as chicken roasted under a brick with peppers, and succulent pastas, like green tortellini—is the finest in the area. Adventurous diners might like to walk the entire 8km (5 miles) back to Florence, with the city lights, twinkling in the distance, to lead the way. You can stop at any point along the way and board bus #7 back to the Centro Storico. *See p 51.*

Masaccio's Trinita, at the Basillica di Santa Maria Novella.

"attractions," the ancient hilltop settlement of Fiesole supplies a welcome change of pace, and an escape from the oppressive heat and crowds of Florence. The little town was here long before its

The Basilica di Santa Maria Novella houses some of Florence's finest frescoes.

Centro Storico

1 Ponte Vecchio
2 Piazza della Signoria
3 Palazzo Vecchio
4 Rivoire
5 Basilica di Santa Croce
6 Vivoli
7 Museo Nazionale del Bargello
8 Cattedrale di Santa Maria del Fiore
9 Campanile di Giotto
10 Battistero San Giovanni
11 Basilica di San Lorenzo

In Florence's flat, compact historic core, you can wander stone streets that remain essentially the same as they were when Michelangelo, Leonardo da Vinci, and Galileo trod them. And even on the street, the art is everywhere you look. Remember, wear comfortable shoes and bring water. And, if you're traveling in July or August, be aware that walking the hot, crowded city streets is an intense, demanding experience. START: **Take bus B to Ponte Vecchio.**

1 ★★ kids **Ponte Vecchio.** Built in 1345 across the Arno's narrowest stretch, the Ponte Vecchio was the only bridge spared destruction by the retreating Nazi army in 1944. Italy's greatest goldsmith, Benvenuto Cellini, ran his business in the middle of the bridge—one of many jewelers to have replaced the medieval butchers and tanners who originally traded here. ⏱ *30 min. Bus: B.*

2 ★★ **Piazza della Signoria.** The center of civic life in Florence for centuries, this landmark square in the shadow of Arnolfo di Cambio's massive Palazzo Vecchio was the site of Savonarola's *Bonfire of the Vanities* in 1497, and then the Dominican zealot's own pyre a year later on the same spot (now marked with a small plaque). Away from the crowd-pulling blockbusters, less celebrated statuary includes

The Ponte Vecchio has been a bustling commercial hub since the 14th century.

Giambologna's equestrian *Cosimo I* and Bartolomeo Ammannati's controversial *Fountain of Neptune* that inspired a chant in the 16th century: *Ammannato, Ammannato, che bel marmo hai rovinato!* (What beautiful marble you've ruined!) *See p 24,* ❷. ⏲ *30 min. Bus: A, B.*

❸ ★★ **kids** **Palazzo Vecchio.** Florence's "Old Palace" became home to Cosimo I and the Medici in 1540, but it dates to the 13th century, when it was built by Gothic master builder Arnolfo di Cambio. (Di Cambio's 92m/308-ft. landmark tower, which still graces the skyline, was an engineering feat in its day.) The highlight of the interior is the "Hall of the 500" (*Salone dei Cinquecento*), frescoed by Giorgio Vasari and his assistants in the 16th century. (Alas, wax-pigment frescoes by Leonardo melted when braziers were brought in to speed up the drying process.) Michelangelo's sculpture *Genius of Victory* survives, thankfully, along with Donatello's bronze group upstairs, *Judith*

Slaying Holofernes, cast in 1455. You can also visit the private apartments of Eleanor of Toledo, the Spanish wife of Cosimo I, and the chamber where religious zealot Girolamo Savonarola endured a dozen torture

Rape of the Sabines *in the Piazza della Signoria.*

The commanding Palazzo Vecchio.

sessions, including "twists" on the rack. 🕐 1½ hr. Piazza della Signoria. 📞 055-2768465. Admission 6€. Mon–Wed and Fri–Sun 9am–7pm; Thurs 9am–2pm. Ticket office closes 1 hr. before palace. Bus: A, B, 23.

4 ★ **Rivoire.** Have a coffee and a snack at this landmark cafe—the best positioned in Florence for taking in the glories of Piazza della Signoria. *See p 13,* **3**.

5 ★★ kids **Basilica di Santa Croce.** The statue of Dante in the square is lifeless, but Santa Croce (the Franciscans' city base) is the pantheon of Florence, with monuments to Galileo, Michelangelo, Dante, Petrarch, and Rossini. Also behind the 19th-century facade is a galaxy of great sculpture, such as Donatello's carved *Crucifixion* and his equally astonishing 1433 relief of the *Annunciation*. Giotto's damaged *Life of St Francis* fresco is inside the **Cappella Bardi,** just right of the apse. Outside in the cloisters is Brunelleschi's ordered Renaissance **Cappella Pazzi,** and the church's small museum. It is host to what's left of Cimabue's once magnificent *Crucifixion*, the most high-profile victim of the Arno flood of 1966. 🕐 1 hr. Piazza Santa Croce 16. Admission 5€. Mon–Sat 9:30am–5pm; Sun 1–5:30pm. Bus: C.

6 ★★★ **Vivoli.** A block northwest of Piazza Santa Croce, this cafe-cum-*gelateria* serves the world's best ice cream. Just choose your exquisite flavor: fig, melon, chocolate-orange, even rice. Or try their

Rivoire is the place to stop for a coffee or snack in Piazza della Signoria.

semifreddi, with a base of cream instead of milk. *Via Isola delle Stinche 7R (at Via della Vigna Vecchia).* ☎ *055-292334. $.*

⑦ ★★ Museo Nazionale del Bargello. This grim Gothic fortress—once a place for public executions—centers around a courtyard with a vaulted loggia and portico. Its sculpture collection is the Renaissance's finest, including Donatello's *David* (the first free-standing nude since the Roman era), and side-by-side bronze reliefs depicting *The Sacrifice of Isaac* by Brunelleschi and Ghiberti. They were judged in a 1401 competition to decide who should get the commison for the north doors of the Baptistery; Ghiberti won. Downstairs, the 1500s room features works by Giambologna, Cellini and another *David* by Michelangelo. 🕐 *1½ hr. Via del Proconsolo 4 (at Via Ghibellina).* ☎ *055-294883. Admission 7€. Daily 8:15am–6pm. Closed 2nd and 4th Mon and 1st, 3rd, and 5th Sun of month. Bus: A, 14, 23.*

⑧ ★★ Cattedrale di Santa Maria del Fiore. The world's largest cathedral in its day, Florence's Duomo still ranks fourth in size. From 1294 to 1436, builders labored and taxpayers paid for the work, but the flamboyant neo-Gothic facade wasn't added until the 19th century. It's a polychrome jumble of marble

The Campinile di Giotto, or bell tower, with the best view of Brunelleschi's dome.

stripes in sugar-cane colors, but few fault the dome Brunelleschi imposed over it, 105m (351 ft.) off the ground; climbing it is one of the joys of visiting Florence. You mount 463 spiraling steps to the ribbed dome for a sublime panoramic view. Afterward, you needn't waste too much time inside; much of the art, frescoes, votive offerings, pews, and memorials were swept away or moved elsewhere for safekeeping. The most noted is Paolo Uccello's 1436 frescoed "statue" of English mercenary Sir John Hawkwood, on the wall of the left aisle. 🕐 *45 min. Piazza del Duomo. www.opera duomo.firenze.it. Free admission to cathedral; 6€ dome. Cathedral Mon–Wed, Fri 10am–5pm; Thurs 10am–4:30pm; Sat 10am–4:45pm; Sun 1:30–4:45pm. Dome Mon–Fri*

Donatello's David, *at the Museo Nazionale del Bargello, was the first freestanding nude to appear after Roman times.*

Lorenzo Ghiberti's Gates of Paradise at the Battistero San Giovanni.

8:30am–6:20pm; Sat 8:30am–5pm. Bus: A, 1, 6, 7, 10, 11, 14, 17, 23, 31, 32, 57.

⑨ ★★ kids Campanile di Giotto. Giotto, Andrea Pisano, and Francesco Talenti collaborated to build this 81m (269 ft.) tricolore marble bell tower next to the Duomo. The tower's bells inside are called *Grossa, Beona, Completa, Cheirica,* and *Squilla* (or Big, Tipsy, Finished, Priestling, and Shrieker). Climb the tower's 414 steps for a panoramic view of Florence and a dazzling perspective on Brunelleschi's dome. When others are queueing around the block waiting to scale the dome, there's often no one waiting here. ⏱ *30 min. Piazza del Duomo (at Via dei Calzaiuoli).* ☎ *055-2302885. Admission 6€. Daily 8:30am–6:50pm; Jun–Oct Fri–Sat until 10:20pm. Bus: A, 1, 6, 7, 10, 11, 14, 17, 23, 31, 32, 57.*

⑩ ★★★ Battistero San Giovanni. This 11th- and 12th-century octagonal baptistery, named after San Giovanni (St. John the Baptist, patron of the city), is visited mainly for the gilded bronze doors on three of its eight sides. The doors are copies hung in 1990; originals are

The Medici

One family, originally pharmacists from the Mugello, has come to symbolize Florence's Renaissance: the **Medici**. Excluding a brief republican interlude, they controled Florence (often as brutal despots) for 3 centuries. The first to rise to public prominence was **Cosimo "il Vecchio"** (1389–1464), papal banker and patron of Donatello, Fra' Angelico, and Filippo Lippi. His grandson **Lorenzo "The Magnificent"** (1449–92), who survived an assassination attempt at Easter Mass (the Pazzi Conspiracy), knew Botticelli and Michelangelo, dabbled in poetry, and funded a Platonic academy. His death signaled the end of Florence's golden age—the baton passed to Rome. **Cosimo I** (1519–74), the first Grand Duke of Tuscany, built the Uffizi and bought the Pitti Palace. The family even spawned three popes, including **Leo X** and his nephew **Clement VII**—nepotism was the other great family business. Long years of dissolute decline ended with the death of drunkard Giangastone in 1737, and Medici treasures passed to Tuscany.

The ceiling of the 11th- and 12th-century Battistero San Giovanni.

exhibited in the Museo dell'Opera del Duomo (p 14). The most photographed are Lorenzo Ghiberti's east doors, facing the Duomo, which the typically critical Michelangelo dubbed "The Gates of Paradise." The panels illustrate scenes from the Old Testament. Ghiberti also cast the north doors, beating Brunelleschi in a 1401 competition for the commission; the job took him 21 years. Andrea Pisano made the Gothic south doors in 1336. Dominated by a figure of Christ, the 13th-century mosaics inside are also worth a peek. ⏱ *15 min. Piazza San Giovanni (off Piazza del Duomo).* ☎ *055-2302885. Admission 3€. Mon–Sat 12:15–6:30pm; Sun and 1st Sat of month 8:30am–1:30pm; Jun–Oct also Fri–Sat 12:15–10.30pm. Bus: A, 1, 6, 7, 10, 11, 14, 17, 23, 31, 32, 57.*

⑪ ★ **Basilica di San Lorenzo.** The overall effect of this basilica, which houses the tombs of many a Medici, is almost Byzantine; one Bulgarian critic called it "a Florentine Hagia Sophia looming over a souk" (a reference to the Mercato di San Lorenzo; p 65). The Medici shelled out big bags of gold for it, however. The taller of the two domes at the chancel shelters the **Cappella dei Principi,** the shallower cupola covering Michelangelo's **New Sacristy.** Commissioned in 1516, Michelangelo's model for the facade was deemed unacceptable to the Medici, who went to Brunelleschi, to design the **Old Sacristy** at the end of the north transept. Donatello created two pulpits with dramatic bronze panels in the nave. ⏱ *30 min. Piazza San Lorenzo.* ☎ *055-216634. Admission 3.50€. Mon–Sat 10am–5pm; Sun 1:30–5pm. Bus: 1, 6, 7, 10, 11, 14, 17, 23, 31, 32, 57.*

Oltrarno

1 La Specola
2 Cappella Brancacci
3 Santo Spirito
4 Borgo Antico
5 Palazzo Pitti
6 Giardino di Boboli
7 Casa Siviero
8 Via dell'Olmo
9 Giardino delle Rose
10 Piazzale Michelangelo
11 San Miniato al Monte

(i) Tourist Information

Oltrarno, Florence's "other side of the Arno," was once the artisan heart of the city. You'll see signs that tradition dies hard in the craft and antique shops lining Borgo San Jacopo and Via Maggio. But workshops and studios aren't all the neighborhood has to offer. This tour takes in the very peaks of Renaissance art and architecture, and quiet corners of a district that still has a real, working feel, before ending up at the finest view in Florence. START: **Take bus 11, 36 or 37 to Via Romana.**

1 ★ kids **La Specola.** This former headquarters of Oltrarno's World War II resistance now houses the Museo di Storia Naturale's zoology exhibits. In addition to the thousands of stuffed and pickled beasts, there's a touch of gore that's perhaps suited to older kids only. The **Cere Anatomiche** are lifelike waxworks of the human body spliced and diced 500 different ways, used to teach anatomy in the 18th century. Grislier still are Giulio Zumbo's 17th century models of Florence during the plague, showing the dead and decomposing strewn across the city streets. They were commissioned to pique the notoriously lurid and puritan interest of Cosimo III, Florence's penultimate Medici grand duke. ⏱ *1 hr. Via Romana 17.*

☎ 055-2288251. www.msn.unifi.it.
Admission 4€. Mon–Tues, Thurs–Fri,
Sun 9am–12:30pm; Sat 9am–5pm.
Bus: 11, 36, 37.

❷ ★★★ Cappella Brancacci.
The frescoes in the right transept
chapel of Florence's Carmelite
church stand on the brink of what
we now call "the Renaissance."
Originally painted by Masaccio and
Masolino between 1424 and 1427,
the *Scenes from the Life of St. Peter*
were finished off by Filippino Lippi in
the 1480s (spot the stylistic differences). It was Masaccio's vivid
realism and mastery of linear perspective, especially in his *Expulsion
from Eden* and *The Tribute Money*,
that artists were still coming to
study a century later. Vasari especially admired Masaccio's lifelike figures, notably their feet. "All those
artisans who have sought to study
the craft of painting have always
gone for instruction in this chapel,"
he wrote in 1550 in his *Lives*. It's a
miracle any of this is still here:
almost the entire remainder of the
church was destroyed by fire in
1771. Get here early and, despite

what it says on the door, you may
not have to have a reservation;
otherwise, book a slot by phone.
🕐 30 min. Piazza del Carmine 14.
☎ 055-2768224. Admission 4€.
Mon, Wed–Sat 10am–4:30pm; Sun
1–4:30pm. Bus: D.

❸ ★ Santo Spirito. This out-
wardly plain church is where
Brunelleschi's ordered architectural
style reached its apotheosis. The
nave and transept are supported by
an unbroken chain of columns, and
supplemented with 38 peripheral
chapels. The whole effect is of a
space filled wth light and grandeur,
that's only partly spoiled by the ludi-
crous Baroque canopy above the
altar. The sacristy houses a carved
wooden *Crucifixion* attributed to
Michelangelo. Fragments attributed
to Andrea Orcagna (1308–68) are
inside the adjacent museum.
🕐 30 min. Piazza Santo Spirito.
☎ 055-287043. Free admission.
Church Thurs–Tues 9:30am–
12:30pm and 4–5:30pm. Museum
Nov–Mar Sat 10:30am–1:30pm;
Apr–Oct Sat 9am–5pm. Bus: D, 6,
11, 36, 37.

Masaccio's Expulsion from Eden *at the Cappella Brancacci.*

One of the many lavish art-filled rooms in the Palazzo Pitti.

4 ★ **Il Borgo Antico.** Stop in for a hearty salad in this most Florentine of squares. Our favorite is made with

Bacchus in the Giardini di Boboli.

shrimp, avocado, and buffalo mozzarella. Pizzas and pasta are great if you're hungrier. *Piazza Santo Spirito 6R.* ☎ *055-210437. $–$$.*

5 ★★ **Palazzo Pitti.** Luca Pitti, a rich importer of French fabrics, wanted a palace to outclass the Medici—and he got his wish. Niccolò Macchiavelli hailed the *palazzo* as "grander than any other erected in Florence by a private citizen." When the Pittis went broke, the Medici moved in, making it the most opulent palace in Europe until Louis XIV built Versailles. In the 19th century, the Pitti sheltered the Italian royal family, when Florence was briefly the country's capital. Victor Emmanuel III gave it to the state in 1919, which turned it into a series of world-class museums.

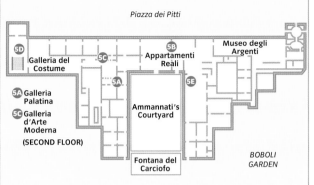

Pitti Palace

Piazza dei Pitti

5D Galleria del Costume
5C Appartamenti Reali
5B Museo degli Argenti
5A Galleria Palatina
5C Galleria d'Arte Moderna
(SECOND FLOOR)
5A
5E
Ammannati's Courtyard
Fontana del Carciofo
BOBOLI GARDEN

After climbing 140 steps, you enter the 5A ★★★ **Galleria Palatina.** Head here if you have to skip everything else. It's filled with masterpieces from the High Renaissance and later eras, collected by the Medici. The most famous resident is Raphael's *Madonna of the Chair,* in the Sala di Saturno, accompanied by several works by Venetian Titian and Flemish Peter Paul Rubens. Baroque sumptuousness defines the 5B ★ **Appartmenti Reali,** home to the Kings of Savoy. Note Caravaggio's *Portrait of a Knight of Malta,* painted before his expulsion from the island in 1608. In the shadow of the Renaissance rooms, the 5C ★ **Galleria d'Arte Moderna**

showcases the Macchiaioli, the 19th-century Tuscan school of pre-Impressionist painters who revolted against academicism. The 5D **Galleria del Costume** is filled with 18th- to 20th-century clothing, including historic wardrobes such as Eleanor of Toledo's burial dress. The ground floor, 5E **Museo degli Argenti** is a camp glorification of the Medici household wares, with treasures in ivory and silver, among other metals. It's ostentatious but fun. 🕐 *2 hr. Piazza de' Pitti.* ☎ *055-2388611. www.firenzemusei.it. Galleria Palatina 12€ including Appartamenti Reali and Galleria d'Arte Moderna. Tues–Sun 8:15am– 6:45pm. Bus: D.*

6 ★ kids **Giardino di Boboli.** Court architect and artist, Niccolò Tribolo (1500–1550), laid out these Renaissance gardens, through which the Medici romped, in the mid-16th century. Since opening to the public in 1776, Boboli has become the most dazzling (and busy) garden in Tuscany, with splashing fountains and elegant

statuary such as *Venus* by Giambologna inside the Buontalenti grotto. The nearby, much-photographed fountain—an obese *Bacchus* astride a turtle—is a copy of a statue depicting Pietro Barbino, Cosimo I's court jester. 🕐 *30 min. Piazza de' Pitti.* ☎ *055-2651838. Admission 10€ including entrance to Museo degli Argenti, Museo delle*

In the Giardino delle Rose.

Porcellane and Galleria del Costume. Jun–Aug daily 8:15am–7:30pm; Mar–May and Sept daily 8:15am–6:30pm; Oct daily 8:15am–5.30pm; Nov–Feb daily 8:15am–4:30pm. Closed 1st and last Mon of each month. Bus: D, 11, 36, 37.

⑦ ★ **Casa Siviero.** Inside a colonial villa right on the Arno is the private collection of resistance fighter and art historian Rodolfo Siviero (1911–1983). The bulk of the paintings are minor works, ancient and modern. Of particular interest is a set of medallions Siviero commissioned after World War II to honor those who helped liberate his city, including Winston Churchill and Dwight D. Eisenhower. 🕐 *30 min. Lungarno Serristori 1–3 (at Piazza Poggi).* ☎ *055-2345219. www. museocasasiviero.it. Free admission. Sat 10am–2pm and 3–7pm (Oct–May 10am–6pm); Sun–Mon 10am–1pm. Bus: D, 12, 13, 23.*

⑧ **Via dell'Olmo.** High on a wall on the western side of this tiny street is a sign that reads: *"Qui arriva la piena del Arno il 4 Novembre 1966."* That's the height the flood waters reached in November 1966 before they began to subside that evening. Countless of the city's treasures were damaged, most famously Cimabue's *Crucifixion* in Santa Croce, and more than 100 residents lost their lives, including several in the underpass by Santa

A view of Florence from the perfectly positioned Piazzale Michelangelo.

San Miniato at Monte is built in the Pisan-Romanesque style.

Maria Novella station. The inundation, Florence's worst since the 16th century, is still known as the Great Amo Flood. ⏱ *5 min. Bus: D, 12, 13, 23.*

⑨ Giardino delle Rose. This little oasis of peace, planted with over 1,000 varieties of rose, makes a perfect pause half-way up the hill to Piazzale Michelangelo. There's also a little Japanese garden donated to Florence by the city of Kyoto. ⏱ *15 min. Viale Poggi 2. No phone. Free admission. May–Jul daily 8am–8pm. Bus: 12, 13.*

⑩ ★ kids Piazzale Michelangelo. Tacky, perhaps; touristy, certainly, but this grand balcony over the city is *the* essential photo stop on any tour of Oltrarno. From where (another) *David* looks out over his city, right at the Palazzo Vecchio that was his first home, you can do the same. ⏱ *15 min. Bus: 12, 13.*

⑪ ★★★ San Miniato al Monte. This most spiritual of Florentine churches is one of the city's truly ancient places. Built from 1018 in the Pisan-Romanesque style, inside and out, it takes its name from Florence's first Christian martyr. St. Minias apparently picked up his severed head and carried it to this spot in 250 AD. The nave and aisles are decorated with Taddeo Gaddi's fading frescoes (from 1341) of the Gospel witnesses, and topped with a soaring, intricate inlaid wooden ceiling. Upstairs, off the raised choir, the Gothic sacristy was frescoed in 1387 with *Stories of the Legend of St. Benedict* by Spinello Aretino, a later follower of Giotto. The only "modern" intrusion is the magnificent, if slightly incongruous, Brunelleschi-inspired Cappella del Cardinale del Portogalle, completed off the left-hand wall of the nave in 1466. It was built as a Renaissance team effort by Antonio Manetti, a pupil of Brunelleschi, and the Rossellino brothers, to serve as a memorial to a young Portuguese cardinal who perished in Florence. ⏱ *45 min. Viale Galileo. ☎ 055-2342731. Free admission (1€ sacristy). Daily 8am–7:30pm (Oct–Easter lunchtime closure depending on weather). Bus: 12, 13.*

The Best of the **Uffizi**

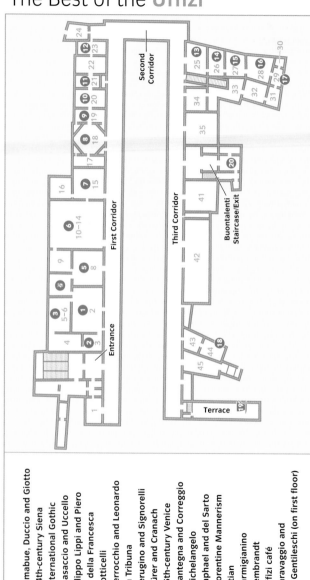

Second Corridor

First Corridor

Third Corridor

Buontalenti Staircase/Exit

Entrance

Terrace

1. Cimabue, Duccio and Giotto
2. 14th-century Siena
3. International Gothic
4. Masaccio and Uccello
5. Filippo Lippi and Piero della Francesca
6. Botticelli
7. Verrocchio and Leonardo
8. La Tribuna
9. Perugino and Signorelli
10. Dürer and Cranach
11. 15th-century Venice
12. Mantegna and Correggio
13. Michelangelo
14. Raphael and del Sarto
15. Florentine Mannerism
16. Titian
17. Parmigianino
18. Rembrandt
19. Uffizi café
20. Caravaggio and Gentileschi (on first floor)

Once the Medici business offices, the Galleria degli Uffizi is now the world's finest museum of Renaissance painting. Reserving tickets is essential: If you don't, expect to queue for up to 6 hours in summer. **Firenze Musei** takes reservations in advance, in English over the phone and online (☎ **055-294883**; www.firenzemusei.it), and also at their office opposite the main entrance. START: **Take bus B or 23 to the Uffizi. Trip length: 3 hr. Admission: 6.50€–10€ plus booking fee 4€. Opening hours: Tues–Sun 8:15am–6:35pm.**

① ★★★ **Room 2.** This opening gallery introduces a trio of great Madonnas. Though still with its roots in Byzantine artistic conventions, Cimabue's *Santa Trinita Maestà* (1280) takes tentative steps towards realistic painting. Duccio di Buoninsegna's *Rucellai Madonna* (1285) influenced a generation of Sienese art. Three decades later, Giotto (1276–1337) painted the most solid *Maestà* (Virgin in majesty) of them all, the *Ognissanti Madonna*.

② ★★★ **Room 3.** This room gives a taste of 14th-century Sienese painting—none finer than Simone Martini's ethereal *Annunciation* (1313), showing a horrified Mary learning of her Immaculate Conception. The Lorenzetti brothers, Pietro and Ambrogio, also created masterpieces displayed in this room, before the Black Death of 1348 claimed their lives; the most sophisticated (and much emulated) work is Ambrogio's *Presentation at the Temple* (1342).

③ ★★ **Room 5–6.** The hyperdecorative style known as "international Gothic" is showcased here. Lorenzo Monaco (1370–1425), Fra' Angelico (1395–1455) and Gentile da Fabriano (1370–1427) were its main Florentine exponents. The latter's 1423 *Adoration of the Magi* is the iconic work of the genre.

④ ★★ **Room 7.** Renaissance innovations in painting were possible in part because of Masaccio (1401–28) and Paolo Uccello (1397–1475) and their revolutionary use of perspective.

The Medici's former offices, the Uffizi has the world's best Renaissance art collection.

Look at the characteristically chaotic foreshortening in Uccello's *Battle of San Romano* (1456), depicting a Florentine victory over the Sienese army. A rare piece by Masaccio (he was dead at 27) is his *Madonna and Child with St. Anne* (1424).

⑤ ★★ **Room 8.** Numerous paintings by Fra' Filippo Lippi (1406–69) are displayed in this early Renaissance salon. His *Madonna and Child with Two Young Angels* is an overtly romantic portrait of the randy monk's mistress. Piero della Francesca's *Portrait of the Duke and Duchess of Urbino* (1472) is as famed for the perspective Tuscan landscape as for the profiles themselves.

⑥ ★★★ **Rooms 10–14.** Sandro Botticelli (1445–1510) authored perhaps the most visited paintings in Florence: his *Birth of Venus* and the enigmatic *Primavera (Allegory of*

Leonardo da Vinci's Annunciation.

Spring). *Primavera*'s varied cast includes (from the left) Mercury, the Three Graces, Venus, and Flora—the godess of spring who was known as Chloris, before her rape by Zephyr (the West Wind), the scene on the right of the panel.

7 ★★ **Room 15.** Leonardo da Vinci (1452–1519) is the main man here. His *Annunciation* (1480) is known for its tricky use of a vanishing point (look at it from the lower-right corner). The nearby *Baptism of Christ* is by his teacher, Andrea del Verrocchio (1435–88).

8 ★ **Room 18.** Octagonal *La Tribuna* is the most lavish salon in the Uffizi, decorated with lapis lazuli for air, red walls for fire, green *pietra dure* for earth, and mother-of-pearl for water. Its focus is the *Medici Venus*, a medieval copy of a Greek original whose pose was copied by Botticelli. Baroque artist Agnolo Bronzino (1503–72) painted the celebrated portrait of Eleonora of Toledo, wife of Cosimo I. When the Medici tombs were opened in 1857, her body was discovered buried in the same satin dress she wore in the painting. You can also just about make out Raphael's *St. John the Baptist in the Desert* (1518) through the gloom.

9 **Room 19.** Perugino's (1446–1523) stern *Portrait of Francesco delle Opere* shines brightest here. Cortonese Luca Signorelli (1445–1523), whose style influenced Michelangelo's Sistine Chapel ceiling, is also represented.

10 ★ **Room 20.** This gallery exhibits paintings by Germans who worked in Florence. Albrecht Dürer (1471–1528) was the undisputed master of the German Renaissance. Contrast his *Adam and Eve* with one by Lucas Cranach (1472–1553). Dürer's work is a study of the body; Cranach's shows a more erotic bent.

11 **Room 21.** Venetian masters of the 15th century shine in this *sala*—especially Giovanni Bellini (1430–1516). His complex *Sacra Allegoria* is the most memorable, showing an advanced understanding of perspective.

12 ★ **Room 23.** This gallery is a showcase for Andrea Mantegna's triptych of the *Adoration of the Magi, Circumcision,* and *Ascension* painted between 1463 and 1470. There are also noted works by Antonio da Correggio (1489–1534).

13 ★★ **Room 25.** Michelangelo's only painting in Florence—a tondo (round painting) of the

Caravaggio's Medusa.

Holy Family, commissioned by the Doni family—is often called the *Doni Tondo* (1506–08). Michelangelo even designed the elaborate frame. The family's muscular forms and contorted poses suggest Michelangelo's preference for sculpture.

⓮ ★ **Room 26.** This salon of High Renaissance compositions is dominated by Raphael's recently restored *Madonna del Cardellino,* in which his usual triangular, hierarchical layout is enlivened by a goldfinch. Also here is the *Madonna of the Harpies* by Andrea del Sarto (1486–1530), a founder of Florentine Mannerism.

⓯ ★ **Room 27.** Florentine Mannerism reaches fever pitch in this room dedicated to Rosso Fiorentino (1485–1541), Del Sarto's pupil. Fiorentino is best appreciated in his *Moses Defends the Daughters of Jethro* (1523), which owes a heavy debt to Michelangelo. Del Sarto's other renowned pupil, Jacopo Pontormo (1494–1557), is represented by *Supper at Emmaus.*

⓰ ★★ **Room 28.** This *sala* is dedicated to Venetian visionary and master colorist, Titian (1488–1566). Of all the postcards sold at the Uffizi,

none—not even Botticelli's *Primavera*—tops the sales of his 1538 *Venus of Urbino,* lounging nude on her bed.

⓱ **Room 29.** The late Mannerist painter Parmigianino (1505–40) dominates this gallery. His *Madonna and Child* is more usually known as the *Madonna with the Long Neck,* for obvious reasons.

⓲ ★ **Room 44.** Compare the two self-portraits by Dutch great Rembrandt van Rijn—one in his prime (1634), the other, more melancholic, as a senior citizen in the year of his death (1669).

⓳ **The Uffizi café,** a bar with a view atop the loggia, serves cold drinks, snacks, and coffee at prices not too out of line with central Florence. *Piazzale degli Uffizi 6.* ☎ *055-23885.* $–$$.

⓴ ★ **1st Floor.** Bad boy of the Baroque, Caravaggio (1571–1610) is the star of these new rooms. His screeching circular *Medusa* (1599), mounted on a circular shield, is a typically deranged self-portrait.

Primavera, by Sandro Botticelli.

Florence's Best Small Museums

1 Sinagoga & Jewish Museum
2 Museo Archeologico
3 Museo Opificio delle Pietre Dure
4 Museo dell'Opera del Duomo
5 Museo Antropologico
6 Buongustai
7 Firenze com'era
8 Museo Horne
9 Gelateria dei Neri
10 Museo Galileo
11 Museo di Santa Maria Novella
12 Museo Stibbert

In the shadow of the Uffizi and Palazzo Pitti, the small museums of Florence are often overlooked. But the city has even more to offer than those vast repositories of great art. Away from the tourist-trodden paths are one of Italy's greatest archaeological museums, an offbeat museum of science, and church museums housing lesser-known Renaissance masterpieces. START: **Take bus C, 6, 31 or 32 to Via della Colonna.**

1 **Sinagoga and Jewish Museum.** This Moorish-Byzantine travertine synagogue was built in the 1870s and badly damaged by the Nazis in 1944. It is used today by Florence's 1,000-strong Jewish community. A small museum upstairs contains an exhibit of the Jewish ghetto that existed in Florence until it was disbanded in 1859. ⏱ *45 min.*

guided tour. Via Farini 4. ☎ *055-2346654. Admission 5€. Jun–Aug Sun–Thurs 10am–6pm, Fri 10am–2pm; Apr–May and Sept–Oct Sun–Thurs 10am–5pm; Nov–Mar Sun–Thurs 10am–3pm. Bus: C, 6, 31, 32.*

2 ★ **Museo Archeologico.** A marvelous *palazzo* is home to one of Italy's greatest (if slightly haphazard) collections of Egyptian and

The Jewish synagogue and museum rises above the surrounding rooftops.

Etruscan artifacts, much of it gathered by the Medici and later Leopold II of Lorraine, in the 1830s. The highlights are all upstairs, including eerie Egyptian sarcophagi in Sala VIII. The 4th-century Arezzo Chimera (a bronze lion with a goat protruding from its back and a serpent for a tail) is the prize exhibit. On Saturday mornings only, you can tour real Etruscan tombs rebuilt in the museum's garden. ⏱ *1 hr. Via della Colonna 38 (at Piazza della SS. Annunziata).* ☎ *055-23575. Admission 4€. Mon 2–7pm; Tues, Thurs 8:30am–7pm; Wed, Fri–Sun 8:30am–2pm. Bus: C, 6, 31, 32.*

❸ **Museo Opificio delle Pietre Dure.** This unique collection grew out of the Medici's passion for *pietre dure,* a type of mosaic work made from semi-precious stones and marble, popular in the 16th century. (The craft is sometimes called "Florentine Mosaic.") Since 1796 this workshop has been dedicated to restoring *pietre dure* works. Attached is a small museum with some examples of the art form, including intricate Tuscan landscapes. ⏱ *30 min. Via degli Alfani 78 (at Via Ricasoli).* ☎ *055-294883. Admission 2€. Mon–Sat 8:15am–2pm (Thurs until 7pm). Bus: C, 1, 6, 7, 10, 11, 17, 31, 32, 57.*

❹ ★ **Museo dell'Opera del Duomo.** The loot from the Duomo, the Baptistery, and Giotto's Campanile (including Ghiberti's "Gates of Paradise") ended up here, behind the Duomo. For openers, Michelangelo carved another *David,* on display in the courtyard. Rarer and more beautiful, Michelangelo's *Pietà,* originally intended for the artist's tomb, is now on the mezzanine. Upstairs are joyous *cantorie*—one by Donatello, the other by Luca della Robbia. With clashing symbols and sounding brass, these *cantorie*

An example of pietre dure, a mosaic of semi-precious stones.

say "praise the Lord" in marble. Sharing the room with the *cantorie* is Donatello's *Magdalene,* one of his most celebrated penitent works, from 1454. 🕐 *1 hr. Piazza del Duomo 9 (at northern end of Via del Proconsolo).* ☎ *055-2302885. Admission 6€. Mon–Sat 9am–6:50pm; Sun 9am–1pm. Bus: 14, 23.*

5 Museo Antropologico. Take a timeout from the Renaissance at this fascinating little anthropological enclave of the University of Florence. Inuit canoes, Japanese *kabuki* masks, Sumatran spears, and Inca mummies from Cuzco, Peru, were all collected during the heyday of European imperialism in the 19th century. Displays are in Italian, but a guide in English is available at the ticket office. 🕐 *45 min. Via del Proconsolo 12.* ☎ *055-2396449. www.unifi.it/ msn. Admission 4€. Sun–Tues and Thurs–Fri 9am–12:30pm; Sat 9am–5pm. Bus: A, 14, 23.*

6 ★ Buongustai. Refuel yourselves where Florentines meet for lunch. Cheap, tasty pasta, *frittata,* or salad is followed by a cheese tasting platter that includes *pecorino di Pienza*. *Via de' Cerchi 15R.* ☎ *055-291304. $–$$.*

7 Firenze com'era. Trace the changing shape of the city at this small museum near the Duomo. Starting with a giant plan of "Fiorenza" in 1490, prints and models are interspersed with landscape paintings, old maps, and Victorian drawings that give a sense of how the medieval center looked before the ancient streets were ripped out to make way

for Piazza della Repubblica. 🕐 *45 min. Via dell'Oriuolo 24.* ☎ *055-2768224. Admission 2.70€. Oct–May Mon–Wed 9am–2pm; Sat 9am–7pm. Jun–Sept Mon–Tues 9am–2pm; Sat 9am–7pm. Bus: 14, 23.*

8 ★ Museo Horne. English-born Herbert Horne, an art historian, immortalized himself by building the nucleus of this collection, including minor masterpieces by some major artists. Works are displayed in his preserved Renaissance home, round a porticoed courtyard. Horne's greatest acquisitions were Giotto's *St. Stephen*, dating from the early 14th century, and a small 1320s diptych by Simone Martini depicting the *Man of Sorrows*. 🕐 *45 min. Via dei Benci 6 (at Corso dei Tintori).* ☎ *055-244661. www.museohorne.it. Admission 5€. Mon–Sat 9am–1pm. Bus: B, C, 13, 23.*

9 ★ Gelateria dei Neri. Plenty of locals think this, rather than the more famous names, is the best ice-cream stop in town. *Via dei Neri 20–22R.* ☎ *055-210034. $.*

10 ★ kids Museo Galileo. The former Museo di Storia della Scienza reopens in late 2009 as the Museo Galileo. It houses such treasures as the lens Galileo used to discover the four moons of Jupiter and the great scientist's right-hand middle finger, stolen at his burial at Santa Croce. A hands-on multimedia approach appeals to older kids. 🕐 *1 hr. Piazza dei Giudici 1.* ☎ *055-2653130. www.imss.fi.it. Admission 6.50€. Call for hours. Bus: B, 23.*

A Renaissance antique sundial in the Museo Galileo.

The frescoes in the Chiostro Verde (Green Cloisters) were nearly destroyed in the 1966 flood.

⓫ ★★ Museo di Santa Maria Novella. Attached to the Basilica di Santa Maria Novella (p 44) are the Green Cloisters (*Chiostro Verde*), open to the public as a museum. Paolo Uccello's 15th-century frescoes were almost destroyed in the 1966 flood, which given their subject matter (Biblical inundation) is perhaps appropriate. Uccello's *Universal Deluge* lunette exhibits his trademark crazy use of perspective. The better preserved **Spanish Chapel** was frescoed earlier (ca. 1365) by Andrea di Bonaiuto. It tells a complex story that places the Dominicans at the center of spreading the word of Christ. ⏱ 45 min. Piazza Santa Maria Novella.

☎ 055-282187. Admission 2.70€. *Mon–Thurs and Sat 9am–2pm. Bus: A, 1, 7, 10, 11, 14, 22, 36, 37, 57, 68, 71.*

⓬ kids Museo Stibbert. Frederick Stibbert (1838–1906), half-Italian, half-Scot, was an eclectic collector, as the 50,000 *objets d'art* (tapestries, antiques, porcelain, paintings) in these 57 rooms testify. As you'll see, Stibbert also had a fetish about war and weaponry: expect lances, swords, and suits of Japanese, European, and Middle Eastern armor. ⏱ 45 min. Via Stibbert 26. ☎ 055-475520. www.museostibbert.it. *Admission 6€. Mon–Wed 10am–1pm; Fri–Sun 10am–5pm. Bus: 4.*

Florence's **Masters of the Renaissance**

① Basilica di Santa Maria Novella
② Cappelle Medicee
③ Cenacolo di Sant'Appolonia
④ Pugi
⑤ Palazzo Medici-Riccardi
⑥ Orsanmichele
⑦ Basilica di Santa Trinita
⑧ Galleria degli Uffizi

ⓘ Tourist Information

For over a century, Florence was the center of the world. The period we now call the Renaissance ("the rebirth") is often dated from Lorenzo Ghiberti's commission for the East Doors of the Baptistery, in 1401, until Michelangelo's final departure for Rome, in the 1530s. This remarkable period of artistic and architectural achievement was initially led by such Tuscan figures as Masaccio, Donatello, and Brunelleschi, later by Leonardo da Vinci, Sandro Botticelli, and Michelangelo himself. It created the city we see today. On this tour, I'll take you to the best works left behind by the sculptors, painters, and architects who changed art forever. START: **Take bus A, 1, 7, 10, 11, 14, 22, 36, 37, 57, 68, 71 to Piazza Santa Maria Novella.**

---

① ★★ **Basilica di Santa Maria Novella.** The iconic green and white marble facade was created in the 15th century, while the dizzying

interior dates to the 13th. (Writer Boccaccio used it for scenes in his *Decameron*.) Of the many interior frescoes, Domenico

Ghirlandaio's adorning the **Cappella Tornabuoni** are the most sumptuous. Ostensibly, they depict *Scenes from the Lives of the Virgin and St. John the Baptist*, but they're also a unique snapshot of wealthy society in 1490 Florence. The adjacent Cappella Stroggi was frescoed by Filippino Lippi in the 1490s with scenes from the Life of St. Philip (Filippino Stroggi's name-sake). On the left wall of the nave, Masaccio's *Trinity* astonished onlookers when it was unveiled in 1425: they'd never seen such realistic recession painted onto a flat wall. By the 1800s, this Romanesque structure in the city of the Renaissance had become "the church for foreigners," attracting expatriate literati, including Percy Bysshe Shelley, Henry James, Ralph Waldo Emerson, and even Henry Wadsworth Longfellow. ⏱ *45 min. Piazza Santa Maria Novella.* ☎ *055-215918. Admission 2.70€. Mon–Thurs and Sat 9am–5pm, Fri and Sun 1–5pm. Bus: A, 1, 7, 10, 11, 14, 22, 36, 37, 57, 68, 71.*

② ★★ **Cappelle Medicee.** Make a fast trek to the **Sagrestia Nuova,** Michelangelo's first

Santa Maria Novella's green cloisters are among Europe's most richly embellished.

realized architectural work—begun in 1520, but left unfinished until 1534. As an architectural space, it echoes the ordered, airy classicism of Brunelleschi's Pazzi Chapel in Santa Croce. From the door, on the left, the tomb of Lorenzo, Duke of Urbino, bears the artist's reclining figures representing *Dawn* and *Dusk*. On the right, the tomb of Giuliano, Duke of Nemours (and youngest son of Lorenzo the Magnificent), features Michelangelo's allegorical figures of *Day* and *Night*. Shrewd observers will note that Michelangelo obviously hadn't seen many naked female bodies. The artist never completed the other two tombs commissioned to him, but in 1521 he did finish a moving *Madonna and Child,* for the tomb of Lorenzo de' Medici the Magnificent. ⏱ *30 min. Piazza Madonna degli Aldobrandini 6 (behind San Lorenzo where Via del Gigli and Via Faenza converge).* ☎ *055-2388602. Admission 6€. Daily 8:15am–5:20pm. Closed 2nd and 4th Sun and 1st, 3rd, and 5th Mon of month. Bus: A, 1, 7, 10, 11, 14, 17, 22, 23, 31, 32, 36, 37, 57.*

③ ★ **Cenacolo di Sant' Appolonia.** Andrea del Castagno (1421–57) first rose to prominence when he was employed to paint the faces of condemned men on the walls of the Bargello. He went on to become, alongside Piero della Francesca (1412–92), one of the great perspective painters of the mid *Quattrocento*. Here, in what remains of the Benedictine convent of Sant'Appolonia, he gives his intense, rather dark take on the *Last Supper* (1447). No prizes for naming the only diner without his halo. ⏱ *15 min. Via XX Aprile 1. No phone. Free admission. Daily 8:15am–1:50pm. Closed 1st, 3rd, 5th Sun and 2nd, 4th Mon of month. Bus: 20, 25, 33.*

Benozzo Gozzoli's Procession of the Magi.

4 ★ **Pugi.** Choose your topping, and your portion size, of freshly baked *schiacciata* (flatbread) and munch it in the square across the street. Closed Sundays. *Piazza San Marco 10.* ☎ *055-280981. www.focacceria-pugi.it. $.*

5 ★ kids **Palazzo Medici-Riccardi.** The onset of the Florentine Renaissance didn't totally kill off the decorative style of painting known as "international Gothic," as this tiny chapel frescoed in 1459 by Benozzo Gozzoli shows. Gozzoli's *Procession of the Magi*

includes a pageant of Medici friends and family, accompanied by a beautifullly rendered menagerie of creatures. Downstairs a giant interactive multimedia display relates to the fresco. ⏱ *30 min. Via Cavour 3.* ☎ *055-2760340. www. palazzo-medici.it. Admission 5€. Thurs–Tues 9am–7pm. Bus: 1, 6, 7, 10, 11, 14, 17, 23, 31, 32, 57.*

6 ★★ **Orsanmichele.** This 1337 Gothic grain warehouse was converted into a church in medieval times. The external

A detail from Andrea Orcagna's Tabernacle at Orsanmichele.

niches were adorned with statuary commissioned by Florence's trades guilds. (Most are originals, still there are reproductions.) The sculptors chosen included such luminaries of the early Renaissance as Lorenzo Ghiberti, Nanni di Bancom and Donatello, whose path-breaking *St George* is now in the Bargello. Inside is Andrea Orcagna's elaborate Gothic Tabernacle (1349–59), housing a *Virgin and Child* (1346) by Giotto's student, Bernardo Daddi. The popular Orsanmichele museum across the street is closed indefinitely. ⏱ *30 min. Via Arte della Lana 1.* ☎ *055-284944. Free admission. Tues–Sun 9.30am–5pm. Bus: A.*

St. Mark, one of several Donatello figures that grace the façade of Orsanmichele.

7 ★★ **Basilica di Santa Trinita.** This oft-missed little gem, founded in the 11th century, was the original home of Gentile da Fabriano's Gothic icon, *The Adoration of the Magi*, now in the Uffizi. Lorenzo Monaco frescoed the **Capella Bartolini Salimbeni** in the 1420s with *Scenes from the Life of the Virgin*; Domenico Ghirlandaio, in uncharacteristically

pious mood, frescoed the **Cappella Sassetti** in the 1480s with a *Life of St Francis*. Comparing them side-by-side paints a picture of progress made in the depiction of space during the early Renaissance. ⏱ *30 min. Piazza di Santa Trinita.* ☎ *055-216912. Free admission. Mon–Sat 7am-noon and 4–7pm; Sun 4–7pm. Bus: A, B, 6, 11, 36, 37.*

8 ★★★ **Galleria degli Uffizi.** If you've still got energy for more Renaissance, finish your day at the planet's greatest repository of 13th, 14th, and 15th century painting. Here you'll find influential works by such important Renaissance figures as Leonardo da Vinci, Paolo Uccello, Raphael, and Piero della Francesca. The building itself was designed in 1560 by Renaissance man Giorgio Vasari, whose *Lives of the Artists* is still the best contemporary text for the greatest period in Western art. Vasari even coined the term Renaissance. A couple of week-nights in summer you'll find the Uffizi open until 10pm. (Exact days change.) *See p 36.*

The Best Dining in Florence

Antellesi 4
Buca dell'Orafo 15
Buca Lapi 8
Buca Mario 7
Cantinetta Antinori 9
Cave di Maiano 26
Cibrèo 25
Da Delfina 6
Don Chisciotte 1
Ganino 18
Garga 10
Giostra 23
Il Cantinone 13
Il Latini 11
Il Pizzaiuolo 24
Le Fonticine 2
Le Mossacce 19

Mamma Gina 14
Nerbone 3
Ora d'Aria 27
Osteria del
  Caffè Italiano 22
Paoli 17
Pennello 19
Quattro Leoni 16
Sabatini 5
Santo Spirito 12
Tijuana 21

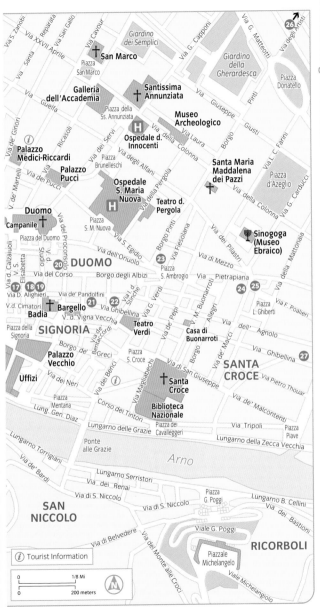

Dining Best Bets

Best for a **Business Lunch**
★ Cantinetta Antinori $$$–$$$$
Piazza Antinori 3 (p 51)

Best for a **Romantic Dinner**
★ Giostra $$$–$$$$ Borgo Pinti
10R (p 52)

Best **Budget Bite**
★ Le Mosacce $–$$ Via del
Proconsolo 55R (p 52)

Best **Seafood**
★★ Don Chisciotte $$$–$$$$$ Via
Ridolfi 4R (p 51)

Best **Steak**
★ Sabatini $$$–$$$$ Via de' Panzani 9A (p 53)

Best **Florentine Family Dining**
★★ Quattro Leoni $$–$$$ Via dei
Vellutini 1R (p 53)

Best **Pizza**
★ Il Pizzaiuolo $–$$$ Via de'
Macci 113R (p 52)

Most **Innovative Cooking**
★★★ Cibrèo $$$$$ Via Verrocchio
8R (p 51)

Best **Sandwich**
★ Nerbone $ Mercato Centrale
(p 53)

Best **Roast Meats**
★ Il Latini $$–$$$ Via del Palchetti
6R (p 52)

Best **Countryside Dining**
★★ Da Delfina $$$ Via della
Chiesa 1, Artimino (p 51)

Best **Modern Tuscan Cuisine**
★★★ Ora d'Aria $$$$ Via Ghibellina 3/cR (p 53)

Best for **Traditional Italian
Cooking**
★ Paoli $$–$$$$ Via dei Tavolini
12R (p 53)

Best **Antipasti**
★ Pennello $$–$$$ Via Dante
Alighieri 4R (p 53)

Best **Ice Cream**
★★★ Vivoli $ Via Isole delle
Stinche 7R (p 26)

Il Latini is a Florence institution.

Florence Restaurants A to Z

Antellesi SAN LORENZO *FLOREN-TINE* Only the finest, freshest Tuscan field and farm ingredients are served at this trattoria in a 15th-century building near the Medici Chapels. *Via Faenza 9R.* ☎ *055-216990. Entrees 12€–18€. AE, DC, MC, V. Lunch, dinner daily. Bus: A, 1, 7, 10, 11, 14, 17, 22, 23, 31, 32, 36, 37, 57.*

★ **Buca dell'Orafo** CENTRO STORICO *FLORENTINE* This cellar trattoria once housed a Renaissance goldsmith. Now, locals and visitors share communal tables and Tuscan peasant food. *Volta dei Girolami 28R (at Piazza del Pesce).* ☎ *055-213619. Entrees 10€–18€. MC, V. Lunch, dinner Sun–Fri. Closed Aug and 2 weeks in Dec. Bus: B.*

Buca Lapi CENTRO STORICO *TUS-CAN* Huddled under the Palazzo Antinori since 1880, this is Florence's most glam *buca* (cellar), under vaulted ceilings. Expect regional classics such as *bistecca alla fiorentina* prepared to decades-old recipes. *Via del Trebbio 1R.* ☎ *055-213768. Main courses 18€–35€. AE, DC, MC, V. Dinner Mon–Sat. Closed 2 weeks in Aug. Bus: A, 6, 11, 22, 36, 37.*

★ **Buca Mario** CENTRO STORICO *TUSCAN* Founded in 1886, this former workman's tavern in the cellar of Palazzo Niccolini turns out classic regional fare. *Piazza degli Ottaviani 16R.* ☎ *055-214179. www.buca mario.it. Entrees 18€–30€. AE, MC, V. Lunch Sat–Sun; dinner daily. Closed Aug. Bus: A, 11, 36, 37.*

★ **Cantinetta Antinori** CENTRO STORICO *FLORENTINE/TUSCAN* For 600 years, the Antinori family has dazzled with ingredients and wines from their own farms and vineyards, served in a 15th-century *palazzo*.

Palazzo Antinori, Piazza Antinori 3. ☎ *055-292234. Entrees 19€–26€. AE, DC, MC, V. Lunch, dinner Mon–Fri. Closed Aug. Bus: A, 6, 11, 22, 36, 37.*

★ **Cave di Maiano** FIESOLE *TUSCAN* This converted farmhouse is known for its reliable kitchen, turning out dishes like herb-flavored roast lamb and homemade ice cream with raspberries. *Via delle Cave 16 (between Florence and Fiesole).* ☎ *055-59133. www.trattoria cavedimaiano.it. Entrees 10€–19€. AE, DC, MC, V. Lunch, dinner daily. Closed 1 week in Feb. Bus: 7.*

★★★ **Cibrèo** SANTA CROCE *MEDITERRANEAN* Fabio Picchi's innovative restaurant remains one of Florence's finest. Simple soups share the menu with ventures like fricasseed roosters' combs and innards in an egg. *Via Verrocchio 8R.* ☎ *055-2341100. Entrees 36€. AE, MC, V. Lunch, dinner Tues–Sat. Closed late July to early Sept. Bus: A, C.*

★★ **Don Chisciotte** SAN LORENZO *ITALIAN/SEAFOOD* The fish served in this old Florentine *palazzo* is the city's freshest, brimming with zesty, unusual flavors. *Via Ridolfi 4R.* ☎ *055-475430. Entrees 18€–30€. AE, DC, MC, V. Lunch Tues–Sat, dinner Mon–Sat. Bus: 20, 33, 25.*

★★ **Da Delfina** ARTIMINO *TUSCAN* In a medieval walled village 9 miles from Florence, this family restaurant draws city folk to feast on dishes made with produce from nearby fields. *Via della Chiesa 1, Artimino.* ☎ *055-8718074. www.dadelfina.it. Entrees 15€–20€. No credit cards. Lunch Tues–Sun, dinner Tues–Sat. From Santa Maria Novella, take the Signa train then a cab for 5 min.*

★ **Ganino** CENTRO STORICO *FLO-RENTINE* Savvy foodies patronize this intimate tavern on a small piazza near the Badia. The chefs deliver reliably praiseworthy victuals, from succulent pastas to Tuscan white beans and juicy T-bones. *Piazza dei Cimatori 4R.* ☎ *055-214125. Entrees 10€–20€. AE, DC. Lunch and dinner Mon–Sat. Bus: A.*

Garga CENTRO STORICO *FLOREN-TINE/TUSCAN* Between Ponte Car-raia and Santa Maria Novella, a young crowd gathers for dishes such as angel-hair with squid and citrus sauce. *Via del Moro 48R.* ☎ *055-2398898. Entrees 21€–25€. AE, MC, V. Dinner Tues–Sun. Bus: A, 6, 11, 36, 37.*

★ **Giostra** SANTA CROCE *TUSCAN* A Hapsburg prince with Medici blood welcomes guests to this inti-mate restaurant, with some dishes based on noble family recipes. *Borgo Pinti 10R.* ☎ *055-241341. www.ristorantelagiostra.com. Entrees 16€–30€. AE, DC, MC, V. Lunch, dinner daily. Bus: 14, 23.*

★ **kids Il Cantinone** OLTRARNO *TUSCAN/ITALIAN* This wine cantina turned bustling osteria is famed for giant bread *crostone*, topped with tomatoes and sausage. For dinner, try regional dishes like wild boar. *Via*

Da Delfina draws Florentines to the countryside.

Santo Spirito 6R. ☎ *055-218898. Entrees 8€–15€. AE, MC, V. Lunch, dinner Tues–Sun. Bus: D, 6.*

★ **Il Latini** CENTRO STORICO *TUS-CAN* At this local dive, diners feast at communal tables on dishes such as *arrosto misto*—slabs of assorted meats cooked on the grill. *Via del Palchetti 6R.* ☎ *055-210916. www. illatini.com. Entrees 10€–20€. AE, DC, MC, V. Lunch, dinner Tues–Sun. Closed 2 weeks in Aug. Bus: A, B, 6.*

★ **kids Il Pizzaiuolo** SANTA CROCE *PIZZA* The only authentic Neapolitan DOC pizzeria inside the old city gates is full most nights—book ahead. They also specialize in seafood. *Via de' Macci 113R.* ☎ *055-241171. www.ilpizzaiuolo.it. Entrees 6€–15€. MC, V. Lunch, din-ner Mon–Sat. Closed Aug. Bus: A, C.*

Le Fonticine SAN LORENZO *TUS-CAN/BOLOGNESE* Silvano Bruci's trattoria is *the* place to go for Italian soul food, based on his wife's Bolog-nese family recipes. *Via Nazionale 79R.* ☎ *055-282106. Entrees 8.50€–19€. AE, DC, MC, V. Lunch, dinner Tues–Sat. Closed 2 weeks in Aug. Bus: 12, 25, 33, 80.*

★ **Le Mossacce** CENTRO STORICO *TUSCAN/FLORENTINE* This noisy, tra-ditional Florentine trattoria has a short menu that only features Tuscan basics like *ribollita* (mixed veg soup-stew) and *spezzatino* (veal stew). *Via del Proconsolo 55R.* ☎ *055-294361. Entrees 5.50€–8.50€. AE, DC, MC, V. Lunch and dinner Mon–Fri. Closed Aug. Bus: A, 14, 23.*

Mamma Gina OLTRARNO *TUSCAN* The food isn't what it was when Mamma Gina was in charge, but her recipes still make this place an excellent choice for lunch near the Pitti Palace. *Borgo San Jacopo 37R.* ☎ *055-2396009. www.mamma gina.it. Entrees 10€–20€. AE, DC, MC, V. Lunch, dinner Mon–Sat. Closed 15 days in Aug. Bus: D.*

A traditional antipasti.

★ **Nerbone** SAN LORENZO *FLORENTINE* Hasten to this 1872 five-table dive for the *bagnato* (boiled beef sandwich) dipped in meat juices. *Mercato Centrale (Via dell'Ariento entrance, stand #292).* ☎ *055-219949. Entrees 4.50€–7€. No credit cards. Lunch Mon–Sat. Closed 2 weeks in Aug. Bus: 12, 25, 33, 80.*

★★★ **Ora d'Aria** SANTA CROCE *MODERN TUSCAN* Florence's chef of the moment Marco Stabile has worked in Sonoma and France, but the flavors in his design-savvy restaurant are staunchly Tuscan and always seasonal. *Via Ghibellina 3/cR.* ☎ *055-2001699. www.oradaria ristorante.com. Entrees 27€; menus 50€–60€. AE, MC, V. Dinner Mon–Sat. Closed Aug. Bus: 8, 13, 14, 31, 32, 33, 80.*

★ **Osteria del Caffè Italiano** SANTA CROCE *WINE BAR/TUSCAN* Umberto Montano's wine bar, in a 13th-century *palazzo*, has the city's best Tuscan *salumi* and fine wines by the glass. *Via Isola delle Stinche 11–13R.* ☎ *055-289368. Entrees 15€–22€. MC, V. Lunch, dinner Tues–Sun. Bus: A, 14.*

★ **Paoli** CENTRO STORICO *TUSCAN/ITALIAN* In an alley almost opposite Orsanmichele, this 1824 restaurant in 13th-century digs is touristy, but the Italian cuisine is superb. *Via dei Tavolini 12R.* ☎ *055-216215. Entrees 13€–28€. AE, DC, MC, V. Lunch, dinner Wed–Mon. Closed 3 weeks in Aug. Bus: A.*

★ **Pennello** CENTRO STORICO *FLORENTINE/ITALIAN* Florence's oldest trattoria is still going strong, with young Tuscan chefs and a vast *antipasti* table. *Via Dante Alighieri 4R.* ☎ *055-294848. Entrees 7.50€–15€. AE, DC, MC, V. Lunch, dinner Tues–Sat. Closed 3 weeks in Aug. Bus: A.*

★★ **kids Quattro Leoni** OLTRARNO *TUSCAN/FLORENTINE* A mixed local and tourist crowd pack this stylish Left Bank trattoria for perfectly executed regional dishes. *Via dei Vellutini 1R.* ☎ *055-218562. www.4leoni.com. Entrees 9€–15€. MC, V. Lunch Thurs–Tues, dinner daily. Bus: D.*

★ **Sabatini** SAN LORENZO *FLORENTINE/INTERNATIONAL* Tripe and beefsteak fans should make for this shrine to Tuscan meat. *Via de' Panzani 9A.* ☎ *055-211559. Entrees 15€–23€. AE, DC, MC, V. Lunch, dinner Tues–Sun. Bus: 1, 6, 7, 10, 11, 14, 17, 22, 23, 31, 32, 36, 37, 57.*

★★ **Santo Spirito** OLTRARNO *ITALIAN/FLORENTINE* Local specialties like salt cod with leeks share menu space with pizzas and large bowls of pasta at this smart little osteria. Service can be slow because everything's cooked from scratch. *Piazza Santo Spirito 16R.* ☎ *055-2382383. Entrees 12€–28€. AE, MC, V. Lunch, dinner daily. Bus: D.*

kids Tijuana SANTA CROCE *MEXICAN* Fajitas, burritos, nachos, and cerveza, and plenty of chili, just like it tastes south of the border. (Well, almost.) *Via Ghibellina 156R.* ☎ *055-2341330. www.tijuanaristorante.it. Entrees 7.50€–12€. Dinner daily. Bus: A, 14.*

The Best Lodging in Florence

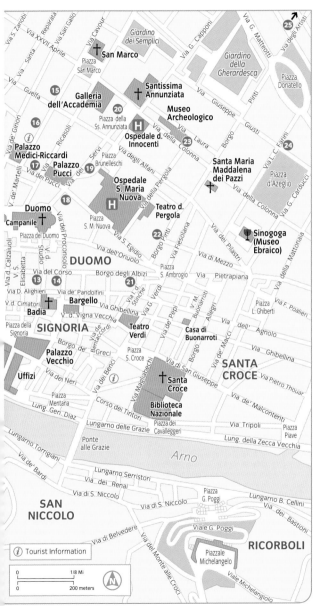

Hotel Best Bets

Best for Families
★★ Residence Hilda $$$–$$$$$
Via dei Servi 40 (p 59)

Best Boutique Hotel
★★ Gallery Hotel Art $$$–$$$$$
Vicolo dell'Oro 5 (p 57)

Most Luxurious Address
★★★ Grand Hotel $$$$$ Piazza
Ognissanti 1 (p 57)

Best Budget Choice
★★ Pensione Maria Luisa de'
Medici $$ Via del Corso 1 (p 58)

Best for a Quiet Night
★★ Regency $$$$$ Piazza M.
D'Azeglio 3 (p 58)

Best for Art Lovers
★ Relais Uffizi $$–$$$$ Chiasso
de' Baroncelli (p 58)

Best for Drivers Touring Tuscany
★ Villa Carlotta $$–$$$$ Via
Michele di Lando 3 (p 59)

Most Luxurious Enclave
★★★ Villa San Michele $$$$$ Via
Doccia 4, Fiesole (p 59)

Best View
★ Grand Hotel Cavour $$$–$$$$
Via del Pronconsolo 3 (p 57)

Best Location
★ Hermitage $$–$$$$ Vicolo
Marzio 1 (p 57)

Most Stylish Hotel
★★★ J. K. Place $$$$$ Piazza
Santa Maria Novella 7 (p 57)

Best B&B
★★ Tourist House Ghiberti $$–$$$
Via Bufalini 1 (p 59)

Best for Great Service
★★ Davanzati $$–$$$$ Via Porta
Rossa 5 (p 57)

Best Palazzo Living
★ Monna Lisa $$$–$$$$ Borgo
Pinti 27 (p 58)

The breakfast area at the Davanzati hotel.

Florence Hotels A to Z

kids Casci SAN LORENZO Antonio Rossini *(The Barber of Seville)* once stayed in this old hostelry near the Duomo. Renovations have upgraded it without destroying the old charm. Some family suites sleep four or five. *Via Cavour 13.* ☎ *055-211686. www. hotelcasci.com. 24 units. Doubles 90€–150€ w/breakfast. AE, DC, MC, V. Bus: 1, 6, 7, 10, 11, 17, 31, 32, 57.*

★★ kids Davanzati CENTRO STORICO From laptops and Play-Stations in each of the tasteful rooms to complimentary drinks with the family proprietors each evening, they've thought of it all at this most welcoming of *palazzo* hotels. *Via Porta Rossa 5 (at Piazza Davanzati).* ☎ *055-286666. www.hoteldavanzati. it. 21 units. Doubles 120€–312€ w/breakfast. AE, DC, MC, V. Bus: A.*

★★ Gallery Hotel Art CENTRO STORICO Florence's original boutique hotel, run by the Ferragamo fashion family, is a bastion of designer comfort. *Vicolo dell'Oro 5.* ☎ *055-27263. www.lungarnohotels.com. 74 units. Doubles 180€–460€ w/breakfast. AE, DC, MC, V. Bus: B.*

★★★ Grand Hotel CENTRO STORICO The Grand is sumptuous—with large bathrooms and Renaissance or Empire bedrooms embellished with silks, brocades, frescoes, and antiques. *Piazza Ognissanti 1.* ☎ *055-27161. www.luxury collection.com/grandflorence. 107 units. Doubles 295€–685€. AE, DC, MC, V. Bus: A, B.*

★ Grand Hotel Cavour CENTRO STORICO Almost opposite the Bargello, this 13th-century *palazzo's* rooftop terrace has stunning panoramic views. Traditional bedrooms are comfy, but some are small. *Via del Proconsolo 3.* ☎ *055-266271.*

www.albergocavour.it. 105 units. Doubles 155€–400€ w/breakfast. AE, DC, MC, V. Bus: 14, 23.

★★ Helvetia & Bristol CENTRO STORICO This luxury Belle Epoque *palazzo*, in the city's elegant fashion quarter, has lavish bedrooms and a Winter Garden. *Via de' Pescioni 2.* ☎ *055-26651. www.royaldemeure. com. 67 units. Doubles 220€–560€. AE, DC, MC, V. Bus: 6, 22.*

★ Hermitage CENTRO STORICO This characterful hotel next to the Museo Diocesano has a divine roof garden above the Ponte Vecchio and small to midsized rooms with 17th- and 19th-century antiques. Ring them for a deal. *Vicolo Marzio 1 (at Piazza del Pesce).* ☎ *055-287216. www.hermitagehotel.com. 28 units. Doubles 120€–245€ w/breakfast. MC, V. Bus: B.*

★★ Il Guelfo Bianco SAN LORENZO Each room in this sympathetically converted 16th-century *palazzo* is different, but the friendly welcome is universal. *Via Cavour 29.* ☎ *055-288330. www.ilguelfobianco.it. 40 units. Doubles 82€–235€ w/breakfast. AE, DC, MC, V. Bus: 1, 6, 7, 10, 11, 17, 31, 32, 57.*

★★★ J. K. Place CENTRO STORICO This architectural gem has elegant rooms with four-poster beds and fireplaces, a glass-covered courtyard, a rooftop terrace, and a splendid library. *Piazza Santa Maria Novella 7.* ☎ *055-2645181. www. jkplace.com. 20 units. Doubles 350€–500€ w/breakfast. AE, DC, MC, V. Bus: A, 11, 36, 37.*

La Scaletta OLTRARNO If you like vintage charm, check into this aging *palazzo* across the Arno and hang out on its flower-decked terrace, with a view down into the Boboli Garden. *Via Guicciardini 13.* ☎ *055-283028. www.hotellascaletta.it. 17 units. Doubles 70€–140€ w/breakfast. MC, V. Bus: D.*

★ **Locanda Orchidea** SANTA CROCE If you need to flop on a tight budget but don't want to compromise on location, there's nowhere cleaner and friendlier at the price. Rooms at the back overlook a quiet garden-courtyard. *Borgo degli Albizi 11.* ☎ *055-2480346. www.hotel orchideaflorence.it. 7 units. Doubles 50€–75€. No credit cards. Bus: A.*

★ **Loggiato dei Serviti** CENTRO STORICO A monastery in 1527, this comfortably elegant hotel has beamed or vaulted ceilings and terra-cotta floors on an iconic Brunelleschi square. Book online for the keenest rates. *Piazza SS. Annunziata 3.* ☎ *055-289592. www.loggiato deiservitihotel.it. 38 units. Doubles 95€–240€ w/breakfast. AE, DC, MC, V. Bus: C, 6, 31, 32.*

★★ **Mario's** SAN LORENZO This spotless, home-style city inn has small to midsized bedrooms stylishly decorated and furnished for comfort. *Via Faenza 89.* ☎ *055-216801. www.hotelmarios.com. 16 units. Doubles 82€–165€ w/breakfast. AE, DC, MC, V. Bus: 12, 25, 33, 80.*

The library at J.K. Place.

★ **Monna Lisa** SANTA CROCE Behind a severe facade, this art-laden 14th-century *palazzo* takes top prize for old-world elegance. Web prices are cheaper than booking direct. *Borgo Pinti 27.* ☎ *055-2479751. www.monnalisa.it. 50 units. Doubles 199€–390€ w/breakfast. AE, DC, MC, V. Bus: C.*

★ **Morandi alla Crocetta** CENTRO STORICO In a 16th-century convent, this quaint *pensione* evokes the era when British travelers sought private homelike lodgings with family heirlooms. Four rooms have their own terraces. *Via Laura 50.* ☎ *055-2344747. www.hotelmorandi.it. 10 units. Doubles 120€–220€. AE, DC, MC, V. Bus: C, 6, 31, 32.*

★★ **Pensione Maria Luisa de' Medici** CENTRO STORICO Step back in time at this B&B inside a 1645 *palazzo* festooned with Baroque art. It's one of the city's most sought-after, with large bedrooms (most with shared baths) up three flights of stairs. *Via del Corso 1.* ☎ *055-280048. 9 units. Doubles 80€–95€ w/breakfast. No credit cards. Bus: A, 14, 23.*

★★ **Regency** SANTA CROCE A citadel of taste and exclusivity away from the center, this intimate hideaway was converted from two posh 19th-century mansions on a leafy square at the eastern edge of town. It's adorned with antiques, carpets, wall fabrics, marble-clad bathrooms, and mirrored wall panels. *Piazza M. D'Azeglio 3.* ☎ *055-245247. www.regency-hotel.com. 34 units. Doubles 330€–500€ w/breakfast. AE, DC, MC, V. Bus: 6, 31, 32.*

★ **Relais Uffizi** CENTRO STORICO Tucked down an alley behind the Loggia dei Lanzi, this hotel is a great value, in a 15th-century building with homey, midsized to large rooms and marble baths. *Chiasso de' Baroncelli.* ☎ *055-2676239.*

Guest quarters at Hotel Torre Guelfa.

www.relaisuffizi.it. 16 units. Doubles 140€–250€ w/breakfast. AE, DC, MC, V. Bus: B.

★★ **kids** **Residence Hilda** CENTRO STORICO These bright, modern apartments come fully equipped and with a great location between the Duomo and SS. Annunziata. No minimum stay. *Via dei Servi 40.* ☎ 055-288021. www.residencehilda.com. 12 units. Apartments 190€–350€. AE, MC, V. Bus: C, 14, 23.

Residenza dei Pucci CENTRO STORICO This restored 19th-century town house close to the Duomo has ample rooms with high ceilings, French tapestries, four-poster beds, and marble baths. *Via dei Pucci 9.* ☎ 055-281886. www.residenza deipucci.com. 12 units. Doubles 80€–170€ w/breakfast. AE, MC, V. Bus: 14, 23.

Tornabuoni Beacci CENTRO STORICO In a 16th-century palace, this timeworn Tornabuoni favorite faces another century with genteel grace. Ask for a recently updated room. *Via de' Tornabuoni 3.* ☎ 055-212645. www.tornabuoni hotels.com. 28 units. Doubles 130€–280€ w/breakfast. AE, DC, MC, V. Bus: A, B, 6, 11, 36, 37.

★ **Torre Guelfa** CENTRO STORICO Florence's tallest privately owned tower hosts this 14th-century *palazzo* hotel near the Ponte Vecchio. Rooms have canopied iron beds. *Borgo SS.* Apostoli 8. ☎ 055-2396338. www. hoteltorreguelfa.com. 15 units. Doubles 150€–210€ w/breakfast. AE, MC, V. Bus: B.

★★ **Tourist House Ghiberti** CENTRO STORICO Large, modern rooms with clean lines but a traditional Florentine flavor characterize this new B&B near the Duomo. There's also a shared guest jacuzzi for tired feet. *Via Bufalini 1.* ☎ 055-284858. www.touristhouseghiberti.com. 6 units. Doubles 93€–158€ w/breakfast. AE, DC, MC, V. Bus: 14, 23.

★ **Villa Carlotta** OLTRARNO This retreat in a residential neighborhood close to the Porta Romana is lavishly renovated with antiques and crystal. One un-Florentine touch: there's a car park. *Via Michele di Lando 3.* ☎ 055-2336134. www. hotelvillacarlotta.it. 32 units. Doubles 110€–320€ w/breakfast. AE, DC, MC, V. Bus: 12, 13, 38.

★★★ **Villa San Michele** FIESOLE Behind a facade designed by Michelangelo, this 15th-century Franciscan monastery is now a swank enclave in the hills, with a heated outdoor pool, lush Italian gardens, and a loggia restaurant with panoramic views over Florence. *Via Doccia 4 (off Via Fra' Angelico), Fiesole.* ☎ 055-5678200. www.villasanmichele.com. 46 units. Doubles 485€–1,070€ w/breakfast. AE, DC, MC, V. Closed mid-Nov to mid-Mar. Bus: 7.

The Best Shopping in Florence

Alice Atelier 13
Babele 7
Beltrami 8
Bojola 12
Brandimarte 2
Coin 19
Cose del '900 3
Emilio Pucci 10
(ethic) 21
Galleria Masini 5
Giovanni Baccani 6
Gucci 9
Il Papiro 16
La Rinascente 18
Mercato Centrale 14
Mercato di
   San Lorenzo 15
Officina Profumo-
   Farmaceutica di
   Santa Maria Novella 4
Paperback Exchange 17
Pineider 20
Richard Ginori 1
Salvatore Ferragamo 11
Vestri 22

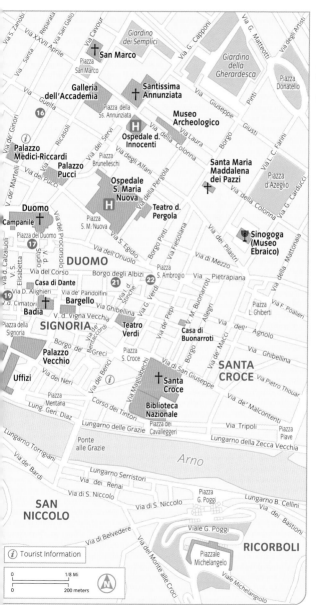

San Marco
Piazza San Marco
Giardino dei Semplici
Giardino della Gherardesca
Piazza Donatello
Galleria dell'Accademia
16
Santissima Annunziata
Piazza della Ss. Annunziata
Museo Archeologico
Palazzo Medici-Riccardi
Palazzo Pucci
Ospedale d. Innocenti
H
Piazza Brunelleschi
Santa Maria Maddalena dei Pazzi
Piazza d'Azeglio
Ospedale S. Maria Nuova
H
Piazza S. M. Nuova
Duomo
Campanile
Piazza del Duomo
17
Teatro d. Pergola
Sinogoga (Museo Ebraico)
DUOMO
Via dell'Oriuolo
Borgo degli Albizi
21
22
Piazza S. Ambrogio
Via Pietrapiana
Piazza L. Ghiberti
Casa di Dante
19
Badia
Bargello
Teatro Verdi
Piazza S. Croce
Casa di Buonarroti
SANTA CROCE
SIGNORIA
Palazzo Vecchio
Uffizi
Piazza Mentana
Lung. Gen. Diaz
Santa Croce
Biblioteca Nazionale
Piazza dei Cavalleggeri
Piazza Piave
Ponte alle Grazie
Arno
SAN NICCOLO
Piazza G. Poggi
Viale G. Poggi
RICORBOLI
Piazzale Michelangelo

Tourist Information

0   1/8 Mi
0   200 meters

Shopping Best Bets

Pucci's outpost in Florence.

Best **Modern Art Gallery**
★★★ Galleria Masini, Piazza Goldoni 6R (p 63)

Best for **Florentine High Fashion**
★★ Gucci, Via de' Tornabuoni 73R (p 64)

Best for **Leather Goods**
★★★ Beltrami, Via della Vigna Nuova 70R (p 64)

Best **Food Market**
★★ Mercato Centrale, Piazza del Mercato Centrale (p 65)

Best for **Young Fashions**
★ (ethic), Borgo degli Albizzi 37R (p 64)

Best for **Paper Goods**
★★ Pineider, Piazza della Signoria (p 65)

Best **Beauty Products**
★★★ Officina Profumo-Farmaceutica di Santa Maria Novella, Via della Scala 16 (p 63)

Best **Shoes for Men and Women**
★★★ Salvatore Ferragamo, Via de' Tornabuoni 14R (p 65)

Best for **Silver**
★★★ Brandimarte, Viale Ariosto 11/cR (p 65)

Best **Local Craftsmanship**
★★ Alice Atelier, Via Faenza 72R (p 63)

VAT Refund

Visitors from non-European Union countries who spend 155€ or more at any one shop are entitled to a value-added tax (VAT) refund worth 11% to 13% of the total. To get a refund, pick up a tax-free form from the retailer. Present your unused purchases for inspection at the airport Customs Office (Dogana) or your point of departure. The inspector will stamp your form, enabling you to pick up a cash refund (minus commission) on the spot.

Florence Shopping A to Z

Florence is known for its showrooms of famous designers and for its artisan workshops, turning out jewelry and leather of the highest quality. The most fashionable shops—and the most expensive—are clustered along **Via de' Tornabuoni.** There you'll find big international names like **Prada** (51R; ☎ 055-283439), **Giorgio Armani** (48R; ☎ 055-219041), **Celine** (26R; ☎ 055-2645521), **MaxMara** (68–70R; ☎ 055-214133), and **Versace** (15R; ☎ 055-2396167). **Via della Vigna Nuova** and **Via degli Strozzi** also pack a high style quotient.

Art
★★★ Galleria Masini CENTRO STORICO Florence's oldest gallery is the best, representing more than 500 of the country's avant-garde oil painters. *Piazza Goldoni 6R.* ☎ *055-294000. www.masiniart. com. AE, DC, MC, V. Bus: A, B, 6, 11, 36, 37.*

Beauty Products
★★★ Officina Profumo-Farmaceutica di Santa Maria Novella CENTRO STORICO Herbal secrets known to the Medici are still sold here in a wonderfully antique atmosphere—potpourris, perfumes, scented soaps, and more. *Via della Scala 16.* ☎ *055-216276. www.smnovella.it/English.html. AE, MC, V. Bus: A, 11, 36, 37.*

Books
★ Babele CENTRO STORICO Florence's best art bookshop also sells homemade stationery and crafts. *Via delle Belle Donne 41R.* ☎ *055-283312. AE, DC, MC, V. Bus: A, 6, 11, 22, 36, 37.*

kids Paperback Exchange CENTRO STORICO New and used titles, all in English. *Via delle Oche 4R.* ☎ *055-2478856. www.papex.it. AE, DC, MC, V. Bus: 14, 23.*

Fashionistas haunt the shops of Via Tornabuoni.

Ceramics & Crafts
★★ kids Alice Atelier SAN LORENZO Handmade theatrical masks in Venetian *Carnevale* and *Commedia dell'arte* styles. *Via Faenza 72R.* ☎ *055-287370. www.alicemasks.com. AE, MC, V. Bus: 12, 25, 33, 80.*

★★ Richard Ginori SESTO FIORENTINO Exquisite designer porcelain and refined bone china are sold in this western suburb outlet. Good buys in Murano glass. *Via Cesare 21, Sesto Fiorentino.* ☎ *055-4210472. www.richardginori1735. com. AE, DC, MC, V. Bus: 18.*

Chocolate

★ kids **Vestri** SANTA CROCE
There's no mistaking the aroma . . .
cocoa, made into all shapes and
sizes, even granita and cold drinking
chocolate, at this artisan choco-
latier. *Borgo degli Albizzi 11R.*
☎ 055-2340374. www.vestri.it.
MC, V. Bus: A, 14, 23.

Department Stores

★ kids **Coin** CENTRO STORICO This
department store in a 16th-century
palazzo sells everything from affordable clothing for men, women and
children, to Italian-designed
kitchenware, to MAC cosmetics.
Via dei Calzaiuoli 56A. ☎ 055-
280531. www.coin.it. *AE, DC, MC,
V. Bus: A.*

★ **La Rinascente** CENTRO
STORICO This six-storey emporium
sells top Italian designers at affordable prices. *Piazza della Repubblica 1.*
☎ 055-219113. *AE, DC, MC, V.
Bus: A.*

Fashion

★★ **Emilio Pucci** CENTRO
STORICO Even Marilyn Monroe left a
request to be buried in her favorite
Pucci dress. Their bright, busy pat-
terns are in fashion again. *Via de'
Tornabuoni 20R.* ☎ 055-2658082.

www.pucci.com. *AE, DC, MC, V.
Bus: A, 6, 11, 36, 37.*

★ kids **(ethic)** SANTA CROCE Edgy
styles for men, women, and children. They also carry the latest CDs,
soaps, fashion magazines, and
more. *Borgo degli Albizzi 37R.*
☎ 055-2344413. *MC, V. Bus: A.*

★★★ **Gucci** CENTRO STORICO
Unforgettable luxury leather goods
and high fashion in the city Gucci
calls home. *Via de' Tornabuoni 73R.*
☎ 055-264011. www.gucci.com. *AE,
DC, MC, V. Bus: A, 6, 11, 36, 37.*

Glass

★★ **Cose del '900** OLTRARNO
Exquisite original Art Deco objects,
including Murano glass. *Borgo San
Jacopo 45R.* ☎ 055-283491. *AE, MC,
V. Bus: D.*

Leather

★★★ **Beltrami** CENTRO STORICO
This world-famous, Florence-based
leathermaker offers stunning
footwear, handbags, belts, brief-
cases, and luggage at good prices.
Via della Vigna Nuova 70R. ☎ 055-
2877779. *AE, DC, MC, V. Bus: 6.*

★★ **Bojola** CENTRO STORICO A
leading retailer of Florentine leather
goods. The store pioneered the
1960s trend of combining leather

Dried fruits and nuts for sale at the Mercato Centrale.

Leather goods are plentiful, well-crafted bargains in the San Lorenzo market.

and cotton fabric. *Via dei Rondinelli 25R.* ☎ *055-211155. www.bojola.it. AE, DC, MC, V. Bus: 1, 6, 7, 10, 11, 14, 17, 22, 23, 31, 32, 36, 37, 57.*

Markets

★★ Mercato Centrale SAN LORENZO Wine, olive oil, porcini mushroons, and pecorino cheese— it's all on sale on two floors of Europe's largest covered food hall. *Piazza del Mercato Centrale. No phone. Bus: 12, 25, 33, 80.*

★ kids Mercato di San Lorenzo SAN LORENZO At the most bustling market in Tuscany, vendors hawk quality leather goods and tacky souvenirs. You might even find designer-label accessories at affordable prices. *Piazza San Lorenzo and streets around. Bus: 1, 6, 7, 10, 11, 14, 17, 23, 31, 32, 57.*

Paper & Stationery

★★ Il Papiro CENTRO STORICO Sumptuous stationery, photo frames, and more at this upmarket chain. *Via Cavour 55R.* ☎ *055-6499151. www.ilpapirofirenze.it. AE, MC, V. Bus: 1, 6, 7, 10, 11, 17, 31, 32, 57.*

★★ Pineider CENTRO STORICO Since 1774 customers from

Napoleon to Elizabeth Taylor have ordered personal stationery, greeting cards, and handcrafted diaries here. *Piazza della Signoria (at Calimaruzza).* ☎ *055-284655. www. pineider.it. AE, DC, MC, V. Bus: A, B.*

Prints & Engravings

★ Giovanni Baccani CENTRO STORICO Collectors have been flocking to "The Blue Shop" since 1903 for exquisite prints, engravings of old Florentine scenes, triptychs, and handmade frames and boxes. *Via della Vigna Nuova 75R.* ☎ *055-214467. AE, DC, MC, V. Bus: 6.*

Shoes

★★★ Salvatore Ferragamo CENTRO STORICO Shoes (and bags) are big news here, with some world-class fashionwear and accessories for men and women. *Via de' Tornabuoni 14R.* ☎ *055-292123. www.salvatoreferragamo.it. AE, DC, MC, V. Bus: A, B, 6, 11, 36, 37.*

Silver

★★★ Brandimarte OLTRARNO Heirloom-quality goods include goblets and flower vases. *Viale Ariosto 11/cR.* ☎ *055-23041. AE, DC, MC, V. Bus: D, 6, 12, 13.*

The Best **Nightlife/A&E** in Florence

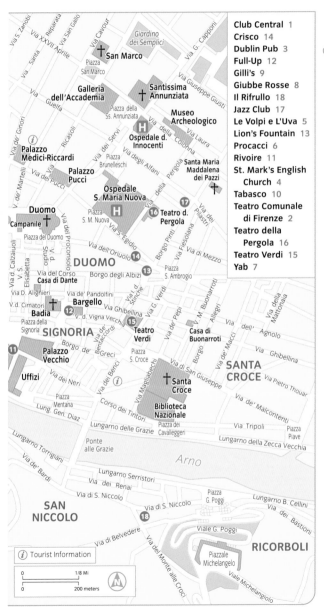

Club Central 1
Crisco 14
Dublin Pub 3
Full-Up 12
Gilli's 9
Giubbe Rosse 8
Il Rifrullo 18
Jazz Club 17
Le Volpi e L'Uva 5
Lion's Fountain 13
Procacci 6
Rivoire 11
St. Mark's English
   Church 4
Tabasco 10
Teatro Comunale
   di Firenze 2
Teatro della
   Pergola 16
Teatro Verdi 15
Yab 7

The Best of Florence

Nightlife/A&E Best Bets

Centro Storico's cafes bustle at night.

Best Wine Bar
★ Le Volpi e l'Uva, Piazza de' Rossi 1 (p 69)

Best Cafe
★★ Gilli's, Piazza della Repubblica 39R (p 69)

Best Dance Club
★ Club Central, Via Fosso Macinate 2 (p 70)

Best Gay Club
★ Tabasco, Piazza Santa Cecilia 3 (p 70)

Best Irish Pub
★ Dublin Pub, Via Faenza 27 (p 69)

Best for Jazz and Blues
★ Jazz Club, Via Nuova de' Caccini 3 (p 70)

Best Theater
★★ Teatro della Pergola, Via della Pergola 12–32 (p 70)

Best Opera & Ballet
★★★ Teatro Comunale di Firenze, Corso Italia 16 (p 70)

Best Cultural Festival
★★★ Maggio Musicale (p 70)

Club & Concert Tips

Italian clubs are cliquey—people usually go in groups to hang out and dance with one another. Plenty of flesh is on display, but single travelers hoping to find dance partners may be disappointed.

Florence is wanting for the musical cachet or grand opera houses of Milan, Venice, and Rome, but the city has two symphony orchestras and a fine music school in Fiesole. Florence's theaters are respectable, and most major touring companies stop in town on their way through Italy. **St. Mark's English Church** (☎ 340-8119192; www.concertoclassico.info), in Oltrarno, also runs an opera and sacred music season. Each summer **Opera Festival** (☎ 055-5978309; www.festivalopera.it) stages operas and musicals in atmospheric locations like the Giardino di Boboli.

Tickets for most cultural and music events are available through **Boxol** (☎ 055-210804; www.boxol.it).

Bars & Pubs

★ **Dublin Pub** SAN LORENZO Irish pubs are the rage in Florence, and this is the best of the lot. *Via Faenza 27.* ☎ *055-2741571. www.dublin pub.it. Bus: 12, 25, 33, 80.*

★ **Il Rifrullo** OLTRARNO This laid-back bar is right at the social center of a buzzy Olttarno corner. It also serves snacks. *Via di San Niccolò 57R.* ☎ *055-2342621. Bus: D, 12, 13, 23.*

Lion's Fountain SANTA CROCE Whatever sports you're missing back home, it's probably on the screens at this popular expat pub hangout. *Borgo degli Albizzi 34R.* ☎ *055-2344412. www.thelions fountain.com. Bus: A, 14, 23.*

★★ **Le Volpi e L'Uva** OLTRARNO Over 50 Tuscan vintages by the glass draw them in to this quirky wine bar in a tiny piazza behind Santa Felicità church. *Piazza de' Rossi 1.* ☎ *055-2398132. www. levolpieluva.com. Bus: D.*

Cafes

★★ **Gilli's** CENTRO STORICO Dating from 1733, this is the oldest, most beautiful cafe in Florence. *Risorgimento* leaders convened here in the 1850s to plot the unification of Italy. *Piazza della Repubblica 39R.* ☎ *055-213896. Bus: A.*

★★ **Giubbe Rosse** CENTRO STORICO This fabled retreat of the Tuscan literati has been going strong since 1888. American breakfasts (8am–11am) are a specialty. *Piazza della Repubblica 13–14R.* ☎ *055-212280. Bus: A.*

★★ kids **Procacci** CENTRO STORICO This darling cafe/bar is beloved by *fashionistas*. Its specialty is *panini tartufati*, egg-shaped rolls filled with white truffle paste. *Via de' Tornabuoni 64R.* ☎ *055-211656. Bus: A, 6, 11, 22, 36, 37.*

★★ **Rivoire** CENTRO STORICO The tables of this classy cafe open onto one of the world's iconic squares. Stick to light snacks and drinks and

Gilli's, the city's oldest cafe, popular by day and night.

ignore the so-so main dishes. *Piazza della Signoria 4R.* ☎ *055-214412. Bus: B.*

Clubs

★ **Full-Up** SANTA CROCE Sugar daddies meet hot models in this old cellar with a small dance floor where DJs play hip-hop, house, or glam depending what night you show up. *Via della Vigna Vecchia 23-25R.* ☎ *055-293006. www.full upclub.com.5€–20€ cover. Bus: A, 14, 23.*

★ **Club Central** WEST FLORENCE This disco lounge close to the Cascine hosts an eclectic bunch of nights, ranging from hip-hop to '80s house. Outside dancefloors really kick off in summer. *Via Fosso Macinate 2.* ☎ *340-3455941. www. centralfirenze.it. 25€ cover. Bus: 1, 9, 12, 16, 26, 27, 72, 80.*

Yab CENTRO STORICO This glamorous hall of mirrors has been a popular dance club since the 1960s. Expect 20-somethings shaking their stuff, beats, and a rope line. *Via Sassetti 5R.* ☎ *055-215160. www.yab.it. 20€ cover. Bus: A, 6, 22.*

A poster outside the Teatro della Pergola.

Gay Bars & Clubs

Crisco SANTA CROCE The most famous men-only cruising bar in Tuscany. Mr. Right is waiting. *Via Sant'Egidio 43R.* ☎ *055-2480580. Bus: 14, 23.*

★ **Tabasco** CENTRO STORICO The oldest gay dance club in Italy lives up to its fiery name, with pumping beats, strobe lights, and Tuscan studs. *Piazza Santa Cecilia 3.* ☎ *055-213000. www.tabascogay. it.13€ cover. Bus: B.*

Jazz

★ **Jazz Club** SANTA CROCE The best live jazz and blues in town, in an atmospheric basement. Closed July and August. *Via Nuova de' Caccini 3.* ☎ *055-2479700. www.jazz clubfirenze.com. Membership 8€. Bus: C.*

Theater

★★ **Teatro della Pergola** SANTA CROCE This is the major classic theater of Tuscany, but you'd better speak Italian. *Via della Pergola 12–32.* ☎ *055-22641. www.pergola. firenze.it. Tickets 14.50€–29€. Bus: C, 6, 31, 32.*

Opera & Ballet

★★★ **Teatro Comunale di Firenze/Maggio Musicale Fiorentino** CENTRO STORICO This is Florence's main cultural venue for opera, ballet, and classical concerts, and home of the Maggio Musicale. *Corso Italia 16.* ☎ *055-2779350. www.maggiofiorentino.it. Tickets 15€–85€. Bus: B.*

★★ **Teatro Verdi** SANTA CROCE Expect everything from Tchaikovsky to *High School Musical* at the home of the Orchestra della Toscana. *Via Ghibellina 99.* ☎ *055-212320. www.teatroverdifirenze.it. Tickets 17€–50€. Bus: A, C, 14, 23.* ●

The Best of Tuscany **in Three Days**

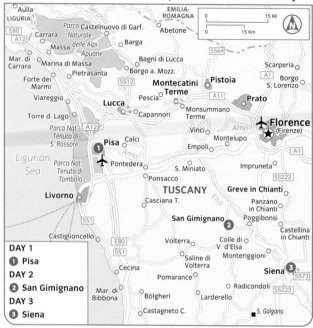

DAY 1
1 Pisa
DAY 2
2 San Gimignano
DAY 3
3 Siena

If you have only 3 days in Tuscany, you'll want to focus on Pisa, with its gravity-defying tower; San Gimignano, known for its medieval "skyscrapers;" and Siena, Tuscany's best repository of Gothic art and architecture. From Florence, you'll shoot 81km (50 miles) west to Pisa, for day 1; 92km (57 miles) southeast to San Gimignano for day 2; and 40km (24 miles) southeast again to Siena. START: **Florence. Trip length: 283km (174 mile) loop.**

Travel Tip

For detailed information on sights and recommended hotels and restaurants in this chapter, see the individual sections on Arezzo, Cortona, Lucca, Montepulciano, Pienza, Pisa, San Gimignano, Siena, and Volterra in chapter 6, "Charming Tuscan Towns & Villages."

Pisa is an hour west of Florence by car. Follow signs for the four-lane FI–PI–LI *raccordo*.

1 ★★★ kids **Pisa.** Pisa is one of the easiest Tuscan cities to explore, because nearly all the major attractions center around Piazza del Duomo (also known as the Campo dei Miracoli—the "Field of Miracles"). Your half-hour in and on the

Previous page: The rooftops of Lucca and beyond.

Leaning Tower, or *Torre Pendente*, is a unique, though expensive, experience. You certainly shouldn't miss the **Duomo** (cathedral) or **Battistero** (baptistery). The **Camposanto** (burial ground) provides a more contemplative contrast. The **Museo dell'Opera del Duomo** (cathedral museum) and **Museo delle Sinopie** are must-sees for anyone with a keen interest in painting and sculpture. Because everything is tightly packed on the Campo, you'll be left with time to enjoy the "real" heart of Pisa, closer to the river. *The tourist office is inside the Museo dell'Opera del Duomo at Piazza Arcivescovado 8 (☎ 050-560464; www.pisaturismo.it).*

Travel Tip

The most economical way to cover the Campo dei Miracoli is with an **Opera pass,** available from ticket offices on the piazza. For 10€, you'll get into everything except the Tower. Alternatively, it's 6€ for any two monuments.

After a night of Pisan fare at a local trattoria (I recommend the seafood at **Porton Rosso**), bed down and head out the following morning to San Gimignano.

For more coverage of sights, hotels, restaurants, shops, and nightlife in Pisa, see p 150 of chapter 6.

From Pisa, head east along the FI–PI–LI *raccordo* until the S429 turnoff at Ponte a Elsa. Take the S429 southeast as far as Certaldo; San Gimignano is signposted on a scenic road south from here.

2 ★★ kids **San Gimignano.** Like Pisa, San Gimignano makes for a doable day trip because its major attractions are tightly packed—as long as you've arrived early. Once you've parked and dropped your bags at the hotel, you can easily get around the town, with its 13 medieval towers, in a day. The Centro Storico centers around the magnificent twin squares of Piazza del Duomo and Piazza della Cisterna. *The tourist office is at*

A view of the Campo from behind bell.

San Gimignano's medieval towers overlooking the hills of Central Tuscany.

Piazza del Duomo 1 (☎ 0577-940008; www.sangimignano.com).
Undoubtedly, the art and architecture highlight is the **Collegiata,**

A cyclist crossing the Arno in Pisa.

no longer a proper "cathedral" because it doesn't have a bishop's seat. **Sant'Agostino** and the **Museo Civico,** as well as the ascent of the **Torre Grossa,** are all within a few minutes' walk. You should have time left for a real-life horror show at the **Museo della Tortura.** Teens will love it, especially if you've paused for an unforgettable ice cream at **Gelateria "di Piazza"** beforehand.

For detailed coverage of sights, hotels, restaurants, shops, and nightlife in San Gimignano, see p 156 in chapter 6.

If you're planning a dose of Slow Food heaven at **Dorandó,** be sure to book ahead. After dinner, stroll the unique historic core: With the day-trippers gone, and just you left in town, it's a place of unparalleled magic.

Siena is 40km (24 miles) southeast of San Gimignano. Head east on the S324 to meet the Firenze–Siena *raccordo* at Poggibonsi, then south to Siena. Enter town via the "Siena Ovest" exit.

③ ★★★ **Siena.** Seeing Siena in a day is the biggest challenge of your trip. Begin at the functional and spiritual heart of town, scallop-shaped

Piazza del Campo, the civic heart of Siena.

Piazza del Campo. The Lorenzetti and Martini frescoes at the **Museo Civico** (inside the Palazzo Pubblico) should be your first stop. Serious Sienese art fans should also stop in at the **Pinacoteca Nazionale,** Siena's picture gallery. After lunch, head for the cathedral complex centered around Piazza del Duomo. You can easily spend 3 hours seeing the **Duomo,** the **Museo dell'Opera Metropolitana** (home of Duccio's *Maestà*), and the **Battistero.** The former hospital of **Santa Maria della Scala,** opposite the Duomo, is a great spot to end your day.

If time remains, squeeze in some shopping and cafe time. Siena is renowned for its bakery products.

For detailed coverage of sights, hotels, restaurants, shops, and nightlife in Siena, see p 162 of chapter 6.

With just 1 night in Siena, sleep close to the center to maximize your time. The **Chiostro del**

Carmine or nearby **Palazzo Ravizza** tick most boxes for travelers on a regular budget.

To return to Florence, where you began this whirlwind tour, take the Firenze–Siena *raccordo* north. Total distance is 70km (43 miles).

Siena's landmark Torre del Mangia.

The Best of Tuscany **in One Week**

DAY 1
1. Lucca
DAY 2
2. Pisa
DAY 3
3. San Gimignano
DAY 4 & 5
4. Siena
5. Monteriggioni
DAY 6
6. Pienza
7. Montepulciano
DAY 7
8. Arezzo

An extra 4 days in Tuscany means you can experience four more towns, because driving distances in the region are short and manageable. This weeklong itinerary expands on the 3-day tour to include Lucca, with its Roman streetplan ensconced behind medieval ramparts; Pienza, the "ideal Renaissance city" commissioned by Pope Pius II in the 15th century; Montepulciano, which yields one of the world's best wines, Vino Nobile; and Arezzo, home of the greatest fresco cycle in Tuscany. This itinerary should leave you time to relax a bit at most of your stops. START: **Florence. Trip length: 407km (282 mile) loop.**

From Florence, Lucca is 72km (45 miles) west on the A11.

1 ★★ **kids Lucca.** At one time, Lucca was the unofficial capital of Tuscany, and a Roman colony known to Caesar and Pompey. Today, it's celebrated for the best-preserved Renaissance ramparts in Europe. I

recommend you start by circumnavigating them on a bicycle.

After your ride, you can see the highlights of Lucca close-up: though it's light on first-class museums, the town shelters some of Tuscany's loveliest churches. Try to visit the **Cattedrale di San Martino,**

San Frediano, and **San Michele in Foro,** if only to check out their Pisan-Romanesque facades. Leave yourselves time for one of Lucca's great pleasures: wandering the main pedestrian shopping street, **Via Fillungo.**

There are plenty of trattorias to choose from to dine on Lucchese fare that evening, before bedding down for the night. Stay inside the walls if you can.

For detailed coverage of sights, hotels, restaurants, shops, and nightlife in Lucca, see p 134 of chapter 6.

Leave early and drive 22km (14 miles) southwest on the S12r to:

➋ ★★★ kids **Pisa.** For detailed suggestions on how to make the most of Pisa in a day, see Day 1 in "The Best of Tuscany in Three Days," p 72.

For detailed coverage of sights, hotels, restaurants, shops, and nightlife in Pisa, see p 150 of chapter 6.

From Pisa, head east along the FI–PI–LI *raccordo* to the S429 turnoff at Ponte a Elsa. Take the S429 southeast as far as Certaldo; San Gimignano is signposted on a road south.

San Gimignano's town square.

➌ ★★ kids **San Gimignano.** Arrive in San Gimignano in the morning and set about exploring the city, with its once-fortified medieval towers. For guidance, see Day 2 in "The Best of Tuscany in Three Days," p 72.

For detailed coverage of sights, hotels, restaurants, shops, and nightlife in San Gimignano, see p 156 of chapter 6.

Siena is 40km (24 miles) southeast of San Gimignano. Head east on the S324 to meet the Firenze–Siena *raccordo* at Poggibonsi, then south to Siena. Enter via the "Siena Ovest" exit.

A cyclist pedals the streets of Lucca.

Casa di Santa Caterina in Siena.

④ ★★★ Siena. With a full week at your disposal, you'll want to spend at least 2 days in Siena. It is the jewel of the Tuscan countryside, more alluring on a summer evening than even Florence. There's no Gothic city like it anywhere in the world.

On your first day, follow the outline for Day 3 in "The Best of Tuscany in Three Days," p 72. For your second day, you shouldn't miss the **Torre del Mangia,** if you haven't climbed it already. Then visit the

Casa di Santa Caterina, with mementos of Italy's patron saint, and **San Domenico,** a church also linked with St. Catherine, where you can see her preserved head.

Allow time in the afternoon for a short drive of 20km (12 miles) to **⑤ Monteriggioni,** the most perfectly preserved fortified village in Italy (full coverage, with driving directions, appears on p 170).

For detailed coverage of sights, hotels, restaurants, shops, and nightlife in Siena, see p 162 of chapter 6.

Leave Siena early, the morning of your sixth day, and drive southeast 55km (33 miles) on the S2 then S146 to:

⑥ ★ Pienza. You can see all of Pienza's major attractions in about 3 hours, before heading out for your next stopover. The highlights of this model Renaissance town are all in **Piazza Pio II,** chiefly the **Duomo, Museo Diocesano,** and **Palazzo Piccolomini.** Wine collectors shouldn't depart without at least looking in at the **Enoteca di Ghino.**

A rear view of Pienza's cathedral, designed by Pope Pius II.

San Biagio, outside Montepulciano.

For detailed coverage of sights, hotels, restaurants, shops, and nightlife, see p 146 of chapter 6.

Montepulciano is 14km (8¾ miles) east, on the S146.

⑦ ★★ Montepulciano. After the morning in Pienza, strike out for an afternoon in Montepulciano. Plan to arrive right after lunch, so you can see Montepulciano's attractions before nightfall. The unmissable sights here are the **Cattedrale,** the **Tempio di San Biagio** (just outside the gates), and the **Palazzo Nobili-Tarugi.** Leave time for tasting some Vino Nobile: **Gattavecchi** is my favorite.

For detailed coverage of sights, hotels, restaurants, shops, and nightlife in Montepulciano, see p 142 of chapter 6.

Leave Montepulciano first thing, driving 53km (33 miles) north to Arezzo. Head northeast on the S327 to the Firenze–Roma autostrada, then north until you reach the signposted exit.

⑧ ★★ Arezzo. For your final look at Tuscany, Arezzo won't disappoint; it's the chief reason to visit the northeastern part of the region. Its steep medieval streets were made for walking (in sensible shoes), but the chief attraction is painted inside the **Basilica di San Francesco:** Piero della Francesca's *Legend of the True Cross.* If you're rushed, you can skip the **Duomo,** but don't miss the **Pieve di Santa Maria,** crazy-sloping **Piazza Grande** or an ice cream at Arezzo's best *gelateria,* **Cremi.** For a memorable meal, a slightly modern end to your Tuscan culinary adventure, dine at **Miseria e Nobiltà.** If you're not due back in Florence until the following day, Arezzo also has a couple of stylish, central boutique hotels.

For detailed coverage of sights, hotels, restaurants, shops, and nightlife in Arezzo, see p 124 of chapter 6.

Arezzo is only 81km (50 miles) southeast of Florence, an easy drive up the A1.

Piazza Communale in Arezzo.

The Best of Tuscany **in Ten Days**

DAY 1
1 Lucca
DAY 2
2 Pisa
DAY 3
3 Volterra
DAY 4
4 San Gimignano   **DAY 8**
DAY 5 & 6   **8** Cortona
5 Siena   **DAY 9**
DAY 7   **9** Arezzo
6 Pienza   **DAY 10**
7 Montepulciano   **10** Greve in Chianti

This tour is similar to **Tuscany in 1 week,** with a few additional stops: Etruscan Volterra, presiding over the rolling Valdicecina; Cortona, another steeply pitched throwback to the Middle Ages; and Chianti Country, where you should have time to visit a vineyard or two before your return to Florence. START: **Florence. Trip length: 510km (305 miles) round-trip.**

From Florence, Lucca is 72km (45 miles) west on the A11.

1 ★★ kids **Lucca.** Head west from Florence for a 1-day visit to Lucca, celebrated for its intact Renaissance walls. A 1-day itinerary is detailed in Day 1, "The Best of Tuscany in One Week," p 76.

For detailed coverage of sights, hotels, restaurants, shops, and nightlife, see p 134 of chapter 6.

Leave Lucca early and drive 22km (14 miles) southwest on S12r to:

2 ★★★ kids **Pisa.** If you arrive early enough, you can see Pisa's sights before twilight, and then spend the night on the town. See Day 1, Pisa, in "The Best of Tuscany in Three Days," p 72.

For detailed coverage of sights, hotels, restaurants, shops, and nightlife, see p 150 of chapter 6.

On Volterra's city walls.

From Pisa, head east toward Florence on the FI-PI-LI and take the turn south at Ponsacco signposted for Volterra. Total distance is 65km (40 miles).

3 ★★ **Volterra.** If you arrive in the morning, you can cover Volterra's attractions in a day. Take in the unobtrusive **Duomo,** a major Etruscan treasure trove in the **Museo Guarnacci, San Francesco;** and best of all, the town's **Pinacoteca,** home of Rosso Fiorentino's iconic *Deposition.*

For detailed coverage of sights, hotels, restaurants, shops, and nightlife, see p 174 of chapter 6.

Head east 17km (11 miles) along the S68 as far as Castelsangimignano, then follow signs 13km (8 miles) north to:

4 ★★ kids **San Gimignano.** Get here early to do San Gimignano in a day. For the 1-day tour, see Day 2 in "The Best of Tuscany in Three Days," p 72.

For detailed coverage of sights, hotels, restaurants, shops, and nightlife, see p 156 of chapter 6.

Siena is 40km (24 miles) southeast of San Gimignano. Head east on the S324 to meet the Firenze–Siena *raccordo* at Poggibonsi, then south to Siena. Enter via the "Siena Ovest" exit.

5 ★★★ **Siena.** As a Tuscan destination, Siena is rivaled only by Florence. Because there is so much to see and do, schedule a 2-night stopover. See "The Best of Tuscany in One Week," p 76, for guidance.

For detailed coverage of sights, hotels, restaurants, shops, and nightlife, see p 162 of chapter 6.

Leave Siena early, the morning of your seventh day, and drive southeast on the S2 and S146 for 55km (33 miles) to:

6 ★ **Pienza.** The Renaissance town is compact enough to cover in a morning. See Pienza, in "The Best of Tuscany in One Week" (p 76). After lunch, continue to Montepulciano for the afternoon and night.

Souvenir gift bags in Montepulciano.

The Cortona countryside.

For detailed coverage of sights, hotels, restaurants, shops, and nightlife in Pienza, see p 146 of chapter 6.

From Pienza, take the S146 east for 13km (8 miles) to:

⑦ ★★ **Montepulciano.** For a half-day itinerary in Montepulciano, see Montepulciano in "The Best of Tuscany in One Week." Spend the night here and head onward in the morning.

For detailed coverage of sights, hotels, restaurants, shops, and nightlife, see p 142 of chapter 6.

From Montepulciano, head for Cortona, a distance of 45km (28 miles), via Bettolle and the Siena–Perugia *raccordo.*

⑧ ★★ kids **Cortona.** This medieval hilltown is major-league steep, but you can still do it in a day. The chief sights are a revamped **Museo dell'Accademia Etrusca e della Città (MAEC)** and sublime panels by Signorelli and Fra' Angelico at the **Museo Diocesano.** If you're fit, take a hike and finish your day with the views from high up on the **Fortezza Medicea.**

For complete coverage of Cortona, see p 128 in chapter 6.

From Cortona, drive north 34km (22 miles) on the S71 to:

⑨ ★★ **Arezzo.** Build your day here round the Piero della Francesca frescoes. For a 1-day itinerary, see Arezzo in "The Best of Tuscany in One Week."

For detailed coverage of Arezzo, see p 124 in chapter 6.

Drive northwest, following signs to Firenze. Take the autostrada northwest toward Florence, to the exit for Figline Valdarno. Follow a signposted route west to:

⑩ ★ **Greve in Chianti.** On your way back to Florence, make a detour to the good living of Chianti Country. Centered around **Piazza Matteotti,** Greve is riddled with wine shops *(enoteche),* and you'll have time to visit a winery or two in the surrounding hills. Our local favorites are **Vignamaggio,** just south of Greve, and **Vicchiomaggio,** just north.

For more coverage of Chianti Country, see p 90, "Tuscany for Food & Wine Lovers," and p 104, "Tuscany Outdoors," both in chapter 4.

Florence is 27km (17 miles) north of Greve on the S222. ●

The fertile vineyards outside Greve, in Chianti country.

4

The Best
Special-Interest
Tours of Tuscany

Tuscany for **Art & Architecture Lovers**

1 Lucca
2 Prato
3 Pisa
4 Volterra
5 San Gimignano
6 Siena
7 Monte Oliveto Maggiore
8 Pienza
9 Montepulciano
10 Arezzo
11 Sansepolcro
12 Monterchi

During the **Middle Ages and Renaissance,** artists who wanted to make a living went to Florence or Siena, where the churches, guilds, and other wealthy patrons were. For the most part, the art stayed where it was created. This doesn't mean you won't find great art elsewhere in Tuscany; Arezzo has the region's finest wall paintings. But in general, art lovers will spend most of their time in and around Florence and Siena. Architecture buffs, on the other hand, have a broader playing field, where the *palazzi* and city plans of provincial towns such as Lucca, Montepulciano, and Pienza attract admirers from all over the world. START: **Lucca is 72km (45 miles) west of Florence on the A11. Trip length: 10 days.**

Travel Tip

For recommended hotels and restaurants, see Lucca, Pisa, San Gimignano, Volterra, Montepulciano, Pienza, Arezzo, and Siena in chapter 6, "Charming Tuscan Towns & Villages."

Previous page: From Piero della Francesca's Legend of the True Cross.

and relief carvings, usually by visiting Lombard and Pisan sculptors. The finest two are the **Cattedrale di San Martino,** with its green and white marble facade by Guidetto da Como; and the exceptionally tall **San Michele in Foro**—another stellar example of Luccan influence on the Pisan-Romanesque style, with its twisted columns and arcades.

The more restrained "Luccan-Romanesque" style of **San Frediano** is graced with white marble plundered from Lucca's Roman amphitheater and embellished with a giant Byzantine-style gold mosaic.

For more on Lucca, see p 134 of chapter 6.

2 ★★ **Prato.** While still based in Lucca, an easy side-trip by train takes you to one of central Italy's outstanding fresco cycles. The apse of Prato's **Duomo** was painted between 1452 and 1466 by Fra' Filippo Lippi, a Dominican monk. The frescoes were reopened to the public, after a dazzling restoration, in 2007. The cathedral's **Assunta Chapel** also has incomplete frescoes by Florentine pioneer of perspective, Paolo Uccello (painted 1435–36). *See p 100,* **1**.

Garden statuary near the San Frediano tower in Lucca.

1 ★ **Lucca.** While light on the art front, for architecture buffs Lucca is one of the most rewarding stops in Tuscany. The facades of the town's many churches exemplify the Pisan-Romanesque style, richly embroidered with polychrome marble insets

Lucca's tall, delicately embellished San Michele in Foro.

Pisa's Duomo, a model of the Pisan-Romanesque style.

Take the S12r south 21km (13 miles), following signs for:

③ ★★★ Pisa. With its **Duomo** and **Leaning Tower,** Pisa introduced the world to the Arab-influenced "Pisan-Romanesque" style of architecture—which flourished from the 11th to the 13th centuries, when the Pisan Republic was a powerful maritime city-state. Gothic sculpture flourished here as well, in the hands of sculptor Nicola Pisano (1220–84) and his son, Giovanni Pisano (1250–1315).

Touring Pisa is easy; its major monuments center around Piazza del Duomo (also known as the **Campo dei Miracoli,** or "Field of Miracles"). Here you'll also find the **Battistero,** with its unusual Gothic dome and Pisano pulpit; and the **Museo dell'Opera del Duomo,** a repository of Gothic sculpture in marble and bronze.

The **Museo Nazionale di San Matteo,** a short trek across town, houses the city's best paintings, notably works by Masaccio (1401–28) and Simone Martini (1284–1344).

For more on Pisa, see p 150 of chapter 6.

From Pisa, head east toward Florence on the FI-PI-LI and take the turn south at Ponsacco signposted for Volterra. Total distance is 65km (40 miles).

④ ★ Volterra. Don't pass by this Etruscan hilltown without stopping in at its picture gallery, the **Pinacoteca.** On the first floor you'll find the exemplar of early Florentine Mannerism, in the form of Rosso Fiorentino's 1521 *Deposition.* It was one of Tuscany's first works of truly "modern" art. Architecture buffs should see the **Palazzo dei**

The skyline of San Gimignano—Tuscany's "medieval Manhattan"—by night.

Priori, the oldest Gothic town hall in Tuscany. It was the template for Florence's Palazzo Vecchio.

For more on Volterra, see p 174 of chapter 6.

Head east 17km (11 miles) along the S68 as far as Castelsangimignano, then follow signs 13km (8 miles) north to:

A fresco from the Collegiata in San Gimignano.

5 ★★ **San Gimignano.** Visitors can journey back to the Middle Ages in San Gimignano, Italy's best-preserved medieval town. Although San Gimignano is today unique in appearance, in the Middle Ages towns throughout central Italy looked like it.

Thirteen of 70+ original towers are left standing from its heyday in the decades before the devastating Black Death. More than defensive strongholds, the towers stood as symbols of a family's prestige and worth. Art outposts not to miss include Benozzo Gozzoli's frescoes inside **Sant'Agostino,** and Domenico Ghirlandaio's *Legend of Santa Fina* inside the **Collegiata.**

For more on San Gimignano, see p 156 of chapter 6.

Siena is 40km (24 miles) southeast of San Gimignano. Head east on the S324 to Poggibonsi and take the Firenze–Siena *raccordo* south to the "Siena Ovest" exit.

6 ★★★ **Siena.** Alongside Florence, the Gothic streets of Siena hold more pleasures for art and architecture lovers than any other Tuscan stop. At least 2 days here are preferable.

In the Middle Ages, Siena rivaled, even outshone, Florence as an art center. Duccio di Buoninsegna and Simone Martini were pioneers in bringing greater realism to the schematic, static Byzantine style, adding flowing lines and expressive human features. Duccio's *Maestà,* inside the **Museo dell'Opera Metropolitana,** is the most important work of this (or any) period in Siena. The Lorenzettis, Pietro and Ambrogio, worked for patrons across Tuscany—and Ambrogio left the greatest work of civic art in Italy on the walls of the **Palazzo Pubblico,** his *Allegories.*

The Black Death of 1348, which decimated Siena's population, also dealt a crippling blow to its artistic aspirations. Florence rose to prominence. But the vitality of Renaissance Siena is evident inside the **Duomo.** The marble intarsia floor, built over centuries, is joined by Pinturicchio's frescoed Libreria Piccolominea as must-sees for any Tuscan art tourist.

The other place to see where Sienese art went with the onset of what we now call "the Renaissance" is the **Pinacoteca Nazionale:** Look out for works by Francesco di Giorgio Martini, Matteo di Giovanni, and Domenico Beccafumi.

For more on Siena, see p 162 in chapter 6.

From Siena, take the S2 southeast for 32km (20 miles) to Buonconvento, then follow signs 9km (5½ miles) northeast to:

7 ★★ **Monte Oliveto Maggiore.** The open-air frescoes of the **Chiostro Grande** ("Great Cloister") at this most bucolic of rural monasteries were executed between 1495 and 1508 by Cortonese painter Luca Signorelli, then Antonio Bazzi, known

Travelers take a break in Pienza's Piazza Pio II.

as Sodoma. (He included a self-portrait, with his pet badger, in panel 3.) They recount *Scenes from the Life of St. Benedict,* based on the biographical *Dialogues* of Gregory the Great. ☎ 0577-707611. www.monteoliveto maggiore.it. Free admission. Daily 9:15am–noon and 3:15–6pm (5pm winter).

Head back to the S2, then 22km (13 miles) southeast to San Quirico d'Orcia. There, turn east on the S146 for 10km (6 miles) to:

⓼ ★★ **Pienza.** This village owes its grandiose look to Pope Pius II, who was born here of Sienese stock in 1405. He set out to transform his modest birthplace of Corsignano into a model Renaissance town: Bernardo Rossellino (1409–64), protégé of the Florentine theorist Leon Battista Alberti, carried out the pope's mandate, creating a cathedral with a classicizing facade, the adjacent Palazzo Piccolomini, and a

piazza that remains a miniature Renaissance jewel. Fifty thousand gold florins poorer, but delighted with the job, Pius renamed the village after himself, hence "Pi-enza."

For more on Pienza, see p 146 of chapter 6.

From Pienza, drive 13km (8 miles) east to Montepulciano, following the S146.

⓽ ★ **Montepulciano.** First on your agenda in this famous wine town should be a parade of the Renaissance *palazzi* flanking its steep main street, known locally as "Il Corso." The meandering climb ends at **Piazza Grande,** where you'll find Michelozzo's **Palazzo Comunale,** Sangallo's **Palazzo Nobili-Tarugi,** and, inside the **Duomo,** Taddeo di Bartolo's dazzling *Assumption* altarpiece. Architecture fans mustn't leave town without a short trek outside the gates to the **Tempio di San Biagio,** an architectural masterpiece of the High Renaissance.

For more on Montepulciano, see p 142 of chapter 6.

From Montepulciano, drive east to the autostrada, taking it north

Detail of the Duomo balcony in Pienza.

toward Firenze for 53km (33 miles) until the Arezzo turnoff.

10 ★★★ Arezzo. This prosperous little jewelry town is home to the greatest fresco cycle in the whole of Tuscany, justly mentioned in the same breath as Michelangelo's Sistine Chapel and Giotto's Cappella Scrovegni in Padua: Piero della Francesca's *Legend of the True Cross* (1452–66), on the apse walls of **San Francesco.** Treated with great realism, these frescoes evoke the Renaissance ideal of serenity and, in their subtle lighting, a sense of timelessness.

Della Francesca was a visionary who imbued his art with an ethereal quality. A master of perspective, he created human figures that seem to have souls, surviving centuries after his death, in the year Columbus reached the Americas. Arezzo is the best base for exploring the "Piero della Francesca trail" further east.

For more on Arezzo, see p 124 of chapter 6.

Head east on the S73 for 39km (24 miles), following signs to:

11 ★★ Sansepolcro. There's hardly a Tuscan town more interwoven with art than Sansepolcro. Sienese School painter Matteo di Giovanni was born here, but it's the local boy and Early Renaissance master Piero della Francesca (1420–92) that draw the art-lovers.

Head for the **Museo Civico,** Via Aggiunti 65 (☎ 0575-732218), to see his masterpieces. During World War II, the British officer commanding the heights over the town remembered he'd read an essay by Aldous Huxley—entitled "The Greatest Picture"—which accorded that status to Piero's 1468 *Resurrection of Christ,* still in the same building. He ordered shelling to cease lest a masterpiece be lost, maybe saving Sansepolcro in the process. Also see

Della Francesca's Resurrection *in Sansepolcro in Arezzo.*

Piero's *Polyptych della Misericordia* (1445–62) in room 3. *Admission 6€. Daily Jun–Sept 9am–1:30pm and 2:30–7:30pm; Oct–May 9:30am–1pm and 2:30–6pm.*

For more on Sansepolcro, see p 95, **6***.*

Head 13km (8 miles) back along the S73 toward Arezzo until you see the turnoff for the village of:

12 Monterchi. Art lovers stop here for one reason: to see Piero's *Madonna del Parto.* It's unusual in that it depicts the Virgin Mary heavily pregnant. One of his most identifiable works, painted after 1459 (dating Piero is notoriously tricky), it rests in a small museum at Via Reglia 1 (☎ 0575-70713). *Admission 3.10€. Tues–Sun 9am–1pm and 2–7pm (until 6pm Oct–Mar).*

After viewing the *Madonna,* stroll this medieval town with its mysterious underground passageway around the apse of the parish church.

Follow the S73 back to Arezzo for the night.

Tuscany for **Food & Wine Lovers**

1. Siena
2. Chianti Country
3. Montalcino
4. Montepulciano
5. Cortona
6. Sansepolcro

Gastronomes celebrate the fertile, sunbaked countryside of Tuscany for its olive groves and the extra-virgin oil they yield; for its Chianina cattle, acclaimed for producing the most succulent beef in Europe; and for its grapes, which give forth the world's best vintages of Chianti, in a region easily explored along the *Chiantigiana* (the "Chianti Road"). With such a bounty of fresh, locally available ingredients, it's only right that Tuscan food be a simply prepared, rural cuisine—known as *cucina povera*. Some recipes you'll taste were known to the Etruscans; others were served at the tables of noble Renaissance families. This moveable feast was designed to help you experience the region at its most delicious. START: **Siena (65km/40 miles south of Florence). Trip length: 5–6 days.**

Travel Tip

For detailed information on sights and recommended hotels and restaurants, see Cortona, Montepulciano, and Siena in chapter 6, "Charming Tuscan Towns & Villages."

1 ★★ Siena. The Sienese are supposedly "cursed with the sweetest teeth in Tuscany." Since the 13th century, locals have been known for their candied fruit-and-almond cakes and other delicious bakery treats.

Panforte and *panpepato* are the two most famous Sienese cakes, baked to ancient recipes. *Panpepato* is a flat, honey-sweetened cake filled with candied fruits and nuts and flavored with spices; the finishing touch is a dusting of ground pepper, cinnamon, and allspice. *Panforte* is dusted with sugar instead. *Ricciarelli* are lozenge-shaped cakes made from almond, sugar, and honey. Originally a jawbreaker dipped in wine at Christmas, *cavallucci* are made with honey-coated, aniseed-flavored walnuts; for modern tastes, they have been softened. *Cantuccini* (almond cookies), so often rounding out a Sienese lunch, are in fact an import from Prato.

All are available at family-run bakeries throughout town:

At a Chianti country wine tasting.

Nannini–Conca d'Oro, Banchi di Sopra 24 (☎ 0577-236009), is the traditional favorite.

Other Sienese goodies like hung hams, extra-virgin olive oil, and local wines are available from the city's best deli: **Pizzicheria de' Miccoli,** Via di Città 95 (☎ 0577-289164).

The town is also home to two of my favorite *gelaterie* in Tuscany. Far too many gelatos later, I still haven't decided which of **Brivido,** Via dei Pellegrini 1–3 (☎ 0577-280058), and **Kopa Kabana,** Via de' Rossi 52 (☎ 0577-223744), I like best.

From Siena, head north on the S222 to Greve in Chianti, a distance of 42km (26 miles).

② ★★ **Chianti Country.** Against a quintessential Tuscan landscape—of medieval wine castles and gray-green olive groves—Chianti Country south of Florence is home to some of Italy's finest food producers, restaurants, and markets. And then there's the wine: First codified by Cosimo III in 1716, and with a history that stretches back at least to the 7th century A.D., Chianti is one of the world's iconic reds. A good base for touring the area is its unofficial capital, **Greve in Chianti.** The whole town is best in September when it hosts the annual Rassegna del Chianti Classico wine fair. *The Greve tourist office is at Piazza Matteotti 11 (☎ 055-8546287).*

From Siena, drive south down the S2 for 42km (25 miles), following signs into Montalcino.

③ ★★★ **Montalcino.** The hills surrounding (largely south of) this medieval town yield **Brunello di Montalcino,** one of the greatest red wines in the world. Many

wineries welcome visitors, and the town itself is filled with *enoteche* (wine shops).

The center of the town's food-stuffs, including gourmet honey and Pecorino cheese, is **Enoteca La Fortezza** (see p 117 in chapter 5). While in Montalcino, you can also sample Brunello's "younger brother," the less noble **Rosso di Montalcino** made of the same Sangiovese grapes as its more famous counterpart. Aged for only a year after harvest, this is a fruity red with hints of Brunello's complex flavor at a third of the price.

Our favorite Brunello estate is **Col d'Orcia,** S. Angelo in Colle (☎ 0577-808942; www.coldorcia.com), which conducts wine-producing experiments with the University of Florence. Over the years, its owners have collected and carefully preserved more than 50,000 bottles of old Brunello vintages. This is one of the largest local wine estates, with about 110 hectares (272 acres) of Sangiovese grapes, called "Brunello." Its star wine is Poggio al Vento. Limited tastings are available in the estate shop, and guided tastings

The vineyards of Badia a Passignano.

Chianti Country

★ **Florence** (Firenze)

Grassina

Rignano sull'Arno

SS222 / A1

San Polo in Chianti / SS69

Impruneta

Strada in Chianti

Incisa in Val d'Arno

Mercatale

Greve in Chianti

Montefioralle / **2A**

2C / **2B**

Figline Valdarno

Castelnuovo dei Sabbioni

2D Panzano in Chianti

SS2

Radda in Chianti / SS408

2G

2E

2F Castellina in Chianti

Gaiole in Chianti

SS222 / Vagliagli

San Gusme

0 2 Mi
0 2 Km

SS408 / SS484

Castelnuovo Berardenga

The Chianti Road (Chiantigiana)

Just south of Greve, **2A Villa Vignamaggio,** Via Petriolo 5 (☎ 055-854661; www.vignamaggio.com), was the first wine to be labeled "Chianti." The estate was once home to Mona Lisa. From Greve, follow signposts west 1km (½ mile) to **2B Montefioralle.** This small hilltop village was the ancestral home of Amerigo Vespucci (1454–1512), the mapmaker and navigator for whom America was named. (Vespucci's niece, Simonetta, was Botticelli's model for his painting *Primavera*.) A signposted, potholed gravel road beyond Montefioralle continues for about 30 minutes to **2C Badia a Passignano** (☎ 055-8071278), a 212-hectare (530-acre) property amid some of the best vineyards for Chianti Classico. ("Classico" denotes the original, and best, Chianti grape zone, and must contain

80% Sangiovese grapes.) In 1049, the Vallombrosan Order, a reformed branch of the Benedictines, took over the property. San Giovanni Gualberto, who established the order here, died in 1073, and his relics are still preserved in the abbey. Antinori, winemakers since 1385, purchased the estate in 1987. You can visit their *Bottega* (small store) on the grounds, purchase wines, and tour the historic cellars. From Montefioralle, follow the signposts south along a secondary road 8km (5 miles) into **2D Panzano.** Foodies flock here to "the Uffizi of Meat," butcher **Dario Cecchini,** Via XX Luglio 11 (☎ 055-852020; www.solociccia.it), the de facto community center, where news is dispensed about food parties, festivals, and markets. The onsite "only meat" eatery **Solociccia** was inaugurated in 2006. *Menu 30€. Lunch Sun, dinner Thurs–Sat.*

From Panzano, follow the signs 13km (8 miles) to **2E Castellina in Chianti,** medieval town and home to a restored stone barn that hosts the region's finest restaurant: **2F Albergaccio,** Via Fiorentina 63 (☎ 0577-741042; www.albergaccio cast.com). Dishes are seasonal and might include ravioli stuffed with salt cod or wood pigeon simmered in Chianti. The wine list is unrivaled in Tuscany. *Entrees 25€.* For our final stop, follow signs toward and past Radda in Chianti for 21km (13 miles), to **2G Badia a Coltibuono,** Coltibuono Nord Est (☎ 0577-744832; www.coltibuono.com), one of the great Chianti estates. Made famous by its owner, Lorenza de' Medici, the maven of Italian cuisine, the estate is celebrated for its Chiantis (try Sangiovetto); first cold-pressed, extra-virgin olive oils; fine restaurant; and cooking school.

and cellar visits are available. *Tours Mon–Fri by appointment. Shop Mon–Sat 8:30am–12:30pm and 2:30–6:30pm.*

For information on other wineries, check with the **Consorzio del Vino Brunello di Montalcino,** Piazza Cavour 8 (☎ 0577-848246; www.consorziobrunellodimontalcino.it).

For more on Montalcino, see p 116, ❶.

From Montalcino, follow the S146 east 32km (23 miles) to:

❹ ★★ **Montepulciano.** This ancient town of Etruscan origin, which perches like an eyrie above the Valdichiana, is celebrated for its violet-scented, ruby wine, **Vino Nobile di Montepulciano,** known since the 8th century. Although Brunello is more beefy and is considered number one by many connoisseurs, the silkier delights of a good Vino Nobile are well worth sampling. On a tighter budget, as in nearby Montalcino, a younger and less expensive **Rosso di Montepulciano** exists. It is aged less and sold sooner. Gattavecchi (p 143) makes an especially noble version.

Pasta with a meat ragout.

One of Montalcino's many enoteche.

For a complete rundown on Montepulciano, including hotels, restaurants, and how to taste its wines, see p 142 in chapter 6.

From Montepulciano, head east to the A1 autostrada, and take it north toward Florence. Continue until the turnoff east for Perugia. Take this road to the junction with the S71 north to Cortona. Total distance is 32km (20 miles).

❺ ★★ **Cortona.** Serious foodies, at least once in their tour of Tuscany, will want to stay at a grand regional inn specializing in the finest Tuscan cuisine and wines. Our candidate is **Il Falconiere** (recommended on p 131 and 133 of chapter 6). The summer dining terrace here opens onto views of the vineyard-covered hillsides. I'll never forget the pumpkin-coated homemade pasta with savory pheasant stuffing and an autumnal *antipasti* of a salt cod tartlet with herb-scented garbanzos.

Husband and wife Riccardo and Silvia Baracchi also offer cooking classes at their restored 18th-century villa 4½km (3 miles) north of Cortona.

Follow the signs out of Cortona west to the S71. Head north toward Arezzo until the junction with the E78 east, for Sansepolcro. The distance to Sansepolcro is 62km (39 miles).

6 ★ **Sansepolcro.** The hometown of Piero della Francesca is also the gastronomic center of eastern Tuscany. For a review of the town's artistic highlights, see p 89, in our "Art and Architecture Lovers" tour, earlier in this chapter.

For gourmet evening dining, head for **Oroscopo di Paola e Marco,** Via Togliatti 68 (☎ 0575-734875; www.relaisoroscopo.com), a restored farmhouse with a creative *cucina* that uses only the finest regional ingredients. Two fixed-price menus—one five courses, another seven—will have you raving about Tuscan food and wine. The owners' enthusiasm is contagious. Winemakers sometimes appear at special gourmet evenings to showcase their wines. You can also spend the night in one of the remodeled, affordable rooms upstairs—which is great if you've had too much *vino*.

When prepared properly, a *bistecca alla fiorentina* is among the best in the world. Authentic versions hail only from the indigenous purebred Chianina cattle. **Carni Shop,** Via dei Lorena 32 (☎ 0575-742924), sells it ready to cook. Rosangela Chieli operates the best pastry shop in town: **Pasticceria Chieli,** Via Fraternità 12 (☎ 0575-742026). Wait until you try the chocolate mousse, pine-nut-studded ricotta tarts, and the almond macaroons.

Classic breads are baked daily in a 15th-century building at **Panificio La Spiga,** Via Santa Caterina 72 (☎ 0575-740522). The most acclaimed *gelateria* is **Gelateria Ghignoni,** Via Tiberina Sud 850 (☎ 0575-741900), 1km (⅔ mile) from the center on the road to Città di Castello. The shop's deep chocolate flavor is worthy of an award. But shrimp gelato? How about porcini mushroom gelato? Perhaps not, but if you're game, they've got it.

The Sansepolcro tourist office (☎ 0575-740536) is at Via Matteotti 6.

Casks of Chianti.

Tuscany for **Families**

① Lucca
② Collodi
③ The Garfagnana
④ Pisa
⑤ Elba
⑥ San Gimignano
⑦ Siena
⑧ Monteriggioni

A n elderly Sienese noblewoman who lived in a decaying palazzo put the damper on this Tuscany for Families tour: "Tell people that Tuscany is an adult attraction," she said. "We have great art and architecture. We are not Disneyland." Fortunately, many of the palaces, castles, and fortified hilltowns of Tuscany look as though they had been created by Walt himself. So kids can be "lured" to cultural attractions—provided you don't call them that. With this tour, I've created a balance between cultural sites and activities that will please the entire family—and added a trip to Tuscany's best beach resort. START: **Lucca, on the A12 autostrada 71km (44 miles) west of Florence, makes the best base for the first part of the tour.**

Travel Tip

For information on sights and recommended hotels and restaurants in Lucca, Pisa, San Gimignano, and Siena, see each town in chapter 6, "Charming Tuscan Towns & Villages."

① ★★ **Lucca.** All family members will delight in walking or biking (or even rollerblading) the 5km (2¾ miles) of Renaissance walls that ring the old town. Lucca is also Italy's comic capital, so fans shouldn't miss the **Museo Nazionale del Fumetto**, Piazza San Romano

Despite all the old churches, Tuscany can appeal to kids.

(☎ 0583-56326; www.museo nazionaledelfumetto.it), with its mixture of Italian cult classics and familiar names like *Batman* and *Topolino* (Mickey Mouse to you and me). *Admission 4€. Tues–Sun 10am–7pm.*

For more attractions, hotels, restaurants, and diversions, refer to *"Lucca"* in chapter 6.

Drive east from Lucca on the S435 for 15km (9 miles); just before Pescia, is the little town of:

2 ★ Collodi. This is the hometown of Carlo Lorenzini, who wrote *The Adventures of Pinocchio* in 1881. (He later adopted the name "Carlo Collodi.") The world-famous children's story is celebrated at the **Parco di Pinocchio** (☎ 0572-429342; www.pinocchio.it/park.htm) with diversions ranging from a giant mosaic about Geppetto and his fibbing puppet to a fantastical maze and a painting corner. Try to read the book with your kids before you go (the Disney movie is significantly different). The park could do with a lick of paint, but is still great fun for tots with imagination. *Admission 10€. Daily 8:30am–sunset.*

While still based in Lucca, go to the Tourist Office, Piazza Santa Maria 35 (☎ 0583-919931; www. luccaturismo.it), and get a map with directions for exploring the Garfagnana, north of town via the S12 and S445.

3 ★ The Garfagnana. Ideal for a day trip with kids, this part of northwestern Tuscany is riddled with chestnut forests, hiking trails, and perfect picnicking pastures tucked between the Apennines and the Apuan Alps. *Maps and local information available from the tourist office in Barga (☎ 0584-724743).*

Our favorite spot is the **Grotta del Vento,** or "Wind Cave," loc. Vergemoli (☎ 0583-722024; www. grottadelvento.com), 16km (10 miles) southwest of Barga. Deep under the karst you'll encounter the most dramatic caves in Tuscany, a subterranean landscape of tunnels, stalactites, stalagmites, and surreal calcite formations. A 1-hour tour guides you and your family safely through; take warm clothing because it's always 52°F (11°C) down there. *Tour*

Pinocchio may well be Tuscany's most famous native son.

The tilt of Pisa's tower has captivated children for centuries.

7.50€. Daily on the hour (except 1pm) 10am–6pm (Nov–Mar Mon–Sat only).

After your day in the hills, return to Lucca for the night.

Just 20km (12 miles) southwest of Lucca, along the S12r is:

④ ★★★ Pisa. At the **Campo dei Miracoli** ("Field of Miracles"), all kids will want to make the memorable climb to the top of the **Leaning Tower,** but the minimum age is 8 years old.

Budding scientists of any age can stray into the Duomo to follow in the footsteps of Galileo Galilei (1564–1642). He supposedly discovered the laws of pendulum motion right there, while watching the chandelier now known as the "Lamp of Galileo." (Who cares if it's a true story?)

From Pisa, head 110km (68 miles) down the coast on the A12 then the S1 to Piombino. From there catch the car ferry (40 min.) to the island of:

⑤ ★★ Elba. The jewel in Tuscany's Mediterranean coast is this island,

where French emperor Napoleon was exiled after the Treaty of Fontainebleau in 1814.

Magical strips of sand include the perfect white crescents at **Fetovaia** and **Cavoli** and the little rockpool-and-sand cove of **Sant'Andrea,** all on the island's west side. There are more family beachfront facilities at **Marina di Campo.** The island is best avoided in packed August, when it becomes party central for young Tuscans.

The main tourist office is at Calata Italia 43 (☎ 0565-914671; www.aptelba.it). Ferries are run by Moby (www.moby.it) and Toremar (☎ 081-0171998; www.toremar.it).

From Piombino, head north on S1 to Cecina, then east on S68 to Castelsangimignano, from where you'll see signs to San Gimignano. It's a journey of 112km (70 miles).

⑥ ★★ San Gimignano. With its preserved medieval towers, San Gimignano is like a stage set for kids, who generally love romping through its pedestrian-only historic core. The adventure begins at the **Torre Grossa,** which everyone can climb for a panoramic sweep of the bucolic countryside that surrounds this hilltown. Then decide

A beach get-away is close by in Elba.

Monterrigioni looks like the figment of a cartoonist's imagination.

whether to subject the children to the **Museo della Tortura**—a Tuscan chamber of horrors, with an authentic collection of instruments of torture. Most older kids find the exhibits fascinating.

For a complete description of hotels, restaurants, and activities, turn to "San Gimignano" in chapter 6.

Travel 11km (7 miles) east on the S324 to Poggibonsi, where you can hook up with the Firenze–Siena *raccordo*. Drive 31km (19 miles) south and turn off at "Siena Ovest."

7 ★★ **Siena.** The Gothic city of Siena is a place kids will never forget. Climb the **Torre del Mangia,** the bell tower of the **Palazzo Pubblico,** for a dramatic view down into the **Campo,** site of summer pageantry and horse racing at the Palio.

At the converted hospital of **Santa Maria della Scala,** under-11s have their own art on-site, too. The **Museo d'Arte per Bambini,** with exhibits by and for young children, moved here in 2008.

If you're in town on a Sunday (not July–Aug), kids will love the **Treno-Natura** (☎ 0577-207413; www.ferrovieturistiche.it). It's an

unforgettable rail round-trip on disused tracks through the UNESCO World Heritage area of the Crete and Val d'Orcia, south of the city. Some weekends it's a steam train. Check the website for dates. *Tickets 16€–27€.*

You'll see a different side of Tuscany, and get to know football Italian-style, if you catch a match at **AC Siena,** Stadio A. Franchi (☎ 0577-281084; www.acsiena.it). The team usually plays in Serie A, Italy's top flight, and games are quite genteel by European standards (except those against Fiorentina). Ask for a seat in the "Gradinata." *Alternate Sun Sept–May. Tickets from TRA.IN, Piazza Gramsci (☎ 0577-204111); Sogno Siena, Via dei Termini 54 (☎ 0577-225703). Prices 20€–45€.*

For more, turn to "Siena" in chapter 6.

The tourist office (☎ 0577-280551; www.terresiena.it) is at Piazza del Campo 56.

8 ★ **Monteriggioni.** For an afternoon adventure, drive your kids to Monteriggioni, 18km (11 miles) north along the Florence road. It's a tiny, perfectly preserved medieval village in its own set of fortified walls. Even Walt couldn't have done it better.

Tuscany by **Rail**

1. Prato
2. Pistoia
3. Lucca
4. Pisa
5. Siena
6. San Gimignano
7. Montepulciano
8. Arezzo

— Railroad

Most of this guide has been written for motorists to discover the Tuscan countryside in their own sets of wheels. But increasing numbers of visitors want to save money in the face of mounting fuel prices, or simply prefer the unique feel you get for somewhere if you arrive by rail. To explore all of Tuscany, you'd have to double back to Florence many, many times and suffer unwieldy transfers. We've designed this 7-day tour to minimize hassle, using Siena as a base for the second half of the week. With a few additional connections made by bus, you can easily see many of the region's highlights. START: **Florence's Santa Maria Novella station.**

Travel Tip

For detailed information on sights and recommended hotels and restaurants, see the Lucca, Pisa, Siena, San Gimignano, Volterra, Montepulciano, and Arezzo sections of chapter 6, "Charming Tuscan Towns & Villages."

1 ★ **Prato.** Tuscany's second city is your ideal first stop, a half-hour west from Florence. Alight at Prato's **Porta al Serraglio** station and the **Duomo** is just a couple of minutes' walk down arrow-straight Via Magnolfi. A one-way ticket is 1.80€. *See p 110,* 1.

Exploring Tuscany by train can be fun and economical.

② ★ **Pistoia.** I love visiting this little city by rail, because my 10-minute walk from the station to Piazza del Duomo takes me right past the best artisan ice cream stop in town: **Chiostri,** Via Vannucci 32 (no phone). Around 3 trains an hour run from Prato, just 20 minutes away. The one-way fare is 1.80€. From the station, walk straight ahead on Via XX Settembre, past the old walls, then take the fifth right on Via degli Orafi into the main square. *See p 111,* **②**.

③ ★★ **Lucca.** Within easy reach of Florence, Lucca receives trains from that city every hour, beginning daily at 5:10am and running up until 10:30pm. (All pass through both Prato and Pistoia.) Trip time is 1½ hours, and a one-way ticket is 5€. Trains pull into the station on **Piazza Ricasoli** (☎ 0583-47013), just south of the city walls.

④ ★★★ **Pisa.** To spend the following night in Pisa, you don't have to double back to Florence: Pisa and Lucca are among the few major tourist sites in Tuscany that share a convenient rail link. Trains leave Lucca every half-hour daily, from

5:40am to 9:40pm, for the 30-minute trip. If you're heading straight for the Campo dei Miracoli, do *not* get off at Pisa Centrale, at the southern end of town; you want **Pisa San Rossore,** just west of the old wall. A one-way fare is 2.40€.

Train travel affords spectacular views of Tuscany.

In Tuscany, poppy fields are a common sight out train windows.

Travel Tip

The golden rule of rail travel in Italy: Don't forget to validate your ticket by inserting it into the yellow machines you find on every platform, often marked "*convalida*." You may be fined if you forget. Regular tickets are valid for 6 hours from validation, so you are allowed to jump off en route (say, at Prato or Pistoia on the way to Lucca).

5 ★★★ **Siena.** To reach our next destination—which you can use as a base for 4 nights—you have to double back from Pisa toward Florence, changing trains for Siena at Empoli. During the day, two trains an hour make the connection. Total journey time is 1¾ hours, and it's 7.10€ one-way. Trains arrive in Siena at **Piazza Rosselli** (☎ 147-80888), 15 minutes by frequent bus north of the center. Buy your local bus ticket from the booth inside the station.

After seeing the sights of Siena, you can break up the trip and return to Florence. Or else you can spend another 3 nights in Siena, taking a series of day trips to some of the enchanting towns of central and southern Tuscany, and return to Siena by nightfall. However, you'll have to rely on the bus instead of the train.

Real rail enthusiasts also shouldn't miss Siena's **Treno-Natura.** *See p 99,* **7**.

6 ★★ **San Gimignano.** This hilltop fortress town with its famous towers is comfortably accessible from Siena. Buy your ticket before travel from **TRA.IN** (☎ 0577-204111; www.trainspa.it), below street level at Piazza Gramsci/Via Tozzi. They run several daily buses linking Siena with San Gimignano (some require a change at Poggibonsi—check when you buy your ticket). A one-way fare is 3.30€ and takes just over an hour. You can see the sights and take a bus back to Siena for dinner.

7 ★★ **Montepulciano.** A bus run by **TRA.IN** (☎ 0577-204111; www.trainspa.it) is also your best bet for a day trip to this precipitous wine town. Buy your ticket, as before, from below Piazza Gramsci. Bus 112 departs from outside Porta Ovile and reaches Montepulciano, via Buonconvento and Pienza, in 1½ hours. A one-way ticket costs 4.70€.

Buses link Montepulciano and Siena at the rate of around five a day. You have a choice of overnighting in Montepulciano or nearby Pienza, or returning to Siena for the night.

Tuscany's highest hill-town also lies on the Siena–Chiusi rail line. But the train station (☎ 0578-20074) is 10km (6 miles) from the center, to which it is connected by local **LFI** buses (☎ 0575-39881; www.lfi.it). However, if you're caught without a bus, it might cost upward of 15€ by taxi.

A ticket validation machine.

8 ★ **Arezzo.** The art city of Piero della Francesca is easily tackled in a day from either Florence (by rail) or Siena (by bus).

From Santa Maria Novella in **Florence,** trains depart for Arezzo at the rate of at least two per hour daily from 5:05am to 11:10pm, taking anything from a half-hour to 1½ hours and costing from 5.60€ for a one-way ticket.

A **TRA.IN** bus (☎ 0577-204111; www.trainspa.it) links Siena and Arezzo every couple of hours, departing the bus terminal at Piazza Gramsci. Journey time is 1½ hours. It's 5.20€ one-way. Buses arrive in Arezzo just by the rail station (and tourist office), in **Piazza della Repubblica.**

Passes & Packages

Rail travel in Italy is inexpensive and easy to navigate. Trip planning is simple using the website for the national rail company, **Trenitalia** (☎ 892021; www.trenitalia.it).

If you're just traveling within Tuscany, it's very unlikely you'll ride enough to get value for any prepaid rail pass. However, passes are available from **Rail Europe** (www.raileurope.com in U.S.; www.raileurope.co.uk in U.K.). From the U.S., the **Italy Pass** offers any 3 days in 2 months for $225 for second-class travel; additional days, up to 10 days, are $30 each. The **Italy Saverpass** is a better deal for two or more people traveling together: $192 each for 3 (not necessarily consecutive) days; $24 each additional day.

The **Italy Rail 'n Drive** package is more expensive but optimal in Tuscany, especially for visiting Volterra with its awkward public transportation links. For $386, you get 4 days of unlimited second-class train travel in Italy and 2 days' Hertz compact car rental with unlimited mileage. Two adults pay $640 ($320 per person) for the same 6-day period.

From the U.K., the **InterRail One Country** pass for Italy costs £93 for any 3 days in a month, £161 for any 6 days, standard class.

Under-26s get discounts on all Italy passes.

Tuscany **Outdoors**

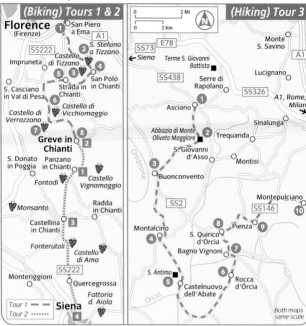

(Biking) Tours 1 & 2

Florence (Firenze)
San Piero a Ema
S. Stefano a Tizzano
A1
SS222
Castello di Tizzano
Impruneta
San Polo in Chianti
Strada in Chianti
S. Casciano in Val di Pesa
Castello di Vicchiomaggio
Castello di Verrazzano
Greve in Chianti
S. Donato in Poggia
Panzano in Chianti
Fontodi
Castello Vignamaggio
Monsanto
Radda in Chianti
Castellina in Chianti
Fonterutoli
Castello di Ama
SS222
Monteriggioni
Quercegrossa
Fattoria d. Aiola
Siena

Tour 1 ———
Tour 2 ········

(Hiking) Tour 3

0   2 Mi
0   2 Km

Monte S. Savino
A1
SS73   E78
←Siena
Terme S. Giovanni Battista
SS438
Serre di Rapolano
Lucignano
SS326
A1, Rome, Milan
Asciano
Abbazia di Monte Oliveto Maggiore
S. Giovanni d'Asso
Sinalunga
Trequanda
Montisi
Buonconvento
Ombrone
SS2
Montepulciano
SS146
Montalcino
S. Quirico d'Órcia
Pienza
Bagno Vignoni
S. Ántimo
Castelnuovo dell'Abate
Rocca d'Órcia
Orcia

Both maps same scale

If you're a biker, hiker, or general outdoor enthusiast, someone who feels the need to spike a visit to old churches with a dose
of fresh country air, these are the tours for you. For a guided cycling
expedition, you could also contact **I Bike Italy** (☎ 347-6383976;
www.ibikeitaly.com). Based in Florence, I Bike Italy offers 1- or 2-day
tours, including from Florence to Siena. The same company also
leads walking tours around Florence.

Tour 1: Cycling Florence–Chianti Country.

The most accessible and scenic
route in Tuscany for cyclists is Chianti Country, immediately south of
Florence. You can extend this tour
by 2 or 3 days by taking the sug-
gested detours. If you're settling for
a beautiful 1-day tour, head straight
south from Florence to Greve in Chianti, the heart of wine country, a full-
day journey of 27km (17 miles). We
recommend a 24-speed mountain

bike for this trip. Stock up on supplies in Florence; you'll find dozens
of idyllic places in the countryside
where you can stop for a picnic.

START: **Florence. Trip length: 27km
(17 miles)/1 day.**

Travel Tip

For more information about stops
along these tours, refer to "Tuscany
for Food & Wine Lovers," earlier in
this chapter.

Tuscany is a challenging, rewarding destination for cyclists.

On your bicycle, cross the Ponte San Niccolò, spanning the Arno River at the eastern end of Florence, and follow the signs from Piazza Ferrucci to the town of Grassina and the S222. This is the Chiantigiana, the celebrated Chianti Road. The route continues south on this road unless otherwise indicated. You'll make your first stop at Ponte a Ema, 4km (2½ miles) south of Florence.

❶ ★ Oratorio di Santa Caterina dell'Antella. A wall fresco of this church at S. Piero a Ema traces the *Life of St. Catherine.* Spinello Aretino completed it in 1390, just before he executed his cycle at San Miniato al Monte, in Florence. The apse displays more frescoes of St. Catherine (ca. 1360), by the "Master of Barberino."

❷ Santo Stefano a Tizzano. Four kilometers (2½ miles) south, on a clearly marked road off the S222, you'll come upon this vine-clad Romanesque church in Petigliolo. It was built by the Buondemontis, a local ruling family.

Nearby, a sign points to:

❸ ★ Castello di Tizzano. This wine estate, set amid vineyards, is a consortium of farms that produce the Gallo Nero label, a prestigious Chianti Classico named after the Chianti's iconic cockerel. Visits are available by appointment only (☎ 055-482737 for reservations). If you've made a reservation, you can explore the 15th-century cellars on-site and purchase a bottle of *vin santo* for your picnic lunch—unless that would interfere with your peddling.

❹ San Polo in Chianti. Two kilometers (1¼ miles) southeast, you'll come upon this little town in the center of Tuscany's iris industry. An annual Iris Festival takes place here each May. You can also visit the ancient church of San Miniato in Robbiana, consecrated in 1077.

From San Polo a byroad points the way west back to:

❺ Strada in Chianti. Taking its name, Strada (street), from an old Roman road that ran through here, this town lies 14km (8½ miles) south of Florence. Immediately to its south, you'll pass the **Castello di Mugano,** one of the best preserved medieval castles in Tuscany. From this point, it's rolling countryside until you reach Vicchiomaggio.

Continue on the S222 for 6km (3¾ miles) to:

❻ ★ Vicchiomaggio. The **Castello di Vicchiomaggio** (☎ 055-854078) once hosted Leonardo da Vinci. Tours of the estate are limited to groups, but you can take part in free tastings at their roadside Cantinetta San Jacopo wine shop, on the S222 at the signposted turnoff to the castle. As well as classic Tuscan wines, pick up a jar of their acclaimed honey. The Vicchiomaggio control 120 hectares (300 acres) of land, of which 28 hectares (70 acres) are devoted exclusively to vines.

7 ★★ **Verrazzano.** This hamlet south of Vicchiomaggio was the birthplace of Giovanni da Verrazzano, the first European colonial to sail into the bay of New York in 1524. His former home, wine estate **Castello di Verrazzano** (☎ 055-854243; www.verrazzano.com), is signposted. Take the route marked "Via San Martino in Valle" to reach it. Its 10th-century tower is surrounded by 15th- and 16th-century buildings. You can purchase bottles, including a Sangiovese–Cabernet blend, on site. *Tour and tasting (1½ hr.) 18€. Mon–Fri. Booking essential.*

Continue south on the S222 for 5km (3 miles) to:

8 ★★ **Greve in Chianti.** On the banks of the Greve River stands wine country's unofficial capital. Head for the central square, **Piazza Matteotti,** and park your bike amidst 17th-century buildings, wine bars, and cafes. Plan to overnight in Greve, unless you have the stamina to bike back to Florence before dark. For more on what to see and do in Greve, see "Tuscany for Food & Wine Lovers," earlier in the chapter.

Tour 2: Cycling Greve in Chianti–Siena.

The following morning, after an overnight in Greve, you can cycle back to Florence or continue on to Siena. The distance of 40km (25 miles) to Siena is longer than Greve to Florence, but with fewer distractions along the route. Leave Greve in the morning and set out along the S222 again, following signs south to Siena. START: **Greve. Trip length: 40km (25 miles).**

1 ★ **Panzano.** This village is 6km (3¾ miles) south of Greve. Besides the medieval castle, the focal point

An invitation to cyclists.

is an *Annunciation* by Michele di Ridolfo di Ghirlandaio (1503–77) inside the church of Santa Maria Assunta.

2 ★ **Fontodi.** Just under 10km (6 miles) south of Greve, this long-neglected estate was recently restored. Now, it's turning out some of the region's finest Chianti Classico. Visits are possible by reservation. *Via San Leolino 89. ☎ 055-852005. www.fontodi.com.*

3 ★★ **Castellina in Chianti.** Castellina is 21km (13 miles) north of Siena. Looking like a postcard left over from the *Quattrocento,* the town is dominated by its imposing, crenellated **Rocca** (fortress) designed in the late 1400s by Giuliano da Sangallo. Walk along **Via delle Volte** a fortified part-tunnel, part-street, and stop in at one of the many *bottegas* for lunch and a glass of Chianti.

The tourist office is at Via Ferruccio 40 (☎ 0577-741392).

4 ★★★ **Siena.** The final destination of most cyclists in Tuscany, this is where you'll want to linger for a while, as your schedule allows. For a complete review of what to see and do here, refer to "Siena" on p 162 of chapter 6. From Siena, you can take your bike on the train back to Florence—unless, of course, you're game to repeat the trip north under your own steam.

Tour 3: Walking in the Crete and Val d'Orcia.

The landscape southeast of Siena—Tuscany's most sculptural—is ideal for covering on foot. You can break this tour at almost any point along the route: At Asciano, Montalcino, Bagno Vignoni, Pienza, or Montepulciano, there are transport options back to Siena. The full Siena–Montepulciano route is comfortably done in 3 to 5 full days, depending on your pace and how many of the stopovers you make. START: **Siena. Trip length: 3–5 full days.**

Leave Siena via the S326, signposted to Perugia. Turn right onto the S438 toward Asciano, 26km (16 miles) southeast of Siena.

1 ★★ **Asciano.** Known as Le Crete ("the clays"), the almost lunar landscape en route to Asciano is among the most memorable and photogenic in Tuscany. The town is girdled by ramparts dating from

1352. Its chief attraction is the sacred art inside the frescoed chambers of the **Museo Corboli,** Corso Matteotti 122 (☎ 0577-719524). *Admission 4€.*

The tourist office is at Corso Matteotti 78 (☎ 0577-718811).

Head south on the S451 and follow the signs for:

2 ★★ **Monte Oliveto Maggiore.** The distance between Asciano and this monastery, founded in 1313 and famed for its frescoed **Chiostro Grande,** is 9km (5½ miles). The monastery's gatehouse trattoria is a pretty spot to pause for a drink or a bite to eat. *See p 87,* **7**.

Continue on the S451, then 9km (6 miles) south down the Via Cassia (S2) to:

3 **Buonconvento.** Ignore the industrial horror surrounding this little town and head for its medieval core. The small **Museo d'Arte Sacra,** Via Soccini 18 (☎ 0577-807181), holds a few Sienese masterpieces, including works by Duccio and Matteo di Giovanni.

Just south of Buonconvento on the S2 is a turnoff for Montalcino. Total journey is 18km (11 miles).

Poppy fields near Abbazia di Sant'Antimo.

There are worse ways to get exercise than a jog through Tuscany.

4 ★ Montalcino. This hilltown has been inhabited since the Etruscans ruled it. *See p 116,* **1**.

Continue south along the Castelnuovo dell'Abate road for 9km (6 miles), to:

5 ★★ Sant'Antimo. This is one of Tuscany's great Romanesque buildings. *See p 121 in chapter 5.*

Continue southeast past Monte Amiata, then turn northeast through Santa Maria to the S323. Bypass Castiglione d'Orcia then approach Rocca d'Orcia. The distance between Sant'Antimo and Rocca d'Orcia is 19km (12 miles).

6 Rocca d'Orcia. From the 11th to the 14th centuries, the **Rocca** (fortress) here was the center of power for the Aldobrandeschi clan, formidable toll collectors along the main road to and from Rome. When you see the view, you'll understand why this was such a strategic location.

Continue along the S323 as it winds north, and turn left at the signposts to Bagno Vignoni on the S2, a distance of 5km (3 miles).

7 ★ Bagno Vignoni. The steaming, sulphurous waters of this curious little village have been frequented since Roman times, notably by Lorenzo "The Magnificent" de' Medici and St. Catherine of Siena. These days it's just as likely to be amateur photographers coming to snap the *piazza d'acqua,* a 49m x 29m (161 ft. x 95 ft.) porticoed Renaissance pool built where the main village square used to be.

Return to the S2 and turn left for 6km (4 miles) to:

8 ★ San Quirico d'Orcia. *See p 117,* **2**.

Walk the S146 10km (6 miles) to:

9 ★★ Pienza. For full details on the sights and services of this model Renaissance town, turn to "Pienza" in chapter 6.

Walk east along the S146 for 13km (8 miles) to:

10 ★★ Montepulciano. The final steep climb to Piazza Grande might just seem like the toughest of your trip for those tired legs. But it's well worth it. See chapter 6 for a full rundown of this magnificent wine town's attractions, hotels, and restaurants.

From here, you can make public transportation connections to Siena, Florence, or even Rome. ●

Northwest Tuscany

1 **Prato**
2 **Pistoia**
3 **Montecatini Terme**
4 **Lucca**
5 **Pisa**
6 **Livorno**
7 **Torre del Lago**
8 **Viareggio**

Northwest Tuscany, land of Puccini, is best known for the ancient maritime republic of Pisa. But beyond the city and its wonky Tower, there's Lucca, with its Renaissance ramparts; the art of Prato and Pistoia; and the great Medici port of Livorno, with the best seafood restaurants in Tuscany. Finally, when you've had enough of old churches and want your music loud, your beach crowd raucous, and your nightlife frantic, there is Viareggio. START: **Prato, 17km (10 miles) west of Florence on the A11, but use Lucca and/or Pisa as a base. Trip Length: 7 days.**

A Note on Hotels & Restaurants

For hotels, restaurants, and detailed information on attractions in Florence, see p 11; in Lucca, see p 134; in Pisa, see p 150.

1 ★★ **Prato.** Known since the 13th century for its textiles, Prato has long lived in the shadow of nearby Florence. The city's reputation for business was well-established before Francesco di Marco Datini, the 14th-century "Merchant of Prato," made his money trading with the Papal

Previous page: Grapes on the vine in a Tuscan vineyard.

A Filippo Lippi fresco in the Prato Duomo.

entourage in Avignon, France. The modern city is home to Italy's largest Chinese community.

Prato's **Duomo,** Piazza del Duomo (☎ 0574-26234; www. diocesiprato.it), alone is reason enough to visit. Housed in an elaborate chapel left of the entrance is the *Sacro Cingolo* (Holy Girdle), reputedly presented to the Apostle "Doubting" Thomas during the Virgin's Assumption. More dazzling still, after a restoration completed in 2007, are the apse frescoes by Fra' Filippo Lippi. Executed between 1452 and 1466, they recount the lives and martyrdoms of St. Stephen and John the Baptist. Prato was the setting for Lippi's seduction of nun Lucrezia Buti, and the birthplace of their son, High Renaissance painter Filippino (1457–1504). *Admission 3€. Mon–Sat 10am–5pm; Sun 1–5pm.*

The cathedral facade sports a circular pulpit by Donatello and his workshop. What you see today is a copy: The original forms the centerpiece of the **Museo dell'Opera del Duomo,** Piazza del Duomo 49 (☎ 0574-29339), next door. The collection is an otherwise modest one, but your ticket gets you into the 12th-century cathedral cloister

and atmospheric vaults under the altar. *Admission 4€. Mon, Wed–Sat 9:30am–12:30pm and 3–6:30pm; Sun 9:30am–12:30pm.*

The tourist office is at Piazza S. Maria delle Carceri 15 (☎ 0574-24112; www.prato.turismo. toscana.it).

Return to the A11 autostrada and continue northwest 17km (10 miles) to Pistoia.

② ★★ **Pistoia.** Around here, if it's green and grows in straight lines, it probably started life somewhere near Pistoia, Tuscany's market garden. The area wasn't always so serene, however: For centuries the Pistoiesi were known for rudeness and bellicosity. Machiavelli described them as "brought up to slaughter and war," and the first pistols were made here in the 1540s.

The core of town, **Piazza del Duomo**, centers around the **Cattedrale di San Zeno** (☎ 0573-25095), rebuilt in the 12th and 14th centuries. Behind a harmonious Pisan-Romanesque facade, the church has a marble porch that makes it look as though it's crouching, ready to pounce. Inside the great treasure is nearly a ton of partially gilded silver, remolded into medieval saints, known as the *Altar of St. James,* the work of an unknown 13th-century silversmith.

The Duomo in Prato.

The octagonal **Baptistery** opposite was built in the 1300s. *Free admission; altar 2€. Mon–Sat 8:30am–12:30pm and 3:30–7pm (no lunch closure May–Sept); Sun 8am–1pm and 3:30–7pm.*

You'll find my favorite Gothic sculpture in all Italy inside the Romanesque church of **Sant' Andrea,** Via di S. Andrea (☎ 0573-21912). Its exquisite pulpit (1298–1301), dripping in Biblical gore with panels including a *Massacre of the Innocents* and *Last Judgment,* is by Giovanni Pisano. *Free admission. Daily 9:30am–12:30pm and 3:30–6pm.*

San Giovanni Fuorcivitas, Via Cavour (☎ 0573-24784), from the 12th to 14th centuries, is famous for the stripes and diamond-shapes covering its north facade, also in the Pisan-Romanesque style. The spartan interior includes a polyptych by Taddeo Gaddi. *Free admission. Daily 7:30am–noon and 5–6:30pm.*

Just north of Piazza del Duomo, the colorful terra-cotta frieze on the **Ospedale del Ceppo,** Piazza Giovanni XXIII, is the work of Giovanni della Robbia (1469–1529). The hospital was originally founded to treat pilgrims, as the frieze depicts.

The tourist office is in Piazza del Duomo (☎ 0573-21622; www.pistoia.turismo.toscana.it).

Travel Tip

An inexplicable lack of tourists means Pistoia's excellent trattorias are priced with locals in mind. For a few euros more, **Abbondanza,** Via dell'Abbondanza 10–14 (☎ 0573-368037), is the best central spot to get to know Pistoiese cooking. *Closed Wed all day and Thurs lunch. $$.*

Drive south to the A11 autostrada and cut west for 19km (12 miles), until you reach:

③ ★ Montecatini Terme. Immortalized in Fellini's *8½,* this is Tuscany's most celebrated spa town. Its waters were known by the Romans for their curative powers, and popularized by Grand Duke Peter Leopold I in the late 1700s. The current buildings sprang up in the early 20th century, as suggested by the eclectic Art Nouveau style of **Viale Verdi.**

Montecatini's waters supposedly have beneficial effects for the liver, intestines, and kidneys. At the oldest

Giovanni della Robbia's frieze on the Ospedale del Ceppo in Pistoia.

A Montecatini Terme spa.

and most alluring of the thermal houses, **Terme Tettuccio,** Viale Verdi 71 (☎ 0572-7781; www.termemontecatini.it), clients arrive every morning to enjoy neoclassical grandeur, a live orchestra, a healthy breakfast, and the rapid laxative effects of the mineral-rich water. *Cure 13€. Open May–Oct.*

Nearby **Excelsior,** Viale Verdi 61 (☎ 0572-7781), the only spa open all year, provides a wide range of treatments including beauty, bathing, and inhaling the water vapors.

From Viale Diaz, a funicular railway ascends to the original Roman settlement, now known as **Montecatini Alto.** Enjoy the summer breezes, an espresso on the piazza, and endless views over the Valdinievole. *Return ticket 6€.*

The tourist office is at Viale Verdi 66 (☎ 0572-772244; www.montecatiniturismo.it).

Take the A11 west 26km (16 miles) to:

④ ★★★ **Lucca.** The *Lucchese* say their city—with its 5km (2¾ miles) of stone ramparts—is more impressive than Florence or Siena, rivals since the Middle Ages. It is worth at least a day of your time.

Leave early and drive 22km (14 miles) southwest on the S12r to:

⑤ ★★★ **Pisa.** The Duomo and the Leaning Tower are triumphs of the Pisan-Romanesque style—and rightly among Europe's top tourist magnets.

Head south on the S1 to Livorno, a distance of 22km (14 miles).

⑥ **Livorno.** Called "Leghorn" by the English (a name later immortalized by a rooster), the freeport of Livorno has a long Anglophile history. Romantic poet Percy Bysshe Shelley wrote *To a Skylark* nearby and sailed to his death from the port—also built by an Englishman, "Roberto" Dudley. The city, though, was heavily bombed in World War II, and is thus short on traditional "sights." The colonial streets and canals of ambitiously named **Venezia Nuova** (New Venice)

The charming town of Lucca.

make the best part of town for a stroll and coffee.

In Piazza Micheli is Livorno's treasure, the Mannerist **Monumento dei Quattro Mori** (1623–26), the contorted bronze masterpiece of Pietro Tacca, crowned by a statue of Duke Ferdinand I.

The Quattro Mori monument in Livorno.

The art highlight is the **Museo Civico** in Villa Mimbelli, Via San Jacopo in Acquaviva 65 (☎ 0586-808001), with an unmatched collection by the Macchiaioli, 19th-century Tuscan forerunners to Impressionism. Native son Giovanni Fattori, who worked from the 1860s until 1908, is the star. *Admission 4€. Tues–Sun 10am–1pm and 4–7pm.*

The city tourist office is a booth in the middle of Piazza del Municipio (☎ 0586-204611).

Fruits of the Sea

If you've made it to Livorno, don't leave without trying its seafood, Tuscany's best. The local specialty is *cacciucco*—a spicy, tomato-based seafood soup-stew. **La Chiave**, Scali delle Cantine 52 (☎ 0586-829865; $$$$), has the finest cuisine in town, with an adventurous menu that changes biweekly. **Antico Moro**, Via Bartelloni 29 (☎ 0586-884659; $$), is blue-collar by comparison—with more rustic, less expensive, but equally tasty fish dishes.

Revisiting Puccini

Music lovers flock to ⑦ **Torre del Lago**, 6km (3½ miles) south of Viareggio along lime-lined Viale dei Tigli, to pay homage to composer Giacomo Puccini (1858–1924). *Turandot*, his masterpiece and swansong, belongs among the great operas of all time. It is often featured at the annual summer, open-air **Festival Puccini** (☎ 0584-359322; www.puccinifestival.it). *Tickets 33€–160€.*

His home on Lago di Massaciuccoli, now the **Museo Villa Puccini** (☎ 0584-341445; www.giacomopuccini.it), holds mementos, autographed scores, and curios from the daily life of the Maestro. The lakeside setting is delightful, with fruit trees and bamboo thickets. *Admission 7€. Apr–Oct Tues–Sun 10am–12:30pm and 3–6pm; Dec–Mar Tues–Sun 10am–12:30pm and 2:30–5:30pm.*

The town also has a reputation as one of the gay-friendliest beach resorts in Italy.

From Livorno, follow the A12 north, bypassing Pisa and taking the exit for Viareggio, a distance of 46km (29 miles).

⑧ **Viareggio.** The Biarritz of the Versilia, an Italian seaside resort *par excellence,* had its heyday in the late 19th century. Its promenade, the **Passeggiata Margherita,** remains one of Italy's most elegant boardwalks—against a backdrop of fashion boutiques, Art Deco bathing establishments *(stablimenti),* cafes, and overpriced seafood restaurants. Its main "sight," the Art Nouveau **Gran Caffè Margherita,** is somewhat of a puffed-up architectural travesty.

What you're really here for is the fine beach—a wide strip of manicured sand with a shallow shelf that's ideal for even little ones to paddle. Viareggio is also one of the few places in Tuscany you'll find things lively and youth-oriented well into the night, in season at least.

The town hosts Italy's second-most important February **Carnevale** (☎ 0584-1840750; www.viareggio. ilcarnevale.com), after Venice.

The tourist office is at Viale Carducci 10 (☎ 0584-962233).

Seafood is Livorno's chief export.

The **Val d'Orcia & Valdichiana**

1 Montalcino
2 San Quirico d'Orcia
3 Bagno Vignoni
4 Radicofani
5 Pienza
6 Montepulciano
7 Sarteano
8 Chiusi
9 Lucignano
10 Monte San Savino
11 Arezzo
12 Castiglion Fiorentino
13 Cortona

Southeastern Tuscany is home to two of the region's great valleys. The silent, cypress-studded landscapes of the Val d'Orcia—emerald green in spring, burnt copper in high summer—have become iconic images that represent Tuscany itself. The sweeping trough cut by the Valdichiana is the only place true *bistecca alla fiorentina* (a T-bone-like beefsteak) can call home: White Chianina cattle are native here. Southeastern Tuscany is also home to fine medieval and Renaissance art and two great wines that surpass even Chianti at its best. START: **Montalcino, 43km (27 miles) southeast of Siena on the S2. Trip length: 7 days.**

A Note on Hotels & Restaurants

For hotels, restaurants, and detailed information on attractions in Arezzo, see p 124; in Cortona, see p 128; in Montepulciano, see p 142; in Pienza, see p 146.

1 ★★ **Montalcino.** As wine lovers well know, this rustic hilltown of cobbled stone streets and narrow stairways is the source of one of the world's greatest red vintages, **Brunello di Montalcino.** The walled town is visible for miles, with the spires of its medieval buildings studding the air like an asparagus

field. The **Enoteca La Fortezza** (📞 0577-849211; www.enote calafortezza.it) is installed in the town's main attraction, a fortress where the Sienese Republic holed up for 4 years after final defeat by Florence in 1555. Within its keep, an abundance of Tuscan foodstuffs are for sale, including Pecorino cheese and Montalcino honey (famous among gourmets). Of course, most come here to stock up on one of 208 Brunellos. Mount the ramparts for one of the great views in Tuscany, a wide sweep from the Val d'Orcia to Monte Amiata. *Admission (ramparts) 4€. Apr–Oct daily 9am–8pm; Nov– Mar Tues–Sun 10am–6pm.*

The town's gathering place is **Caffè Fiaschetteria Italiana,** Piazza del Popolo 6 (📞 0577- 847113), an Art Nouveau cafe, with Thonet chairs, red-velvet banquettes, and marble tables. It has served the celebrated local wine since 1888. *Closed Thurs and Feb.*

Don't leave town without a stop at the magical little **Museo di Montalcino,** Via Ricasoli 31 (📞 0577-864014), with its collection of mostly Sienese sacred art. *Admission 4.50€. Tues–Sun 10am– 1pm and 2–5:50pm.*

The tourist office is at Costa del Municipio 1 (📞 0577-849331. www.prolocomontalcino.it).

The Valdichiana.

The fortress in Montalcino is the town's main attraction.

Follow signs back to the S2 then south; it's 12km (7 miles) to:

② ★ **San Quirico d'Orcia.** This little walled farming village, with its magnificent travertine Gothic-Romanesque **Collegiata dei Santi Quirico e Giulitta,** was once an important stopover along the Via Francigena, the pilgrim route that linked Canterbury (in England) with Rome. Its quaint streets and formal 1540 gardens, the **Horta Leonini,** Piazza della Libertà, are an easy spot to kill a couple of hours.

Continue south on the S2 5km (3 miles) to the turnoff for:

3 ★ **Bagno Vignoni.** See p 108, **7**.

Keep heading south on the S2 for 23km (14 miles) to the turn for:

4 **Radicofani.** It's all too easy to pass 2 hours wandering the steep cobblestone lanes and tiny piazzas of this atmospheric town. Pick up a couple of *fiorentina* steaks from **Macelleria Rossi** (☎ 0578-55864; www.macelleriarossi.it) for a DIY BBQ. On the road below town, **La Posta** is a crumbling 1587 inn and posthouse that once hosted Grand Tourists like Charles Dickens. Its fountain bears the Medici coat of arms.

On the hill above, visible for miles, is Radicofani's 9th-century **Fortezza** (☎ 331-4103303), reinforced by Pope Hadrian IV in the 12th century. It was the home of the "gentleman outlaw" Ghino di Tacco that Boccaccio immortalized in his *Decameron.* Views from its **Torre**

The 9th-century Fortezza rises above the picturesque town of Radicofani.

stretch almost to the sea. *Admission 4€. Daily 9am–8pm.*

Take the Sarteano road east out of town, then cut north along the S53, following signs for Pienza. It's a journey of 27km (17 miles).

5 & **6** ★★★ **Pienza and Montepulciano.** Two of the great art cities of Tuscany—Montepulciano and Pienza—can be visited in a day, but a lazy day in each would be preferable. Don't leave Pienza without taking in its breathtaking view over the Val d'Orcia from **Via del Casello.** Both towns are covered in depth in chapter 6, which presents a complete range of hotels, restaurants, shops, attractions, and nightlife. You can overnight in either Montepulciano or Pienza.

Head south on the S146 past Chianciano, then follow signs for Sarteano, a total of 19km (12 miles). Next stop is the Valdichiana, the broadest valley in the Apennines and the so-called "breadbasket of Italy."

7 ★ **Sarteano.** Distinctly off the regular tourist trail, this little walled town remains one of my favorite places to while away a morning in southern Tuscany. Come on a Saturday and you can join a tour run by the **Museo Civico,** Via Roma 24 (☎ 0578-269261), to see the **Tomba della Quadriga Infernale.** This unique Etruscan tomb frescoed with a demonic charioteer was only discovered in 2003. Other tombs in the spectacularly-sited **Pianacce** necropolis are open daily (and free). *Tour 5€ inc. museum admission. Sat only. Booking essential.*

Also worth tracking down is a 1545 *Annunciation* by the last great Sienese painter, Mannerist Domenico Beccafumi. It's in the boxy little church of **San Martino,** Piazza San Martino.

Val D'Orcia, outside Pienza.

The tourist office is at Corso Garibaldi 1 (☎ 0578-269204).

Follow signposts out of town for Chiusi, 12km (7 miles) away.

⑧ ★ **Chiusi.** If you're on the trail of the Etruscans, head here to see what's left of one of the most powerful cities in their 12-city confederation (the *Dodecapoli*). Chiusi was then known as Clevsin; so powerful was the city, that its king, Lars Porsenna, attacked Rome in 508 B.C. What's left of Clevsin is buried under the little town today. Explore it for yourself with a subterranean tour of the **Labirinto di Porsenna,** Piazza Duomo (☎ 0578-226490). *Admission 3€. Guided visits Jun–Sept daily 10:10am–12:10pm and 4:10–6.10pm; Oct–May Tues, Thurs, Sat–Sun 10:10am–12:10pm, Sun also 4:10–6:10pm.*

Chiusi's **Museo Archeologico Nazionale,** Via Porsenna (☎ 0578-20177), is one of Italy's outstanding Etruscan museums. Wander back in time as you take in the alabaster funerary urns, black and orange Attic-style ceramics, Bucchero pottery, and a 6th-century B.C.

sphinx. Most were recovered from necropoli around the town; the tombs are open daily for visits (ask at the museum desk). *Admission 4€. Daily 9am–8pm.*

The tourist office is at Piazza Duomo 1 (☎ 0578-227667; www. comune.chiusi.siena.it).

Take the A1 bound for Florence for 25km (15 miles) until the exit for Sinalunga/Lucignano. Follow signs for another 14km (9 miles).

⑨ ★ **Lucignano.** In an ideal world, you'd get your first sight of this little place from the air: Its elliptical street layout is unique in the annals of Tuscan town planning. Like a simplified maze, the village is laid out in four concentric ellipses with quaint little squares in the center. One is dominated by the **Collegiata,** with its 18th-century double half-oval staircase by Andrea Pozzo.

The highlight of the tiny **Museo di Lucignano,** Piazza del Tribunale 22 (☎ 0575-838001), is the *Albero della Vita* (Tree of Life), a complex 14th-century reliquary made by Sienese goldsmiths. The *Tree,* and

Lucignano, in the Valdichiana.

the atmospheric, frescoed room that houses it, is a popular spot for wedding vows. *Admission 3€. Mid-Mar to Oct Thurs–Mon 10am–1pm and 2:30–5:30pm; off season Fri 10am–1pm, Sat–Sun 10am–1pm and 2:30–5:30pm.*

The tourist office (☎ 0575-836899; www.comune.lucignano.ar.it) is inside the Museo.

Drive 8km (5 miles) north to:

⑩ ★ **Monte San Savino.** The birthplace of High Renaissance sculptor Andrea Sansovino (1460–1529) is another quiet little Valdichiana hilltown that's managed to avoid the perils (and riches) of commercial mass tourism. Dotted with medieval and Renaissance *palazzi*, it invites an afternoon of exploration and aimless wander.

As you hoof it around the town, you can see some of Sansovino's works, notably his altarpiece at the little church of **Santa Chiara.** The Della Robbia brothers are believed to have glazed this altarpiece for him, depicting the *Madonna and Child with Saints. Free admission. Wed–Fri (Apr–Oct also Tues) 9am–1pm; Sat–Sun 9am–1pm and 4–7pm.*

The **Loggia dei Mercanti,** Corso Sangallo, with its Corinthian columns, is also attributed to Sansovino. Across the street is Antonio da Sangallo the Elder's **Palazzo di Monte.** Further up the hill, at the Piazza di Monte, is the church of **Sant'Agostino.** Sansovino renovated the building in 1532, adding the cloister and gallery.

The seasonal tourist office is in Piazza Gamurrini (☎ 0575-849418).

Take the E78 20km (12 miles) northeast to:

⑪ ★★ **Arezzo.** The most landlocked of all the towns of Tuscany, Arezzo was originally an Etruscan settlement and later a Roman center. The city flourished in the Middle Ages before its capitulation to Florence.

The city's treasures are covered in depth in chapter 6, which presents a complete range of hotels, restaurants, shops, attractions, and nightlife.

The tourist office is at Piazza della Repubblica 28 (☎ 0575-377678).

Drive south on the S71 for 19km (12 miles) to the turnoff for:

⑫ **Castiglion Fiorentino.** You can't miss Castiglion Fiorentino: as you approach the **Torre del Cassero,** a pronglike tower, looms over the skyline. Wandering into the little hilltown takes you through a medieval girdle of fortified walls, leading to its hub, **Piazza del Municipio.** Dominating the square is the (now somewhat tattered) **Loggia di Vasari** reputedly designed by Renaissance man Giorgio Vasari in the 16th century.

The town's chief attraction is the **Pinacoteca Comunale** at Piazza del Municipio 12 (☎ 0575-659457), a repository of precious goldsmithery and notable paintings including Taddeo Gaddi's *Madonna and Child* and Bartolomeo della Gatta's bizarre *St. Francis Receiving the Stigmata. Admission 3€. Open Tues–Sun 10am–12:30pm and 4–6:30pm.*

The tourist office is in the car park opposite Porta Fiorentina (☎ *0575-658278*).

Continue south on the S71 for 12km (7 miles) to:

⓭ ★★ **Cortona.** This art city is your final Valdichiana stopover: There's no better spot to survey the entire "breadbasket of Italy" than the ramparts of its **Fortezza Medicea.** For a complete list of its attractions, hotels, restaurants, shops, and nightlife, see the Cortona section in chapter 6.

Sant'Antimo

Devotees of Romanesque architecture should take the southern road out of Montalcino and follow signs for Sant'Antimo for 9km (5 miles), until they come upon an idyllic glade that's home to the unmistakable **Abbazia di Sant'Antimo,** below Castelnuovo dell'Abate (☎ *0577-835659*; www.antimo.it). In the 12th century, it became a Cistercian abbey, and French monks still sound their Gregorian chants here daily. It's one of Tuscany's best examples of Romanesque architecture in the Lombard French style, with a semi-circular apse and 30m (100-ft.) bell tower. *Free admission. Mon–Sat 10:30am–12:30pm and 3–6:30pm; Sun 9:15–10:45am and 3–6pm.*

The Sant'Antimo Abbey.

Where to **Stay & Dine**

A Note on Hotels & Restaurants

For recommended hotels and restaurants in Arezzo, Cortona, Montepulciano, and Pienza, refer to the coverage of each town in chapter 6, "Charming Tuscan Towns & Villages."

★ **Posta Marcucci** BAGNO VIGNONI This family-run spa hotel is modern, with comfortable communal spaces and well-equipped rooms with views across the Val d'Orcia. Access to the adjacent geothermal spa pool is included. *Via Ara Urcea 43.* ☎ *0577-887112. www.hotelpostamarcucci.it. 36 units. Doubles 164€–204€ w/breakfast. MC, V.*

La Sfinge CHIUSI Of a lackluster lot, this slightly characterless cube emerges as the winner, thanks to the prime location, friendly owners, and simple but spacious bedrooms. Some units open onto panoramas of the valley. *Via Marconi 2.* ☎ *0578-20157. www.albergolasfinge.com. 14 units. Doubles 85€. MC, V. Closed Feb.*

★★ **Il Pama** RADICOFANI *TUSCAN GRILL* For a taste of where Tuscans eat lunch, grab a plastic table in the makeshift garden at this roadside inn. Food is market fresh, simple, and a great value. Order a *frittura mista* (mixed fried seafood), some roast suckling pig, and sides for the table—then get your fingers dirty. *Via Marconi 3.* ☎ *0578-55919. Entrees 4€–6.20€. No credit cards. Lunch daily (winter not Mon), dinner Tues–Sun.*

★★ **Zaira** CHIUSI *SOUTHERN TUS-CAN/ETRUSCAN* The finest food in a town that punches above its weight when it comes to cooking: Try meat dishes like rabbit with lemon or duck cooked in Vino Nobile. Then ask to see the underground wine cellar, inside an Etruscan well that dates to 500 B.C. *Via Arunte 12.* ☎ *0578-20260. www.zaira.it. Entrees 8€–15€. AE, DC, MC, V. Lunch, dinner Tues–Sun.*

★★ **Porta Castellana** MONTAL-CINO It's well worth booking ahead at this stylish three-room B&B built into former brickvaulted storehouses on the edge of Montalcino. Breakfast in the garden as the mists rise from the Val d'Orcia below is unforgettable. *Via S. Lucia 20.* ☎ *0577-839001. www.portacastellana.it. 3 units. Doubles 75€. MC, V.*

Re di Macchia MONTALCINO *MONTALCINESE* Local cooking around here means one thing: meat, especially game such as wild boar and hare, for *antipasto, primo,* and *secondo* if you dare. The powerful flavors, and warren-like setting, are just right to wash down a bottle of the iconic Brunello. *Via Saloni 21.* ☎ *0577-846116. Entrees 8€–16€. MC, V. Lunch, dinner Fri–Wed.* ●

Arezzo

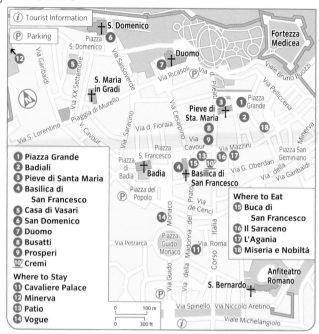

Tourist Information

Parking

1 Piazza Grande
2 Badiali
3 Pieve di Santa Maria
4 Basilica di
   San Francesco
5 Casa di Vasari
6 San Domenico
7 Duomo
8 Busatti
9 Prosperi
10 Cremi

Where to Stay
11 Cavaliere Palace
12 Minerva
13 Patio
14 Vogue

Where to Eat
15 Buca di
   San Francesco
16 Il Saraceno
17 L'Agania
18 Miseria e Nobiltà

Young Aretines are proud and prosperous, racing their Vespas through the Etruscan-era streets of this bustling town amid fertile Valdarno and Valdichiana farmlands. Famous native sons include the poet Petrarch (1304–74); architect and author Giorgio Vasari (1512–74); and Roberto Benigni, who brought Arezzo to a world audience as director and star of *Life Is Beautiful*. Time here is best spent strolling the steep streets of the medieval core, but don't miss the frescoes by Piero della Francesca in the Basilica di San Francesco. START: **Arezzo is southeast of Florence, well signpposted from the A1. Trip length: 81km (50 miles).**

Previous page: A rooftop view of Cortona.

1 ★★ kids **Piazza Grande.** This lopsided square began sinking at one end almost as soon as it was laid out around 1200, and it's been unstoppable since. The **Loggia di Vasari,** on the eastern (high) side was designed by the man himself, with obvious similarities to Florence's Uffizi. Note the semicircular apse of

the Pieve di Santa Maria, typical of the Romanesque style. ⏱ *15 min.*

2 **Badiali.** A charming jumble of a shop to pick up a *faux*-ancient print, small watercolor, or souvenir calendar complete with all the saints' days. *Piazza Grande 2.* ☎ *0575-354720. No credit cards.*

Shopping Tip

Diehard shoppers should time their visit to coincide with the **Arezzo Antique Market,** running for over 40 years. It takes over Piazza Grande on the first Sunday of each month and the Saturday before. Bargains and rare finds usually disappear by 10am.

3 ★ **Pieve di Santa Maria.** This 12th-century church backing onto Piazza Grande is a stellar example of the Pisan-Romanesque style, with each of 88 external arches on the facade uniquely sculpted. Its chief treasure inside is Pietro Lorenzetti's 1320 polyptych of the *Madonna and Child with Saints,* on the high altar above the crypt. Notice how St. Luke on the pinnacle panels looks up at the *Annunciation* and writes it down in his Gospel, a unique narrative feature. ⏱ *20 min. Corso Italia 7.* ☎ *0575-22629. Free admission. Daily 8am–noon and 3–6pm.*

4 ★★★ **Basilica di San Francesco.** Between 1452 and 1466, Piero della Francesca painted *The Legend of the True Cross* inside San Francesco's Cappella Bacci—a cycle of frescoes based on Jacopo da Varazze's 1260 *Golden Legend.* They are rightly talked about in the same art-historical league as the Sistine Chapel. Each of the 10 panels is remarkable for its grace, ascetic severity, narrative detail, compositional precision, and dramatic light effects—"the most perfect morning light in all Renaissance painting," wrote art historian Kenneth Clark. They also feature some of the strangest hats ever frescoed. The church's rose window, from 1520, is by Guillaume de Marcillat. ⏱ *45 min. Piazza San Francesco 4.* ☎ *0575-352727. www.pierodellafrancesca.it. Admission 6€. Nov–Mar Mon–Sat 9am–6pm, Sun 10am–6pm; Apr–Oct until 7pm.*

5 **Casa di Vasari.** The first art historian—who chronicled the lives of Michelangelo, da Vinci, Masaccio, and others—Vasari (1511–74) bought this house in 1540. He decorated it with Mannerist artworks, often by his students, and executed the allegorical frescoes himself—all of which goes to prove he was a much better architect than he was painter. *Via XX Settembre 55.* ☎ *0575-409040. Admission 2€. Wed–Mon 8:30am–7pm; Sun 8:30am–1pm.*

Ceiling frescoes from Arezzo's 13th-century Duomo.

⑥ ★ **San Domenico.** The curious lopsided facade of this 13th-century basilica, which Vasari claimed was by Nicola Pisano, hides one of Arezzo's most ancient treasures: a crucifix painted around 1260 by a young Cimabue, teacher of Giotto and "father" of Tuscan art. Fragmentary frescoes by Spinello Aretino (1350–1410) adorn both walls of the nave. *Piazza San Domenico 7.* ☎ *0575-23255. Free admission. Daily 9am–6:30pm.*

Detail from Constantine's Dream, *from one of Francesca's frescoes in the Duomo.*

⑦ ★ **Duomo.** At the highest point in town, Arezzo's 13th-century cathedral is a rare Tuscan Gothic-style construction that symbolically towers over the civic Palazzo del Comune opposite. Don't miss Della Francesca's 1459 *Mary Magdalene* and the aisle stained-glass windows (1521–26) recounting the *Life of Christ*, by Guillaume de Marcillat. The adjacent park, **Il Prato,** is a good spot to take a breather, or let the kids run about. *Piazza del Duomo.* ☎ *0575-23991. Free admission. Daily 7am–12:30pm and 3–6:30pm.*

⑧ ★★ **Busatti.** Since 1842, the Busatti-Sassolini family has been selling exquisite textiles and handmade fabrics—including sumptuous linens; and hemp, cotton, and wool items such as curtains, towels, cushions, tablecloths, and rugs in several colors. You'll also find lace, earthenware, and glassware. *Corso Italia 48.* ☎ *0575-355295. www. busatti.com. AE, MC, V.*

⑨ **Prosperi.** This is one of Tuscany's finest jewelry stores, since 1816, with an impressive range of silver, gold, and platinum jewelry. Prosperi is also an authorized Rolex dealer. *Corso Italia 76.* ☎ *0575-20746. AE, DC, MC, V.*

⑩ ★ **Cremì.** Interrupt your shopping with a stop for the best artisan *gelato* in town. They also sell pancakes with a choice of sweet fillings. *Corso Italia 100. No phone. $.*

Arezzo's Piazza della Liberte.

Where to Stay

Cavaliere Palace CENTRO STORICO This patrician mansion from 1600 is now a modern hotel convenient for the railway station. Midsized rooms are well sound-proofed, half with showers, half with tubs. *Via Madonna del Prato 83.* ☎ *0575-26836. www.cavaliere hotels.com. 29 units. Doubles 150€ w/breakfast. AE, DC, MC, V.*

Minerva NORTH AREZZO In a squeeze (no centrally located options are available), go for this 1960s structure just beyond the walls. Inside it's a bastion of modern comfort, with a touch of Italian style and elegance. The town's best fitness center is free to guests. *Via Fiorentina 4.* ☎ *0575-370390. www. hotel-minerva.it. 130 units. Doubles 91€–103€ w/breakfast. AE, DC, MC, V.*

★★ **Patio** CENTRO STORICO For atmosphere, this ambitious hotel in the 18th-century Palazzo de' Giudici is our local favorite. Each of the large units is dedicated to one of Bruce Chatwin's travel tales, with furniture from the country it represents—like Emperor Wu-Ti accessories from China. *Via Cavour 23.* ☎ *0575-401962. www.hotelpatio.it. 7 units. Doubles 155€–176€ w/breakfast. AE, DC, MC, V.*

★★ **Vogue** CENTRO STORICO An ultra-stylish refit has transformed this well-located boutique hotel into your best bet for a sexy room in central Arezzo. Outside high season, always haggle over price. *Via Guido Monaco 54.* ☎ *0575-24361. www.voguehotel.it. 26 units. Doubles 150€–230€ w/breakfast. AE, MC, V.*

Where to Dine

★ **Buca di San Francesco** CENTRO STORICO *TUSCAN/ARETINE* Arezzo's best formal dining is in the frescoed cellar of a *palazzo* from the 1300s. In its 7th decade, it's still keeping alive "the memory of the old Tuscan flavors." Try its *la saporita di bonconte*, a platter including baked rabbit, sausages, and tripe. *Via San Francesco 1.* ☎ *0575-23271. Entrees 10€–17€. AE, DC, MC, V. Lunch Wed–Mon, dinner Wed–Sun. Closed 2 weeks in Aug.*

★ **Il Saraceno** CENTRO STORICO *TUSCAN/ARETINE* This trattoria serves consistently good, cheap, regional food, with an excellent wine list, and friendly service. Specialties include stewed wild boar with polenta and Tuscan pork with rosemary. *Via Mazzini 6A.* ☎ *0575-27644. Entrees 8€–18€. www.il saraceno.com. AE, DC, MC, V. Lunch, dinner Thurs–Tues. Closed Jan.*

L'Agania CENTRO STORICO *ARETINE* Locals pack this place for rib-sticking *ribollita*, hand-rolled pasta, and robust, value fare such as *fegatelli* (pig's liver). A bottle of local Chianti is just 4€. *Via Mazzini 10.* ☎ *0575-295381. www.agania.com. Entrees 6€–10€. AE, DC, MC, V. Lunch, dinner Tues–Sun.*

★★ **Miseria e Nobiltà** CENTRO STORICO *MODERN ITALIAN* A short menu, funky decor, and soft jazz set this restaurant apart from the Aretine average. Modern offerings might include pasta with zucchini, saffron, and cherry tomatoes or lard-wrapped roast pork with radicchio. After hours, it morphs into a wine bar that also sells Tuscan-brewed beers. *Piaggia San Bartolomeo 2.* ☎ *0575-21245. Entrees 10€–16€. MC, V. Lunch Wed–Sun, dinner Tues–Sun.*

Cortona

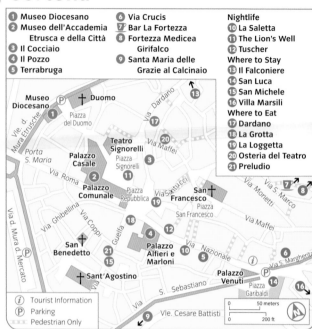

1 Museo Diocesano
2 Museo dell'Accademia
   Etrusca e della Città
3 Il Cocciaio
4 Il Pozzo
5 Terrabruga
6 Via Crucis
7 Bar La Fortezza
8 Fortezza Medicea
   Girifalco
9 Santa Maria delle
   Grazie al Calcinaio

Nightlife
10 La Saletta
11 The Lion's Well
12 Tuscher
Where to Stay
13 Il Falconiere
14 San Luca
15 San Michele
16 Villa Marsili
Where to Eat
17 Dardano
18 La Grotta
19 La Loggetta
20 Osteria del Teatro
21 Preludio

Map labels: Museo Diocesano · Duomo · Piazza del Duomo · Via d. Mura Etrusche · Porta S. Maria · Via Roma · Palazzo Casale · Teatro Signorelli · Piazza Signorelli · Via Dardano · Via Maffei · Palazzo Comunale · Piazza Repubblica · Via Santucci · San Francesco · Piazza San Francesco · Via Monetti · Via S. Marco · Via Maffei · Via d. Mura d. Mercato · Via Ghibellina · Via Coppi · Guelfa · San Benedetto · Sant'Agostino · Palazzo Alfieri e Marloni · Via Nazionale · Palazzo Venuti · Piazza Garibaldi · Via S. Margherita · S. Sebastiano · Vle. Cesare Battisti

(i) Tourist Information
(P) Parking
▪▪▪ Pedestrian Only

0   50 meters
0   200 ft

Cortona, as much as anywhere in Tuscany, has a fair claim to the title "city of art." Luca Signorelli (1445–1523) and Sassetta (1392–1451) were both Cortonese; Fra' Angelico lived here for a decade. At its peak Cortona rivaled Arezzo and Perugia, and almost Florence, in power and prestige. Memories of its heyday linger in its art collections and medieval architecture, making it one of Tuscany's most romantic hilltowns. Despite this embarrassment of cultural riches, it was a much more recent phenomenon that placed Cortona on the tourist map: Frances Mayes' bestseller *Under the Tuscan Sun*. START: **Cortona is southeast of Florence on the S71. From Arezzo, take the S71 south and follow the signs. Trip length: From Florence 105km (63 miles); from Arezzo 34km (22 miles).**

1 ★★ **Museo Diocesano.** Cortona's outstanding collection of sacred art reflects the town's former glory, and its position at the crossroads of influences from Florence, Siena, and even the neighboring region of Umbria. Native son Luca

Signorelli is the predictable star, in particular his monumental 1502 *Lamentation,* complete with surreal background scenes including the Crucifixion and Resurrection. Elsewhere in this deconsecrated church turned museum, Fra' Angelico's

Fra' Angelico's Annunciation, *in the Museo Diocesano.*

gentle *Annunciation* (1436) over the former baptismal font reveals him in top form, on his favorite subject. The narrative scenes from the *Life of the Virgin* on the predella are especially charming. Also represented are Sienese master Pietro Lorenzetti (1280–1348) and Florentine Bartolomeo della Gatta (1448–1502), and a fine Greco-Roman sarcophagus from the 2nd century even pops up. ⏱ *1 hr. Piazza del Duomo 1.* ☎ *0575-62830. Admission 5€. Apr–Oct daily 10am–7pm (Nov–Mar closes 5pm).*

② ★ **Museo dell'Accademia Etrusca e della Città.** Cortona's revamped civic museum, housed in the 13th-century Palazzo Casali, traces the history of the *città* from its earliest origins, through a sequence of multimedia displays from the area's Etruscan and Roman digs. Upstairs, the eclectic collection of the Accademia Etrusca meanders through Egyptian mummies to 17th-century celestial globes, *Quattrocento* ivories, and Etruscan bronze figurines. The prize find is an intact Etruscan bronze lamp from the 4th century B.C., in Room 5. A new archeology and paleontology floor opened in late 2008. ⏱ *1 hr. Piazza Signorelli 9.* ☎ *0575-637235.*

www.cortonamaec.org. Admission 7€. Apr–Oct daily 10am–7pm; Nov–Mar Tues–Sun 10am–5pm.

Farmers' Market

Saturday is market day. Head to **Palazzo Casali** (home of MAEC) in the morning, when local farmers start hawking fresh produce. You'll also find an annual Antiques Fair in late August and early September. ☎ *0575-630610.*

③ ★ **Il Cocciaio.** Cortona is known for its ceramics, and Il Cocciaio is the oldest and best of the town's outlets. The traditional patterns in green, cream, and dark yellow are prominent. Look for the symbolic stylized daisy, a design created by Gino Severini. This shop is unbelievably stuffed—don't bring your pet bull. *Via Benedetti 24.* ☎ *0575-605294. www.toscumbria. com/cocciaio. AE, DC, MC, V.*

④ Il Pozzo. This converted 11th-century courtyard is a quaint spot to pick up souvenir prints, stationery, or small gift items, all of Tuscan provenance. *Via Nazionale 10–12.*

Tuscan produce for sale at the farmers' market at Palazzo Casali.

☎ 0575-603730. www.cortonagift shop.com. MC, V.

⑤ ★ Terrabruga. I marginally prefer shopping at Il Cocciaio, but the serious pottery shopper should also consider its major rival, Terrabruga. Here, you will also find a wide array of terra-cotta ceramics in traditional Cortonese colors. These authentic craftwares are designed and manufactured by hand in owner Giulio Lucarini's workshop. *Via Nazionale 56.* ☎ *0575-605099. www. terrabruga.com. AE, DC, MC, V.*

⑥ ★ kids Via Crucis. The torturous, stepped ascent up Cortona's Via Santa Margherita is known as the "Path of the Cross": 15 mosaics by Cortonese Futurist Gino Severini (1883–1966) depicting the *Stations of the Cross* line the route. The climb also passes the Porta Berarda, through which Margherita di Laviano entered Cortona in 1277, on her way to sainthood as St. Margaret of Cortona. Take water, and don't attempt the route if you have asthma or a heart condition: It's major-league steep. ⏱ *45 min.*

Santa Maria della Grazie al Calcinaio.

A typical cobblestone street in medieval Cortona.

Pause for sustenance at the simple **⑦ Bar La Fortezza**, Piazza Santa Margherita (no phone), next to the Santuario di Santa Margherita. You earned it.

⑧ ★ kids Fortezza Medicea Girifalco. Built in 1556 by a relative of Pope Pius IV, Cortona's fortress has unmatched views over the Valdichiana, as far as Monte Amiata and Lago Trasimeno in Umbria. It's a magnificent sight—and makes the energy-sapping climb worthwhile. ⏱ *20 min.* ☎ *0575-637235. Admission 3€. Daily 10:30am–12:30pm and 2:30–6pm.*

⑨ Santa Maria delle Grazie al Calcinaio. Three kilometers (2 miles) downhill from the center, this monument to High Renaissance architecture was built by Sienese polymath Francesco di Giorgio Martini between 1485 and 1513. Laid out on a Latin cross plan, the church enjoys a bucolic setting amid olive groves below the ancient walls. The 1516 rose window is by Guillaume de Marcillat; a late 16th-century *Madonna and Saints*, by Alessandro Allori, is in the right transept. ⏱ *30 min. Via del Calcinaio. No phone. Free admission. Mon–Sat 4–7pm (3–5pm winter); Sun 10am–12:30pm.*

Where **to Stay**

★★ Il Falconiere SAN MARTINO
Just 4½km (3 miles) north of Cortona
is one of Tuscany's best country
inns. A restored series of 17th-cen-
tury buildings have the feeling of
a family house in the Valdichiana
countryside, with original furnishings, four-poster iron beds, and a
large pool amid an olive grove. *Loc.
San Martino 370.* ☎ *0575-612679.
www.ilfalconiere.it. 19 units. Doubles 270€–360€ w/breakfast. AE,
DC, MC, V.*

San Luca TOWN GATE   If you'll
settle for standard, yet comfortable,
bedrooms, San Luca will put you at
the heart of Cortona at an affordable price. The reputable on-site
restaurant has great views over
the Valdichiana and the bars, craft-
stores, and street cafes of Via
Nazionale and Piazza Repubblica are
just 2 minutes' (flat) stroll away.
Piazza Garibaldi 1. ☎ *0575-630460.
www.sanlucacortona.com. 60 units.
Doubles 120€ w/breakfast. AE, DC,
MC, V.*

★★ San Michele CENTRO STORICO
This central hotel in an 11th-century
palace has vaulted ceilings with
pietra serena arches, small to midsize
rooms under wood-beamed ceilings,
and antique furnishings. The tower
rooms are ideal for lovers. Email them
for the best prices.

In 2007, the same owners also
opened the tranquil Relais Borgo
San Pietro (www.borgosanpietro.
com) 3 miles northwest of Cortona.
This 17th century farmhouse was
converted to host 35 hotel rooms
and 5 full-equipped apartments
amid 7 acres of landscaped garden,
in San Pietro a Cegliolo, just off the
road to Castiglian Fiorentino. *Via
Guelfa 15.* ☎ *0575-604348. www.
hotelsanmichele.net. 50 units. Doubles 135€–150€ w/breakfast. AE,
DC, MC, V.*

★★ Villa Marsili TOWN GATE
With dignified lounges and finely furnished, frescoed bedrooms, this former gentleman's residence from
1786 is the coziest nest close to

A look inside a room at the San Michele hotel.

Palazzo Communale at night.

town, with outdoor gardens. Most rooms are elaborately furnished (bordering on campy), some with Murano glass chandeliers, and most with views of the Valdichiana. *Via C.* *Battisti 13.* ☎ *0575-605252. www.villamarsili.net. 27 units. Doubles 110€–230€ w/breakfast. AE, DC, MC, V.*

Cortona After Dark

La Saletta is the best wine bar in town with live jazz on Saturday nights in winter. Patrons of all ages come for excellent Tuscan wines by the glass and elegant surroundings. *Via Nazionale 26–28.* ☎ *0575-603366.* **The Lion's Well** is Cortona's Irish pub. Attracting a crowd in their 20s and 30s, it sells some wines by the glass. *Piazza Signorelli 28.* ☎ *0575-604918.* Centrally located **Tuscher** is Cortona's most elegant bar-cafe, with an attractive mix of visitors and locals. Excellent pastries, snacks, coffee, and tea are available Tuesday to Sunday from breakfast until midnight. *Via Nazionale 43.* ☎ *0575-62053.*

Where **to Dine**

★ **Dardano** CENTRO STORICO *TUSCAN* Visitors often overlook this family-owned, budget trattoria with Tuscan fare made with bounty from the Cortonese countryside. The cooks are known for their roasts— duck, chicken, and guinea hen (our favorite). In season, Mr. Castelli hunts game for the menu. *Via Dardano 26.* ☎ *0575-601944. Entrees 5€–8€. No credit cards. Lunch, dinner Thurs–Tues. Closed Jan–Feb.*

★★★ **Il Falconiere** SAN MARTINO *MODERN TUSCAN* This converted 17th-century *limonaia* affords one of Tuscany's best dining experiences. Silvia Baracchi, the owner, supervises every detail, and her well-trained staff will dazzle your palate with innovations on old recipes. Many ingredients come from the hotel garden. *Loc. San Martino 370.* ☎ *0575-612679. Entrees 18€–28€. AE, DC, MC, V. Lunch, dinner daily. Closed Jan 10–Feb 10 and Mon–Tues lunch in Nov.*

Wine Tip

The local wine to order, if you can track it down, is the light white **Vergine della Valdichiana.**

La Grotta CENTRO STORICO *TUSCAN* Come to this trattoria on a dead-end alley for tasty *casalinga* (home-cooking) and grotto-style dining, at tables in cozy chambers lined with stone and brick. Don't miss the thick *ribollita* (vegetable soup-stew) and tender, flavorful *fiorentina* steaks—the most affordable in town. *Piazza Baldelli 3.* ☎ *0575-630271. Entrees 8€–17€. AE, MC, V. Lunch, dinner Wed–Mon.*

★ **La Loggetta** CENTRO STORICO *TUSCAN* Abandoning the pizza menu has sharpened up the cooking at this visitors' favorite. Innovative pasta dishes like *tagliolini* with cabbage and truffle or *pici* (thick, short spaghetti) with duck *ragù* complement the setting under a loggia above Piazza della Repubblica. Alternatively, dine inside under the wood-beamed ceilings of the 16th-century Palazzo Pocetti. *Piazza di Pescheria 3.* ☎ *0575-630575. www. locandanelloggiato.it. Entrees 7€– 15€. AE, DC, MC, V. Lunch, dinner Thurs–Tues. Closed Jan.*

★★ **Osteria del Teatro** CENTRO STORICO *CORTONESE* An atmospheric alley just uphill from Piazza Signorelli is the setting for a creative take on Cortonese cuisine. Come in season (summer through October-ish), and you can eat a full *porcini* mushroom route through the menu. *Via Maffei 2.* ☎ *0575-630556. www.osteria-del-teatro.it. Entrees 8.50€–20€. AE, MC, V. Lunch, dinner Thurs–Tues.*

Preludio CENTRO STORICO *MODERN TUSCAN* Your best bet for semi-formal dining in the historic core, this spot draws regulars for fine seasonal food, great service, and cozy surrounds. Try the *pici* with game *ragù. Via Guelfa 11.* ☎ *0575-630104. Entrees 9€–18€. AE, DC, MC, V. Lunch, dinner Tues–Sun. Closed early Jan.*

A table at Il Falconiere, one of Tuscany's finest restaurants.

Lucca

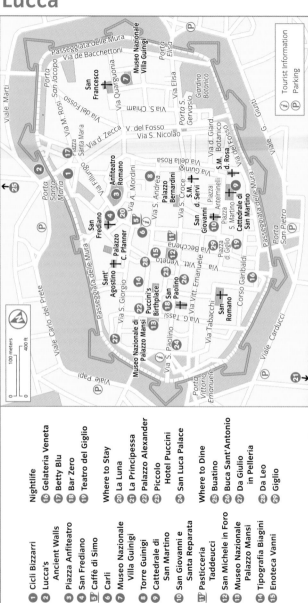

① Cicli Bizzarri
② Lucca's
    Ancient Walls
③ Piazza Anfiteatro
④ San Frediano
⑤ Caffè di Simo
⑥ Carli
⑦ Museo Nazionale
    Villa Guinigi
⑧ Torre Guinigi
⑨ Cattedrale di
    San Martino
⑩ San Giovanni e
    Santa Reparata
⑰ Pasticceria
    Taddeucci
⑫ San Michele in Foro
⑬ Museo Nazionale
    Palazzo Mansi
⑭ Tipografia Biagini
⑮ Enoteca Vanni

Nightlife
⑯ Gelateria Veneta
⑰ Betty Blu
⑱ Bar Zero
⑲ Teatro del Giglio

Where to Stay
⑳ La Luna
㉑ La Principessa
㉒ Palazzo Alexander
㉓ Piccolo
    Hotel Puccini
㉔ San Luca Palace

Where to Dine
㉕ Buatino
㉖ Buca Sant'Antonio
㉗ Da Giulio
    in Pelleria
㉘ Da Leo
㉙ Giglio

Lucca is the most graceful provincial city in Tuscany, set within a ring of massive medieval and Renaissance walls. At the heart of one of Europe's richest agricultural regions, locals eat and drink well, and have a deserved reputation for politeness. Hometown to Puccini, who celebrated his 150th birthday in 2008, the entire city is dotted with grand *palazzi* and churches. Plus the popularity of the bike as the preferred form of local transport makes Lucca a pleasure to wander. START: **Lucca is west of Florence on the A11, north of Pisa on the S12r. Trip length: from Florence 72km (45 miles); from Pisa 21km (13 miles).**

① **kids Cicli Bizzarri.** A bike rental shop (next door to the tourist office) might seem like a curious first stop, but you'll need wheels where we're heading. Rent yours here for 2.50€– 3.50€ per hour.

Antonio Poli (www.biciclettepoli. com), a few doors down at number 42, is a competitively-priced bike-hire alternative. *Piazza Santa Maria 31.* ☎ *0583-496031. No credit cards.*

② ★★★ **kids Lucca's Ancient Walls.** Planted with plane, chestnut, and ilex trees, Lucca's ramparts make for one of Tuscany's great bike rides. Now a city park stretching for 5km (2¾ miles), the **Passeggiata delle Mura** gives Lucca its special charm, and walking or cycling the circular route is the best way to get yourselves oriented. The only question is: clockwise or counterclockwise? I prefer the former, starting from Piazza Santa Maria and heading east, so my last view before descending is down into the manicured Baroque garden of the **Palazzo Pfanner.** ⏱ *1¼ hr.*

Flower vendors in Piazza dell' Anfiteatro.

3 ★ **kids** **Piazza Anfiteatro.** If you want to hang out at a street cafe, make it one near the lovely Piazza Anfiteatro, off the northern end of the main shopping street, Via Fillungo ("long thread"). A 2nd-century Roman amphitheater stood here until its destruction in the 1100s: Locals used it as a quarry for the stone to construct Lucca's palaces and churches. The foundations of what were the grandstands today support an ellipse of medieval houses. ⏱ 15 min.

4 ★ **San Frediano.** The original 6th-century basilica, built to honor an Irish hermit who became Bishop of Lucca, was reconstructed in the 12th century in the Lucchese-Romanesque style, using marble from the dismantled Roman amphitheater. The dazzling 13th-century *Ascension* mosaic on the facade, possibly by local painter Bonaventura Berlinghieri, was restored in the 1800s. Just inside the entrance is the church's treasure, a 12th-century Romanesque baptismal font depicting the story of

A cyclist on Lucca's massive ramparts.

Moses. ⏱ 20 min. Piazza San Frediano. ☎ 0583-493627. Free admission. Mon–Sat 7:30am–noon and 3–5pm; Sun 10:30am–5pm.

5 **Caffè di Simo.** On Lucca's main shopping drag, this is the most famous cafe in town. Puccini came here for a drink, perhaps contemplating his next opera. *Via Fillungo 58.* ☎ 0583-496234. $.

6 ★ **Carli.** One of the oldest jewelry stores in Tuscany, from 1655, Carli specializes in exquisite antique jewelry, silver, and watches. *Via Fillungo 95.* ☎ 0583-491119. AE, DC, MC, V.

7 ★ **Museo Nazionale Villa Guinigi.** Once owned by Paolo Guinigi, who ruled Lucca from 1400–1430, this museum displays the best from local archaeological digs as well as Romanesque, Gothic, and Renaissance sculpture. Its painting collection is strong on works by regional artists. Highlights include a tomb slab by Jacopo della Quercia, and Zainobi Machiavelli's *Madonna and Child.* ⏱ 30 min. *Via della Quarquonia.* ☎ 0583-496033. Admission 4€; 6.50€ with Palazzo Mansi. Tues–Sat 8:30am–7pm, Sun 8:30am–1pm.

8 ★ **kids** **Torre Guinigi.** This tower, rising 44m (146 ft.) with trademark ilex growing from the roof, was built by the city's ruling family in the 15th century. Climb its 230 steps to get a proper picture of Lucca enclosed by its ring of walls, with the Apennine mountain range beyond. ⏱ 20 min. *Via Sant'Andrea (at Via Chiave d'Oro).* ☎ 0583-48524. Admission 3.50€. Mar–mid to Sept daily 9am–7:30pm; mid-Sept to Oct daily 9:30am–8pm; Nov–Feb daily 9:30am–5:30pm.

A sidewalk cafe in Lucca.

⑨ ★★ Cattedrale di San Martino. Pope Alexander II consecrated Lucca's Duomo in 1070, but it took 4 centuries to finish. This ornate, asymmetrical structure was constructed around its *campanile* (bell tower) with an arched facade in the Pisan-Romanesque style. This facade was never completed; the topmost loggia and tympanum have yet to be built. Look for the reliefs under the portico, a stellar example of 13th-century stonework, including a fascinating 12-panel calendar of peasant life. The interior was given a Gothic dress in the 14th to 15th centuries, but remains dark and a touch grim. A highlight, in the sacristy, is Jacopo della Quercia's *Tomb of Ilaria del Carretto* (ca. 1406), his earliest surviving work and the first sculptural creation of the Renaissance to use Roman decorative motifs. Ruskin called it "the loveliest Christian tomb in Italy."

Adjacent to the cathedral is the **Museo della Cattedrale,** housing among its sacred art, the fine golden accoutrements worn by the *Volto Santo* on Lucca's Feast of the Luminara, September 13th. 🕐 *45 min. Piazza San Martino.* ☎ *0583-490530. www.museocattedrale lucca.it. Free admission to cathedral;* 2€ *sacristy;* 6€ *sacristy, Museo and San Giovanni. Mon–Fri 9:30am–5:45pm, Sat 9:30am–6:45pm, Sun 9:30–10:45am and noon–6pm.*

⑩ ★ San Giovanni e Santa Reparata. The main structure of the present church dates from the 1100s, although the facade is largely from the 1500s. Its roots, however, stretch much further back: Foundations under the nave, baptistery, and

The San Pietro gate is one of several medieval gates in Lucca.

Lucca After Dark

Lucca is a typically drowsy Tuscan town after dark, with just a few nightspots. Strolling the center with a gelato is perhaps the best way to pass a warm evening. In business since 1927, **Gelateria Veneta,** Via Vittorio Veneto 74 (☎ 0583-467037; www.gelateria veneta.net), is the traditional choice. There's usually some bar life at **Betty Blu,** Via Gonfalone 16–18 (☎ 0583-492166; closed Wed), where young locals gather to drink moderately, smoke copiously, and talk—to each other or on their cellphones. The recorded soundtrack spans everything from Radiohead to Europop. Summer drinkers at **Bar Zero,** Via S. Paolino 58 (no phone), usually spill out onto the steps of San Paolino church opposite. Beers, spirits, and wines by the glass are all popular as is the adjacent late night kebab take-away. October to March is the season at the **Teatro del Giglio,** Piazza del Giglio (☎ 0583-467521; www.teatrodelgiglio.it), one of Tuscany's major houses. Rossini premiered William Tell here in 1831. The program has a mix of classical dance, theater, opera, and modern musical shows.

altar have been opened up to show an archeological history that heads back past the 7th-century Lombard mausoleum, past the Paleochristian 5th-century church to the 1st-century B.C. mosaic floor of Lucca's Roman baths. ⏱ 30 min. Piazza

A detail of San Michele in Foro.

San Giovanni. ☎ 0583-490530. Admission 2.50€. Mar–Oct daily 10am–6pm; Nov–Feb Sat–Sun 10am–5pm.

⓫ ★ **Pasticceria Taddeucci.** This pastry shop, founded in 1881, created a legendary confection called *Buccellato Taddeucci,* still sold today. Even Prince Charles dropped in for a taste of the anise-flavored cake studded with raisins. *Piazza San Michele 34.* ☎ *0583-494933. $.*

⓬ ★★ **San Michele in Foro.** The *foro* in the name of this 12th-century church comes from the fact that it was built atop the Roman forum. The facade, with its four galleries, blind arcades, and individually unique, almost pagan columns, represents the zenith of the form that Romanesque architecture took around here. While the internal architecture is much altered, and

The rooftops of Lucca and the surrounding countryside.

disappointing after that blockbuster facade, worth a peek is Filippino Lippi's *Saints* in the right transept. ⏱ *20 min. Piazza San Michele.* ☎ *0583-48459. Free admission. Daily 9am–noon and 3–5:30pm.*

⑬ Museo Nazionale Palazzo Mansi. It's almost a case of the frame outshining the painting at this lavishly decorated 16th-century palace, formerly owned by the powerful Mansi family. Fans of Baroque portraiture, though, should head upstairs to the gallery for works by Pontormo, Bronzino, Beccafumi, Correggio, Veronese, and others. ⏱ *45 min. Via Galli Tassi 43 (at Via del Toro).* ☎ *0583-55570. Admission 4€; 6.50€ with Villa Guinigi. Tues–Sat 8:30am–7:30pm, Sun 8:30am–1:30pm.*

Puccini, Lucca's favorite son.

⑭ ★ Tipografia Biagini. The highest quality paper is turned into bespoke stationery at this traditional typography workshop. Orders are designed and set by hand, and can be shipped home. *Via S. Giustina 20–24.* ☎ *0583-54292. www.tipografiabiagini.it. AE, MC, V.*

⑮ ★★ Enoteca Vanni. Founded in 1965 this is Lucca's best wine cellar with great examples of the respectable local DOC, Montecarlo. Lucca's hills are also acclaimed for olive oil: Renzo Baldaccini's Organic Lucca DOP is the finest in town and produced in limited quantities and stocked here. *Piazza S. Salvatore 7.* ☎ *0583-491902. www. enotecavanni.com. MC, V.*

Where **to Stay**

La Luna CENTRO STORICO   You'll find problems here if you look hard enough, but no one complains about the price, as long as you duck the overpriced breakfast buffet. Rooms come in all sizes—from spacious to tiny; ditto for the bathrooms. Still, the hotel offers a consistently warm and welcoming atmosphere. *Corte Compagni 12 (off Via Fillungo).* ☎ *0583-493634. www. hotellaluna.com. 29 units. Doubles 100€–115€. AE, DC, MC, V.*

★★★ La Principessa MASSA PISANA   The poshest digs around Lucca are in a luxurious villa with roots that date to 1320, 3km (2 miles) south of the walls on the road to Pisa. The present building dates largely from an 18th-century reconstruction, complete with serene gardens and swimming pool. *Via Nuova per Pisa 1616, Massa Pisana.* ☎ *0583-370037. www.hotel principessa.com. 41 units. Doubles 180€–264€. AE, DC, MC, V. Closed Nov–Apr.*

★ Palazzo Alexander CENTRO STORICO   The 12th-century building became a girls' boarding school in the 1800s then was restored and reopened as an intimate hotel in 2000. Modern conveniences like whirlpool baths and computer hookups have been installed discreetly, and timbered ceilings left intact. *Via S. Giustina 48 (at Via Gialli Tassi).* ☎ *0583-583571. www. palazzo-alexander.com. 12 units. Doubles 120€–190€ w/breakfast. AE, MC, V.*

★ Piccolo Hotel Puccini CENTRO STORICO   The city's best value and most conveniently located hotel takes its name from the composer, who was born across the street. Small and friendly, the hotel offers clean, cozy bedrooms with modern furnishings. Some bedrooms open onto a small square. *Via di Poggio 9 (off Piazza San Michele).* ☎ *0583-55421. www.hotelpuccini.com. 14 units. Doubles 93€. AE, DC, MC, V.*

★★ San Luca Palace CENTRO STORICO   Opened in 2007, this crisp conversion of a 1540 *palazzo* has upped the ante for comfort within the walls. Modern, well-equipped rooms have retained some antique character. *Via San Paolino 103.* ☎ *0583-317446. www.sanlucapalace.com. 26 units. Doubles 170€–290€ w/breakfast. AE, DC, MC, V.*

La Principessa, Lucca's most luxurious hotel.

Where to Dine

Tuscan crostini.

★★ **Buatino** NORTH LUCCA *ITAL-IAN/LUCCHESE* It's worth the walk 10 minutes north of Piazza Santa Maria to this slightly funky bar-cum-trattoria. *Antipasti* include Italian classics like *bruschetta,* and unfussy pasta dishes are all made fresh on the premises. For *secondi,* expect Lucchese ingredients like rabbit, *baccalà* (salt cod), and *farro* (spelt wheat) to make an appearance. *Borgo Giannotti 508.* ☎ *0583-343207. Entrees 8€–10€. AE, MC, V. Lunch, dinner Mon–Sat.*

★★ **Buca Sant'Antonio** CENTRO STORICO *TUSCAN* The finest, most reliable cuisine in Lucca is served in a 1782 building where Puccini used to dine. The classic Tuscan dishes are prepared with flavor, flair, and superb simplicity. Reservations recommended. *Via della Cervia 3.* ☎ *0583-55881. Entrees 15€. AE, MC, V. Lunch Tues–Sun, dinner Tues–Sat.*

★ **Da Giulio in Pelleria** CENTRO STORICO *LUCCHESE* There's no more authentic Lucchese dining within the city walls. Local special-ties include horse tartar, veal snout, and Tuscan sausages with stewed white beans, plus, as ever, there are grilled meats and pasta. *Via delle Conce 45.* ☎ *0583-55948. Entrees 7€–11€. MC, V. Lunch Sat and 3rd Sun of month, dinner Mon–Sat.*

★ **Da Leo** CENTRO STORICO *TUS-CAN/LUCCHESE* The Buralli family makes everyone feel welcome at their unpretentious tavern in a 16th-century building. Guests come not for the 1930s decor, but for the affordable regional menu, including homemade pastas prepared daily and seasonal game roasts. *Via Tegrimi 1 (at Piazza San Salvatore).* ☎ *0583-492236. www.trattoria daleo.it. Entrees 9€–12€. No credit cards. Lunch, dinner Mon–Sat; Jun–Aug dinner Sun.*

Giglio CENTRO STORICO *ITALIAN/ TUSCAN* Time-honored recipes are prepared authentically at this traditional dining room, using farm products from the Lucca region. Meals begin with steaming bowls of minestrone and proceed to classic Tuscan mains such as stewed rabbit with olives. *Piazza del Giglio 2 (off Piazza Napoleone).* ☎ *0583-494058. Entrees 13€–16€. AE, MC, V. Lunch Thurs–Tues, dinner Thurs–Mon. Closed 2 weeks in Nov.*

Montepulciano

(i) Tourist Information
(P) Parking

1 Palazzo Comunale
2 Cattedrale di Santa Maria
3 Palazzo Nobili-Tarugi
4 Museo Civico
5 Contucci
6 Gattavecchi
7 Santa Maria dei Servi
8 Mazzetti Albo Mosaics
9 Caffè Poliziano
10 Tempio di San Biagio

Where to Stay
11 Duomo
12 Il Borghetto
13 Meublé Il Riccio
14 San Biagio

Where to Dine
15 Acquacheta
16 Pulcino
17 Il Cantuccio
18 La Grotta

The garnet colored Vino Nobile, beloved by epicures, put the medieval town of Montepulciano on the map. At an altitude of 605m (1,985 ft.), Montepulciano is also Tuscany's loftiest hill town, with remarkable views over the vineyards from up there on its volcanic crag. Before checking out individual sites, climb its steeply graded, serpentine main street—it has many names, but locals call it simply "Il Corso." Piazza Grande is at the summit of the Corso, where you can begin your tour of the individual attractions. START: **From Florence, take the A1 south to the Chianciano Terme exit, then the S146 for 18km (11 miles). From Siena, head south on the S2 to San Quirico d'Orcia, then follow the S146 east to Montepulciano. Trip length: 124km (74 miles) from Florence; 67km (40 miles) from Siena.**

---

1 ★ kids Palazzo Comunale. The highest point in town is **Piazza Grande,** enveloped by Renaissance *palazzi* and this Gothic town hall. The crenellated clock tower was added by Michelozzo (1396–1472), inspired by the Palazzo Vecchio (built in the 1200s), in Florence. A climb up the tower gives you a chance to get your Montepulciano geography straight—and take in expansive views over the Valdichiana below. *⏱ 20 min. Piazza Grande.* ☎ *0578-7121. Admission 1.60€. Mon–Sat 10am–6pm.*

Piazza Grande in Montelpulciano.

the 13th to 17th centuries. Other gems include 15th-century illuminated choir books, enameled terra cottas by Andrea Della Robbia (1435–1525), and Etruscan funerary urns. ⏱ *30 min. Via Ricci 10.* ☎ *0578-17300. Admission 4.13€. Tues–Sun 10am–7pm.*

Vino Nobile

Montepulciano's vintners have organized a consortium-cum-show-room, the **Consorzio del Vino Nobile di Montepulciano** (☎ 0578-757812; www.consorzio vinonobile.it). The public can visit, at the Palazzo del Capitano del Popolo on Piazza Grande, and sample members' wines. *Three tasting glasses 5€.* Mon–Sat 1–5pm.

Montepulciano is littered with *enoteche* and *cantine* (wine cellars) where you can sample and purchase Vino Nobile and other local products.

2 ★ Cattedrale di Santa Maria. To the world, this uncompleted Duomo presents a blank facade, but the sparse interior is not without its treasures. I visit just to gaze at Taddeo di Bartolo's 1401 triptych, *Assumption of the Virgin*, above the high altar. It glows, with the artist's use of subtle pinks, blood orange, eggplant purple, and plenty of gold leaf. ⏱ *20 min. Piazza Grande. No phone. Free admission. Daily 9am–12:30pm and 3:15–7pm.*

3 ★★ Palazzo Nobili-Tarugi.
Facing the Duomo across Piazza Grande, this *palazzo*—with its half-moon arches, Ionic columns, great portico, and entryway with pilasters—is attributed to Antonio da Sangallo the Elder. The much-photographed 1520 fountain out front incorporates two Etruscan columns, topped by two griffins and two lions bearing the Medici coat of arms. The interior is closed to the public. ⏱ *15 min. Piazza Grande.*

4 Museo Civico. The Sienese-Gothic Palazzo Neri-Orselli houses most of Montepulciano's art treasures. Its collection of some 200 Tuscan paintings features works from

5 ★★ Contucci. In Montepulciano's main square, this renowned winery occupies the cellars of the 13th-century Palazzo Contucci, home to popes and Grand Dukes over the years. Contucci was one of the first makers of Vino Nobile, still a proud tradition today. *Palazzo Contucci, Piazza Grande.* ☎ *0578-757006. www.contucci.it. AE, DC, MC, V.*

6 ★★ Gattavecchi. The Riserva here, aged for an extra 6 months in oak *barriques,* was the best Vino Nobile I tasted in Montepulciano. Ask to see the cellars: They have been in continuous use since before 1200, originally by the friars of the church next door. *Via di Collazzi 74.* ☎ *0578-757110. www. gattavecchi.it. AE, MC, V.*

7 Santa Maria dei Servi. The little parish church next to Gattavecchi is notable for a curious little *Madonna and Child* inserted smack

in the middle of another painting, to the left of the altar. The *Madonna* has been attributed to the 13th-century Sienese workshop of Duccio di Buoninsegna. ⏱ *10 min. Piazza di Santa Maria. No phone. Free admission. Irregular hours.*

⑧ ★ Mazzetti Albo Mosaics. Large framed mosaics, of scenes from Montepulciano and around, all handmade by Albo in his workshop. Prices from 450€. *Via di Cagnano 4 (workshop around corner on Corso).* ☎ *0578-757272. No credit cards.*

Ceramics for sale along the Corso.

⑨ ★★ Caffè Poliziano. This cafe, which opened in 1868, has bounced back after decades of slumber, since the days when Pirandello and Fellini quaffed here. Restored to some of its former glory, it is the center of sleepy Montepulciano's nighttime activities. You can sip Noble wines on an outdoor terrace; in the off season there's a winter garden dining room. *Via Voltaia nel Corso 27.* ☎ *0578-758615. www.caffepoliziano.it. $–$$$.*

⑩ ★★ Tempio di San Biagio. This masterpiece of High Renaissance architecture was the greatest achievement of architect Antonio da Sangallo, who finished it in 1529. He was obviously inspired by Bramante's design for St. Peter's in Rome. Built on a Greek cross plan, it was designed to house a statue of the Madonna. Crowned by its dome, the church has two *campaniles* or bell towers—one left unfinished. When shadows start to lengthen, the yellow travertine structure shines like gold. ⏱ *20 min. Via di San Biagio (10 min. downhill walk from Porta di Grassi). No phone. Free admission. Daily 9am–12:30pm and 3:30–7:30pm.*

San Biagio and the surrounding countryside.

Where to Stay

Duomo CENTRO STORICO   Small to midsized rooms at this family-run favorite, named for the cathedral opposite, are decorated in Tuscan *arte povera* style. All have renovated private bathrooms. *Via San Donato 14.* ☎ *0578-757473. www.albergoduomo.it. 13 units. Doubles 94€. AE, DC, MC, V.*

★ **Il Borghetto** CENTRO STORICO This rustic hostelry in a 16th-century building has midsized rooms with panoramic views, old brick floors, Tuscan antiques, and modern amenities. *Via Borgo Buio 7.* ☎ *0578-757535. www.ilborghetto.it. 17 units. Doubles 105€. AE, DC, MC, V. Closed Aug.*

Meublé Il Riccio CENTRO STORICO   Rooms are a bit featureless, but the unique setting above a 13th-century cloister in Montepulciano's oldest street, and the best roof terrace in town, ensure a memorable stay. *Via Talosa 21.* ☎ *0578-757713. www.ilriccio.net. 6 units. Doubles 100€. AE, DC, MC, V.*

★ **San Biagio** SAN BIAGIO   The town's most comfortable inn is a restored nobleman's house outside the walls. The best rooms have Tuscan decor and balconies with postcard views over the vines. The seasonal indoor pool almost evokes Pompeii's baths. *Via San Bartolomeo 2.* ☎ *0578-717233. www.albergo sanbiagio.it. 27 units. Doubles 100€–115€ w/breakfast. MC, V.*

The rooftop terrace at Meublé Il Riccio.

Where to Dine

★★ **Acquacheta** CENTRO STORICO *TUSCAN GRILL*   The menu's short at this informal little osteria inside a converted wine *cantina*: pasta five ways, grilled meat, salads, plus a lengthy pecorino list. Their *fiorentina alla brace* is the best steak in town. *Via del Teatro 22.* ☎ *0578-758443. www. acquacheta.eu. Entrees 5.50€–12€. MC, V. Lunch, dinner Wed–Mon.*

★ **kids Pulcino** TOWARD CHIANCIANO *SOUTHERN TUSCAN*   The restaurant outlet of Montepulciano's artisan food empire. Go for grilled meats straight from the farm, like the half-chicken or succulent veal, or *pici*, hand-rolled, short, thick spaghetti. One downer: Service is usually slow. *S146 per Chianciano 37.* ☎ *0578-758711. www.pulcino.com. Entrees 10€–16€. AE, DC, MC, V. Lunch, dinner daily. Closed Jan–Easter.*

Il Cantuccio
CENTRO STORICO *TUSCAN*   Many dishes here, such as the chicken and rabbit platter, are based on Etruscan recipes; all are Poliziana, the local cuisine. Try the tagliatelle in duck *ragù* or grilled Florentine steak with Tuscan white beans, finished with the ricotta torte. *Via delle Cantine 1–2.* ☎ *0578-757870. Entrees 9€–22€. AE, DC, MC, V. Lunch, dinner Tues–Sun. Closed 2 weeks in Nov, first 2 weeks of July.*

★ **La Grotta** SAN BIAGIO *ITALIAN* Across the street from San Biagio, this old-fashioned brick-vaulted tavern serves upmarket Italian classics, most of it harvested from the local countryside. I return for pasta with guinea fowl *ragù* and pork filet flavored with coffee beans and served with carrot-and-onion flan. *Via San Biagio 2.* ☎ *0578-757607. Entrees 19€–21€. MC, V. Lunch, dinner Thurs–Tues. Closed Jan 10–Mar 10.*

Pienza

Parking ℗

Tourist Information ⓘ

1. Piazza Pio II
2. Duomo
3. Museo Diocesano
4. Palazzo Piccolomini
5. Ferro Biagiotti
6. Nannetti e Bernardini
7. Enoteca di Ghino
8. Bar Il Casello

Where to Stay
9. Castello di Ripa d'Orcia
10. Chiostro di Pienza
11. San Gregorio
12. Piccolo Hotel la Valle

Where to Eat
13. La Chiocciola
14. La Porta
15. Latte di Luna

This model Renaissance town was the creation of Pope Pius II, who wanted to transform his village of Corsignano into a place that would glorify his name. He was born here as Silvio Piccolomini, in an impoverished branch of a noble Sienese family; he later added "Aeneas" as a first name out of love of the tales of Virgil, and after years as a humanist scholar, gout sufferer, and itinerant diplomat, served as pope from 1458 to 1464. His envisioned city never grew beyond a few blocks, but it remains a masterpiece. Zeffirelli recognized it for the stage setting it is, deserting Verona to film *Romeo and Juliet* here in 1968. START: **From Siena, take the S2 south to the S146 and follow the signs east. Trip length: from Siena 55km (33 miles).**

① ★ **Piazza Pio II.** Begin in the center of town: Virtually all the sights are on this set-piece piazza or nearby. The square is enclosed by the Duomo, Palazzo Piccolomini, and Palazzo Vescovile (Bishop's Palace).

The fourth side features the distinctly non-Renaissance **Palazzo Comunale,** home to the town hall and municipal offices. The bell tower, added later, was built lower than the Duomo's to emphasize the power of the Church over civil authority. 🕐 *10 min.*

2 ★★ **Duomo.** The classicized Renaissance facade complete with Roman arches and pediment conceals a Gothic interior influenced by the Austrian "hall churches" Pius admired on his travels. The Piccolomini family is honored with a coat-of-arms (cross and five upturned crescents) in the rose window and all over the church. Pius commissioned four leading Sienese artists to paint devotional altarpieces, and they're all still here: counterclockwise from the right aisle, Giovanni di Paolo, Matteo di Giovanni, Vechietta, and Sano di Pietro. Alas, the whole thing is built on clay and sandstone, and may one day collapse: Check out the slope to the altar and ceiling cracks. ⏱ *30 min. Piazza Pio II.* ☎ *0578-748548. Free admission. Daily 7am–1pm and 2:30–7pm.*

3 ★ **Museo Diocesano.** This neat little collection housed inside the Bishop's Palace looted local churches for its array of 14th- and 15th-century Sienese paintings, including a *Madonna and Child* by Pietro Lorenzetti (ca. 1280–1348). More surreal is the lifesized carved *San Regolo* holding his own severed

The Pienza Cathedral on Piazza Pio.

A virgin and child by Matteo di Giovanni.

head. ⏱ *40 min. Corso Rossellino 30.* ☎ *0578-749905. Admission 4.10€. Mid-Mar to Oct Wed–Mon 10am–1pm and 3–7pm; off season Sat–Sun 10am–1pm and 3–6pm.*

4 ★ **Palazzo Piccolomini.** The papal home of Pius II is architect Bernardo Rossellino's masterpiece, although it's obviously influenced by Alberti's Palazzo Rucellai in Florence. In Tuscany most facades are the star attraction. Not here: At the rear is a three-story loggia overlooking a hanging garden above the Val d'Orcia. Descendants of Pius lived here until 1968. ⏱ *30 min. guided tour only. Piazza Pio II.* ☎ *0577-286300. www.palazzopiccolomini pienza.it. Admission 7€. Mid-Mar to mid-Oct Tues–Sun 10am–6:30pm; closes 4:30pm otherwise. Closed 2nd half of Nov, 2nd half of Feb.*

5 ★ **Ferro Biagiotti.** Come for quality wrought-iron handcrafts, based on ancient designs. The products are made by an ancient technique, using fire, anvil, and hammer. *Corso Rossellino 67 (at Piazza Pio II).* ☎ *0578-748666. MC, V.*

Pecorino is Pienza's most famous export.

6 Nannetti e Bernardini.
Italy's most famous Pecorino, a sheep's-milk cheese, is sold in shops along Corso Rossellino, among which this artisan deli is the best. Fancier varieties are soaked in wine or dusted with truffles. For a lunchtime bite, try their Porchetta (salty herbed pork) *panino. Corso Rossellino 81.* ☎ *0578-748506. www.nannettiebernardinipienza. com. No credit cards.*

7 ★★ Enoteca di Ghino. Outstanding vintages of the very best wines from Tuscany and beyond. Bottles from 25€ to 10 times that. *Via del Leone 16.* ☎ *0578-748057. www.enotecadighino.it. MC, V.*

8 Bar Il Casello. This sleek, air conditioned bar and cafe is the social center of town, with snacks during the day, Tuscan reds and whites by the glass, and devastating views over the Val d'Orcia. It's open daily until midnight, shockingly late by local standards. *Via del Casello 3.* ☎ *0578-749105. $.*

Pienza's Via dell'Amore (Lover's Lane).

Where to Stay

★★ Castello di Ripa d'Orcia

RIPA D'ORCIA   Huge rooms with stone walls, beamed ceilings, and plush beds in a medieval castle. The owners run a restaurant and *enoteca* on the premises and require a minimum 2-night stay. *Loc. Ripa d'Orcia (signposted from San Quirico).* ☎ *0577-897376. www.castello ripadorcia.com. 6 units, 8 apts (sleep 2–4). Doubles 125€–168€ w/breakfast; apt. for 2 550€–780€ per week. MC, V. Closed Nov to mid-Mar.*

★★ Chiostro di Pienza CENTRO

STORICO   Converted to a hotel in 2005, this 15th-century convent and cloister is the best choice within the walls, with a pool overlooking the wilds of the Val d'Orcia. Spacious rooms have frescoes; those in the wing are best. *Corso Rossellino 26.* ☎ *0578-748400. www.relaisil chiostrodipienza.com. 37 units. Doubles 170€–230€ w/breakfast. AE, DC, MC, V.*

★ San Gregorio WEST PIENZA

This hotel adjacent to Piazza Dante opened in 1997 in a former cultural center bombed in World War II. Standard doubles are elegant and comfortable. There's an outdoor pool and restaurant serving traditional Tuscan fare. *Via della Madonnina 4.* ☎ *0578-748175. www.hotels angregorio.com. 16 units. Doubles 90€–116€ w/breakfast. MC, V.*

Piccolo Hotel la Valle NORTH

PIENZA   Our third choice in town, this modern hotel has spacious rooms, comfortably furnished, and with fridges. In good weather ask for breakfast on the terrace overlooking the Val d'Orcia. *Via Circonvallazione 7.* ☎ *0578-749402. www.piccolo hotellavalle.it. 15 units. Doubles 100€–130€ w/breakfast. MC, V.*

Where to Dine

La Chiocciola NORTH PIENZA

TUSCAN   Dishes at this rustic tavern with outdoor tables have stood the test of time. Try the pappardelle with wild boar or hare sauce, or the ravioli stuffed with local pecorino cheese. The cooking, with its abundant use of regional flavors, is never mannered. *Viale Mencattelli 2.* ☎ *0578-748683. www.trattoriala chiocciola.it. Entrees 7€–13€. AE, MC, V. Lunch, dinner Thurs–Tues. Closed 2 weeks in Jan.*

★ La Porta MONTICCHIELLO

TUSCAN   For a special treat, drive 6km (3¾ miles) southeast to the medieval village of Montichiello to this renowned osteria. The restaurant is at the main town gate, in an elegant room furnished in typical Tuscan style. There's terrace dining in fair weather (book ahead to ensure a berth). Regional fare includes favorites like wild boar carpaccio and ravioli stuffed with spinach and ricotta, served with a truffle sauce. *Via del Piano 3, Monticchiello.* ☎ *0578-755163. www.osterialaporta.it. Entrees 11€–18€. MC, V. Lunch, dinner Fri–Wed. Closed last 3 weeks of Jun and Jan.*

★ kids Latte di Luna CENTRO

STORICO *SOUTHERN TUSCAN*   This laid-back trattoria near the eastern town gate draws a diverse regular crowd—from foreign exchange students to local *carabinieri*. Don't miss the homemade *semifreddi* (similar to ice cream) for dessert. *Via San Carlo 2–4.* ☎ *0578-748606. Entrees 7€–15€. MC, V. Lunch, dinner Wed–Mon. Closed Feb to mid-Mar and July.*

Pisa

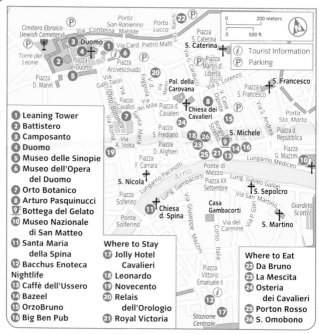

1 Leaning Tower
2 Battistero
3 Camposanto
4 Duomo
5 Museo delle Sinopie
6 Museo dell'Opera del Duomo
7 Orto Botanico
8 Arturo Pasquinucci
9 Bottega del Gelato
10 Museo Nazionale di San Matteo
11 Santa Maria della Spina
12 Bacchus Enoteca

Nightlife
13 Caffè dell'Ussero
14 Bazeel
15 OrzoBruno
16 Big Ben Pub

Where to Stay
17 Jolly Hotel Cavalieri
18 Leonardo
19 Novecento
20 Relais dell'Orologio
21 Royal Victoria

Where to Eat
22 Da Bruno
23 La Mescita
24 Osteria dei Cavalieri
25 Porton Rosso
26 S. Omobono

W hen Pisans discuss the good old days, they're talking about the 12th century. Buildings such as the Duomo and Leaning Tower, were created in those heady days of Pisan power. Pisa enjoyed great maritime influence because of its harbor at the mouth of the Arno River, and the Pisan-Romanesque architecture that developed through the rich years of the 13th century is the reason so many outsiders pass through today. The city began to decline following its defeat at sea by the Genovese in 1285 and the silting up of its vital harbor, and eventually succumbed to Florence. I suggest you spend the night here, and get to know its charming center beyond the Campo dei Miracoli. START: **From Florence, take the A11 and A12 west and follow signs. Trip length: 76km (47 miles).**

1 ★★★ kids **Leaning Tower (Torre Pendente).** The freestanding *campanile*, or bell tower, of the cathedral, the most famous building in Italy, was begun in 1173. It was intended to be vertical but started to lurch almost immediately: You just can't stack that much marble on sinking subsoil. However, construction continued, with two long interruptions, until 1350, and in December 2001 it was righted to

Pisa's oft-photographed 12th-century tower.

② ★★ **Battistero.** This stunning example of the Pisan-Romanesque style (with its own distinct lean) was begun in 1152 by Diotisalvi, and finally crowned with a Gothic dome in the 14th century. Don't miss the hexagonal pulpit (1260) by Nicola Pisano; it's supported by pillars resting on the backs of three marble lions, and carved with five scenes from the *Life of Christ*. ⏱ *20 min. Piazza del Duomo.* ☎ *050-3872211. www.opapisa.it. Admission 5€; 10€ for entire Campo exc. Tower. Nov–Feb daily 10am–5pm; Mar daily 9am–6pm; Apr–Sept daily 8am–8pm; Oct daily 9am–7pm.*

lean a mere 4m (14 ft.)—but you'll still notice the disorienting effects as you climb spiral steps to the top. It was supposedly from here that Galileo dropped balls of different masses, disproving Aristotle's theories about the acceleration of falling bodies. ⏱ *30 min. Piazza del Duomo.* ☎ *050-3872211. www.opapisa.it. Admission 15€. Nov–Feb daily 10am–5pm; Mar and Oct daily 9am–6pm; Apr–Sept daily 8:30am–8:30pm. Minimum age 8.*

③ ★ **Camposanto.** In 1278, Giovanni di Simone designed this cemetery, allegedly over dirt from the Holy Land shipped to Pisa by the Crusaders. Some 600 members of medieval Pisan nobility are interred here. The entire building was once decorated with frescoes by Benozzo Gozzoli, Andrea di Bonaiuto, and others, almost all destroyed when the Camposanto was hit by a U.S. incendiary bomb in 1944. Best of what remains is Buffalmacco's sobering *Triumph of Death*, painted in the late 1330s. ⏱ *40 min. Piazza del Duomo.* ☎ *050-3872211. www.opapisa.it. Admission 5€; 10€ for*

The Battistero.

entire Campo excluding Tower. Nov–Feb daily 10am–5pm; Mar daily 9am–6pm; Apr–Sept daily 8am–8pm; Oct daily 9am–7pm.

④ ★★ Duomo. This cathedral, started by Buschetto in 1063 using a mix of classical and Arab styles, became the most influential Romanesque building in Tuscany. The facade was erected by Rainaldo in the 1200s, with arches that diminish in size as they ascend. The pulpit by Giovanni Pisano (1302–11) even outshines the one by his dad in the baptistery. ⏱ *40 min. Piazza del Duomo.* ☎ *050-3872211. www.opapisa.it. Admission 2€ (free Nov–Feb). Nov–Feb Mon–Sat 10am–1pm and 2–5pm, Sun 1–5pm; Mar and Oct Mon–Sat 10am–6pm, Sun 1–6pm; Apr–Sept Mon–Sat 10am–8pm, Sun 1–8pm.*

⑤ ★ Museo delle Sinopie. The sketches (or *sinopie*) displayed here survived beneath the Camposanto's ruined frescoes after the 1944 bombardment. (Fresco artists drew in red-brown pigment before applying their paint.) Compare the different drawing styles of such painters as Benozzo Gozzoli, Taddeo Gaddi, and Andrea di Bonaiuto. ⏱ *30 min. Piazza del Duomo.* ☎ *050-3872211. www.opapisa.it. Admission 5€; 10€ for everything in Campo. Nov–Feb daily 10am–5pm; Mar daily 9am–6pm; Apr–Sept daily 8am–8pm; Oct daily 9am–7pm.*

⑥ ★ Museo dell'Opera del Duomo. Mostly Romanesque and Gothic art removed for safekeeping from the monuments of Piazza del Duomo is showcased here, including Bonnano Pisano's 12th-century San Ranieri door from the Duomo and plenty of *famiglia* Pisano sculpture. The courtyard has a unique view of the Campo dei Miracoli. ⏱ *45 min. Piazza Arcivescovado 6.* ☎ *050-3872211. www.opapisa.it. Admission 5€; 10€ for entire Campo exc. Tower. Nov–Feb daily 10am–5pm; Mar daily 9am–6pm; Apr–Sept daily 8am–8pm; Oct daily 9am–7pm.*

⑦ ★ kids Orto Botanico. Europe's oldest botanical garden, founded in 1543, is the perfect spot to breathe deep and wander unbothered after the chaos of the Campo. ⏱ *45 min. Via Ghini 5.* ☎ *050-2211316. Admission 2.50€. Sept–Jun Mon–Fri 8:30am–5:30pm, Sat 8:30am–1pm; Jul–Aug Mon–Sat 8:30am–1pm. Closed 1 week Aug.*

⑧ Arturo Pasquinucci. This kitchenware outlet, dating from 1870, sells an eclectic mix of crystal, glass, and ceramics. Dedicated shoppers will find plenty more to occupy them in the arcades of **Borgo Stretto** between here and the river. *Via Oberdan 22.* ☎ *050-580140. AE, DC, MC, V. Closed Aug.*

Bustling, modern shopping amid medieval architecture.

Santa Maria della Spina, on the quay.

9 ★ **Bottega del Gelato.** Pisa's best gelato. Enough said. *Piazza Garibaldi 11.* ☎ *050-575467. $.*

10 ★ **Museo Nazionale di San Matteo.** An old convent that was once a prison today houses sacred art and sculpture gathered from Pisa's holy places. It's memorable largely for many minor works by some major artists, like Masaccio's *St. Paul* (1426), the only piece of his much-studied *Pisa Altarpiece* still in Pisa. ⏲ *40 min. Piazzetta San Matteo 1.* ☎ *050-541865. Admission 5€. Tues–Sat 9am–7pm, Sun 9am–2pm.*

11 ★★ **Santa Maria della Spina.** All the truly ancient churches of Pisa face the sea, the original source of the maritime city's protection and wealth. This extravagant Gothic masterpiece, wrought by Pisa's leading Gothic sculptors including Giovanni Pisano, is no exception. There's little point going inside. ⏲ *10 min. Lungarno Gambacorti (at Via Sant'Antonio). No phone. Admission 1.50€. Mon–Fri 10am–2pm and 3–6pm; Sat–Sun 10am–6:45pm.*

12 ★ **Bacchus Enoteca.** This is the best wine shop in Pisa, especially strong on Tuscan vintages. Wines can be shipped worldwide. *Via Mascagni 1.* ☎ *050-500560. AE, MC, V.*

Pisa After Dark

Caffè dell'Ussero, Lungarno Pacinotti 27 (☎ 050-581100), is one of Italy's oldest literary cafes, installed in 1775 on the ground floor of Palazzo Agostini. Young men of the Risorgimento drank and plotted here as students. Ice creams, pastries, and cafe-style fare are served daily. A few doors down, stone-clad **Bazeel,** Lungarno Pacinotti 1 (☎ 349-1902586; www.bazeel.it), is the bar of the minute, attracting Pisa's fashionable set for live music and DJs. For beer lovers, lively **OrzoBruno,** Via Case Dipinte 6 (☎ 050-578802; www.ilbirrificio artigiano.it), has a selection of locally-brewed light and dark ales. The sedate, English-style **Big Ben Pub,** Via Palestro 11 (☎ 050-581158), is still popular with visitors and locals alike.

Where to Stay

★ **Jolly Hotel Cavalieri** STATION This smart, modern chain hotel is the most convenient for rail and air arrivals. Rooms are clean and well equipped—ask for one that's been recently renovated. *Piazza della Stazione 2.* ☎ *050-43290. www.jolly hotels.it. 100 units. Doubles 80€– 137€ w/breakfast. AE, DC, MC, V.*

Leonardo CENTRO STORICO The best budget hotel in town, in the heart of "real" Pisa. Rooms are simply furnished but comfortable; ask for an upper floor. *Via Tavoleria 17.* ☎ *050-579946. www.hotel leonardopisa.it. 27 units. Doubles 85€–115€ w/breakfast. AE, DC, MC, V.*

★★ **Novecento** CENTRO STORICO This immaculately converted colonial villa set round a courtyard garden is Pisa's new boutique offering. Rooms are small-ish, but ooze style, and so close to the Campo are great value. *Via Roma 37.* ☎ *050-500323. www.hotelnovecentopisa.it. 13 units. Doubles 130€ w/breakfast. AE, MC, V.*

★★ **Relais dell'Orologio** CENTRO STORICO A former private home of a noble family is the most intimate hotel in town, with a sophisticated yet welcoming ambience. Some rooms are small. The same family runs a B&B, the **Relais dei Fiori,** for tighter budgets. Check the website for discounts. *Via della Faggiola 12.* ☎ *050-830361. www.hotelrelaisorologio.com. 21 units. Doubles 136€–350€. AE, DC, MC, V.*

★ **Royal Victoria** CENTRO STORICO In business since 1839, this traditional hotel blends harmoniously with Pisa's colonial-style quayside. Opt for a room overlooking the Arno—or, even better, in the 10th-century tower. *Lungarno Pacinotti 12.* ☎ *050-940111. www.royalvictoria.it. 48 units. Doubles 80€–140€ w/breakfast. AE, DC, MC, V.*

The facade of the Royal Victoria hotel.

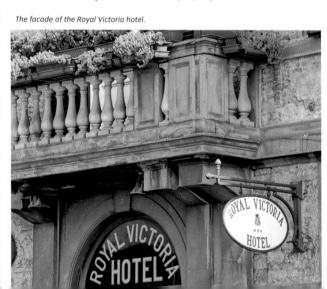

Where to Dine

Da Bruno PORTA A LUCCA
CASALINGA PISANA Your best bet
within 5 minutes' walk of the Leaning Tower, this popular trattoria has
been feeding visitors for half a century. Baked rabbit, roast garlic-stud-
ded lamb, and salt cod with leeks
and tomatoes are a few of the chef's
favorites. *Via Luigi Bianchi 12.*
☎ *050-560818. Entrees 10€–16€.*
*AE, DC, MC, V. Lunch Wed–Mon, din-
ner Wed–Sun.*

La Mescita CENTRO STORICO *TUS-
CAN* Simple, fine cuisine near the
Piazza Vettovaglie marketplace. The
menu changes monthly, and after
hours the place becomes an
enoteca with a long wine list. *Via
Cavalca 2.* ☎ *050-957019. Entrees
16€–20€. AE, DC, MC, V. Dinner
Tues–Sun, lunch Sat–Sun. Closed 3
weeks in Aug.*

★ **Osteria dei Cavalieri** CENTRO
STORICO *TUSCAN* At this temple of
Tuscan cuisine, the menu is traditional, but skilled chefs manage to
lighten and modernize many of the
region's robust classics. Try simple
grilled fish or *tagliata* (slivers of rare
beef). *Via San Frediano 16.* ☎ *050-
580858. www.osteriacavalieri.pisa.it.
Entrees 11€–15€. AE, DC, MC, V.
Lunch Mon–Fri, dinner Mon–Sat.
Closed Aug.*

★ **Porton Rosso** CENTRO
STORICO *TUSCAN/SEAFOOD*
Tucked down a tiny alley near the

Traditional crostini.

market, this seafood joint is highly
rated by fish-loving locals. There's
always a *"menu terra"* and pasta if
you prefer the land-based route.
Vicolo del Tidi. ☎ *050-580566.
Entrees 10€–16€. AE, MC, V. Lunch,
dinner Mon–Sat. Closed 3 weeks
in Aug.*

★ **S. Omobono** CENTRO STORICO
CASALINGA PISANA Dine among
locals right on Pisa's market. Expect
rustic Pisan classics such as *bro-
chette alla renaiaola* (pasta squares
in a puree of turnip greens and
smoked fish) or *baccalà alla livornese* (salt cod stewed with tomatoes). *Piazza S. Omobono 6.* ☎ *050-
540847. Entrees 8€–9€. MC, V.
Lunch, dinner Mon–Sat. Closed 2
wks. in Aug.*

San Gimignano

1 Sant'Agostino
2 I Ninnoli
3 Collegiata
4 Pinacoteca & Torre Grossa
5 Gelateria "di Piazza"
6 Museo della Tortura
7 Galleria Gagliardi
8 Tinacci

Nightlife
9 Da Gustavo
10 Birreria Avalon

Where to Stay
11 Antico Pozzo
12 Bel Soggiorno
13 La Cisterna
14 La Collegiata
15 Leon Bianco
16 Pescille
17 Relais Santa Chiara

Where to Eat
18 Chiribiri
19 Dorandó
20 La Mangiatoia
21 Le Vecchie Mura
22 Osteria delle Catene

ⓘ Tourist Information
Ⓟ Parking

Tuscany's best-preserved medieval town, named after a 6th-century Bishop of Modena, once had more than 70 towers, symbols of clan rivalry and one-upmanship, and a visible sign of the town's wealth in the years running up to the Black Death. That devastating 1348 plague called time on San Gimignano's good times—riches dried up, building stopped and the town slowly became magically frozen in time. The painter Benozzo Gozzoli was born here, and novelists and film directors have used it as a stage (E. M. Forster in *Where Angels Fear to Tread* and Franco Zeffirelli in *Tea with Mussolini*). Try to stay overnight: The place can feel like a theme park during the day, but San Gimignano at dusk is one of Tuscany's special places. Also seek out a glass of Tuscany's only white DOCG wine, Vernaccia di San Gimignano. START: Take the raccordo to "Poggibonsi nord" from Florence, or "Colle Val d'Elsa sud" from Siena, then follow signs. Trip length: 40km (24 miles) from Siena, 52km (32 miles) from Florence.

With its dramatic skyline, San Gimignano has been called the medieval Manhattan.

1 ★ Sant'Agostino. In 1464, a plague swept San Gimignano and the citizens prayed to St. Sebastian to end it. When the sickness passed, they dutifully hired native son Benozzo Gozzoli to paint a thankful scene on the nave's left wall showing this patron saint of plagues and his cloak of angels breaking the plague arrows being thrown down by a vengeful God. The town liked the results, so they commissioned Gozzoli to spend the next 2 years frescoing the apse of their Romanesque-Gothic church with *Scenes from the Life of St. Augustine.* Right in front, Piero del Pollaiuolo's 1483 *Coronation of the Virgin* sits on Benedetto di Maiano's sculpted 1494 marble altar. ⏱ *20 min. Piazza Sant'Agostino.* ☎ *0577-907012. Free admission. Daily 7am–noon and 3–7pm (Nov–Mar 6pm).*

2 I Ninnoli. Portable home goods and souvenirs include boxes inlaid with gold, reproductions of famous paintings, and an array of mirrors, lamps, plaster bas-reliefs, and chandeliers. *Via San Matteo 3.* ☎ *0577-943011. AE, MC, V.*

3 ★★★ Collegiata. The city's main church dates from the 11th century, but its present look is mostly from the 1400s. Inside, it's among Tuscany's most richly decorated churches, with scenes from the Old and New Testaments facing each other across the nave. Above the main door is an especially graphic *Last Judgement* (1410) by Sienese painter Taddeo di Bartolo. Nearby is native son Gozzoli's 1465 *St Sebastian.* The saint, martyred during the reign of Roman emperor Diocletian, is a traditional protector from plague. At the end of the nave on the right is one of my favorite spots in all Tuscany: Guiliano da Maiano's Renaissance Caphel of Santa Fina, frescoed in 1475 by Domenico Ghirlandaio with 2 scenes from the life of the local saint, a young girl named Fina. Look for the towers of 15th century San Gimignano in the background of her funeral, on the left. ⏱ *30 min. Piazza del Duomo.* ☎ *0577-940316. Admission 3.50€. Apr–Oct Mon–Fri 9:30am–7:10pm, Sat until 5:10pm, Sun 12.30–5:10pm; Nov–Mar Mon–Sat 9:30am–4:40pm, Sun 12:30–4:40pm; closed 2nd half Nov, 2nd half Jan.*

Two Beautiful Squares & Market Days

Two of Tuscany's loveliest squares, **Piazza del Duomo** and **Piazza della Cisterna**, stand side by side in the heart of town. On Thursday and Saturday mornings, country vendors hawk their wares in Piazza del Duomo, in the long shadows of Gothic palaces and seven towers. Piazza della Cisterna, named for its 13th-century well, is lined with 13th- and 14th-century buildings and hotels that make a fine choice for an overnight stay in this special town.

④ ★ Pinacoteca & Torre Grossa. Climb 54m (175 ft.) up the highest tower in town for one of Tuscany's best panoramas, over the bucolic hills around San Gimignano and across the whole Val d'Elsa. (Though if you climb the hill to the right of the Collegiata, you'll get almost the same view for free from San Gimignano's ruined fortress.) The same ticket includes the art at the 13th-century **Palazzo del Popolo.** Lippo Memmi's impressive *Maestà* (from 1317) dominates the Council Chamber. Slightly racier are frescoes by his father, Memmi di Filippuccio, showing scenes from a wedding night. ⏱ *40 min. Piazza del*

Backstreets in San Gimignano.

Duomo 1. ☎ *0577-990312. Admission 5€. Nov–Feb daily 10am–5:30pm; Mar–Oct daily 9:30am–7:30pm.*

⑤ ★★ Gelateria "di Piazza." The queues out the door tell their own story: This place has been named Gelato World Champion multiple times for a reason. My top choices are Vernaccia wine flavor and Crema di Santa Fina, made with saffron. (But not on the same cone.) *Piazza della Cisterna 4.* ☎ *0577-942244. www.gelateriadipiazza.com. $.*

⑥ kids Museo della Tortura. Though certainly not for young or easily frightened children, San Gimignano's original torture museum provides a fascinating, and reasonably scientific, presentation of some grim subject matter. The setting, in the Torre del Diavolo (Devil's Tower), and implements like the "Iron Maiden of Nuremberg" and "Heretic's Fork" might just give you nightmares. Commentary in English completes the grisly experience. Note: There are other, more gratuitous "torture museums" in town; this is the original and best. ⏱ *30 min. Via del Castello 1–3 (at Piazza della Cisterna).* ☎ *0577-942243. Admission 8€. Apr–Oct daily*

Domenico Ghirlandaio's The Funeral of Saint Fina *in Collegiata.*

10am–8pm (until midnight in mid-summer); Nov–Mar daily 10am–6pm.

7 ★★ Galleria Gagliardi.
Despite its berth on tourism Main St., this is a serious (and seriously good) gallery for contemporary art and sculpture. Gagliardi represents artists from across the northern half of Italy and displays a range of work on canvas, and in ceramics, marble, and bronze. *Via San Giovanni 57.* ☎ *0577-942196.*

www.galleriagagliardi.com. AE, MC, V.

8 Tinacci. Three generations of the Tinacci family have sold high-quality local artisania—leather goods, ceramics, pottery, terra cottas, wooden trays, sacred art images, and carnival masks—from these ancient cellars. *Via San Giovanni 41A.* ☎ *0577-940345. www. tinacci.com. AE, DC, MC, V.*

San Gimignano After Dark

Da Gustavo, Via San Matteo 29 (☎ 0577-940057), the town's best wine bar, draws a mixed crowd of visitors and locals. Vernaccias and Chiantis (from 2.50€) are usually good, often sold by the glass, with snacks such as crostini or bruschette, and Panforte for the sweet-toothed. **Birreria Avalon,** Viale Roma 1–5 (at Porta San Giovanni; ☎ 0577-940023), is one of the most popular pubs, with a restaurant menu, the best selection of national wines and international beers, occasional live music, Internet access, and a terrace.

Where **to Stay**

★★ **Antico Pozzo** CENTRO STORICO Dante slept in this 15th-century *palazzo*, now the old town's best hotel. Rooms vary in size, many with antiques and some with frescoes. *Via San Matteo 87.* ☎ *0577-942014. www.anticopozzo.com. 18 units. Doubles 130€–150€ w/breakfast. AE, DC, MC, V.*

Bel Soggiorno CENTRO STORICO Family-run since 1886, this hotel is a fine choice near the major sites, with grand public areas and comfy, basic rooms; three open onto a terrace. *Via San Giovanni 91.* ☎ *0577-940375. www.hotelbelsoggiorno.it. 22 units. Doubles 95€–120€. AE, DC, MC, V. Closed Jan–Feb.*

★ **La Cisterna** CENTRO STORICO Rooms vary—from spacious with views to small and cramped—at this converted palace right on Piazza della Cisterna. Views from the breakfast room are jaw-dropping. *Piazza della Cisterna 24.* ☎ *0577-940328. www.hotelcisterna.it. 50 units. Doubles 87€–140€ w/breakfast. AE, DC, MC, V.*

★★★ **La Collegiata** NORTH SAN GIMIGNANO One of the town's top two hotels, this Relais & Châteaux property in a 16th-century convent amid the cypresses has tapestries, frescoes, and über-tasteful rooms. Ask to stay in the main building. *Loc. Strada 27.* ☎ *0577-943201.*

Guest quarters at Antico Pozzo.

La Collegiata hotel is located in a former convent.

www.lacollegiata.it. 21 units. Doubles 210€–450€. AE, MC, V.

★ **Leon Bianco** CENTRO STORICO This 11th-century, family-run townhouse has many original features, views of the Val d'Elsa, and medium to large rooms, most with beamed ceilings. *Piazza della Cisterna 8.* ☎ *0577-941294. www.leonbianco. com. 26 units. Doubles 85€–150€ w/breakfast. AE, DC, MC, V.*

★ **kids Pescille** PESCILLE This modern country hotel has a tranquil garden, pool, and tennis court. Rooms are sharply designed, some with balconies (our favorite is the Tower). *Loc. Pescille.* ☎ *0577-940186. www.pescille.it. 50 units. Doubles 90€–130€. AE, DC, MC, V.*

★★ **Relais Santa Chiara** SOUTH SAN GIMIGNANO For facilities and elegance, this modern hotel just outside the walls is one of the town's top two, with terra-cotta floors, marble mosaics, and large rooms, many with balconies or terraces. Superior doubles have hydromassage tubs. *Via Matteotti 15.* ☎ *0577-940701. www.rsc.it. 41 units. Doubles 150€–240€ w/breakfast. AE, DC, MC, V.*

Where to Dine

★ **kids** **Chiribiri** CENTRO STORICO *RUSTIC TALIAN* What this little (eight tables) brick-vault lacks in size, it more than makes up for in character. The noisy kitchen knocks out Italian and regional meat and pasta classics with gusto. A bonus: It's open 11am to 11pm nonstop, so if you or yours have odd meal times, they can feed you. *Piazzetta della Madonna 1.* ☎ *0577-941948. Entrees 8€–15€. No credit cards. Lunch, dinner daily.*

★★★ **Dorandó** CENTRO STORICO *MODERN TUSCAN* The city's top restaurant, with stone walls and a vaulted roof, serves creative, light seasonal dishes based on medieval and Etruscan recipes. All with a Slow Food ethos. *Vicolo dell'Oro 2.* ☎ *0577-941862. www.ristorante dorando.it. Entrees 22€–27€; tasting menu 60€. AE, DC, MC, V. Lunch, dinner daily; Nov closed Mon. Closed Dec to mid-Feb.*

★★ **La Mangiatoia** CENTRO STORICO *TUSCAN* Many dishes at this intimate old-town restaurant—

like venison with pine nuts, raisins, vinegar, and chocolate—derive from ancient Sangimignanese recipes. *Via Mainardi 5.* ☎ *0577-941528. Entrees 14€–18€. MC, V. Lunch, dinner Jul–Aug Wed–Mon, otherwise Mon–Sat. Closed Jan to mid-Feb.*

★ **Le Vecchie Mura** CENTRO STORICO *TUSCAN* Seasonal, quintessentially Tuscan dishes—*ribollita*, wild boar in Vernaccia wine—are served in a cavernous 18th-century interior or on the knockout terrace. *Via Piandornella 15.* ☎ *0577- 940270. www.vecchiemura.it. Entrees 9€–17€. AE, DC, MC, V. Dinner Wed–Mon. Closed Nov–Feb.*

★ **Osteria delle Catene** CENTRO STORICO *TUSCAN* Tuscan wines and food reign in this medieval setting with modern lighting. Expect saffron soup from a medieval recipe, tagliatelle with boar, or duck with cavolo nero. *Via Mainardi 18.* ☎ *0577-574998. Entrees 13€–15€. MC, V. Lunch, dinner Thurs–Tues. Closed Jan to mid-Mar.*

The small, but charming Chiribiri.

Siena

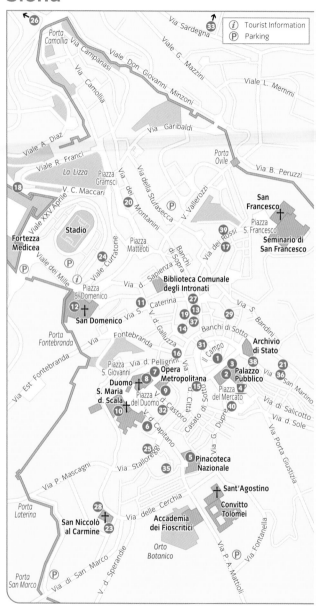

i Tourist Information
P Parking

1. Piazza del Campo
2. Palazzo Pubblico
3. Torre del Mangia
4. Gino Cacino
5. Pinacoteca Nazionale
6. Martini Marisa
7. Battistero
8. Duomo
9. Museo dell'Opera Metropolitana
10. Santa Maria della Scala
11. Casa di Santa Caterina
12. San Domenico
13. Cortecci
14. Vitra
15. Sena Vetus

Nightlife
16. Brivido
17. Kopa Kabana
18. Enoteca Italiana
19. Enoteca i Terzi
20. The Dublin Post
21. Gallery

Where to Stay
22. Certosa di Maggiano
23. Chiostro del Carmine
24. Chiusarelli
25. Duomo
26. Garden
27. Grand Hotel Continental
28. Palazzo Ravizza
29. Piccolo Hotel Etruria
30. Santa Caterina

Where to Eat
31. Al Mangia
32. Al Marsili
33. Botteganova
34. Cane e Gatto
35. Castelvecchio
36. Gallo Nero
37. Guido
38. Le Logge
39. L'Osteria
40. Papei

I f you have time for only one stop besides Florence, make it Siena. Dominating the medieval trade routes between France and Rome, the city in its day had Italy's richest banks and finest Gothic architecture, a quasi-democratic government under "the Nine," and its own constitution. Once Florence's rival in might and artistic patronage, Siena never fully recovered from the Black Death, which mowed down the population from 100,000 to 30,000 in 1348. Now, the medieval character of its public features is frozen in time—the city is a living museum for art, architecture, and history buffs, with a vibrant civic culture. START: **Siena is southeast of Florence along the Firenze–Siena raccordo. Trip length: From Florence 70km (43 miles).**

1 ★★★ kids **Piazza del Campo.** The most dramatic piazza in Italy is Siena's "Campo." First laid out in the early 12th century on the site of the Roman forum, it is shaped like a sloping scallop shell or fan. By 1340, the city's leaders had paved the square in brick and divided it into nine sections in honor of the Council of Nine (the *Nove*), who ruled Siena during its golden age. Today it's the setting for the **Palio** (see below).

At the upper end of the square stands the **Fonte Gaia,** created from 1408 to 1419 by Jacopo della Quercia. What you see today is an inferior copy from 1868. ⏱ *15 min.*

2 ★★★ **Palazzo Pubblico.** This Gothic *palazzo*, the finest in Italy, was constructed in a crenelled style from 1297 to 1310 to house the city's government. Siena's remaining faithful added the loggia chapel by the entrance, the **Cappella della Piazza,** to thank God for delivering them from the Black Death.

Inside is one of Europe's outstanding civic museums, two rooms in particular marking the pinnacle of artistic achievement in Siena. In the **Sala del Mappamondo** is Simone Martini's 1315 *Maestà,* showing the city's protector under a huge canopy. It's not just a religious work: Christ's scroll reads: *Love Justice, ye who judge the Earth.*

Siena's medieval Piazza del Campo.

Palio, Siena's biannual horserace and medieval pageant.

Next door in the **Sala del Pace** (where "the Nine" sat), the walls are covered by Ambrogio Lorenzetti's *Allegories of Good and Bad Government* (1338). It's a work of civic art without parallel, commissioned to remind rulers of the qualities of good government and a prosperous city: Justice, Wisdom, and Peace all appear. Alas, in the wake of the Black Death that killed Lorenzetti, *Bad Government* on the opposite wall came to pass: Fear, Treason, and War stalked Siena for decades. ⏱ *1½ hr. Piazza del Campo.* ☎ *0577-292263. Admission 7.50€; 12€ with Torre del Mangia. Mid-Mar to Oct daily 10am–7pm, otherwise 10am–6pm.*

❸ ★★ kids Torre del Mangia. The 14th-century tower of the Palazzo Pubblico was named after a gluttonous bell-ringer, Giovanni di Duccio, nicknamed "Mangiaguadagni" or "eater of profits." At 102m (336 ft.), it is the tallest secular monument from the Middle Ages remaining in Tuscany, so if you're expecting a great view you won't be disappointed. ⏱ *30 min. Piazza del Campo.* ☎ *0577-292262. Admission 7€; 12€ with Palazzo Pubblico. Mid-Mar to Oct daily 10am–7pm, otherwise 10am–4pm.*

❹ Gino Cacino. This venerable deli, suppliers to some of Siena's notable restaurants, will load you a sandwich from whatever's behind the counter. *Piazza del Mercato 31.* ☎ *0577-223076. $.*

❺ ★ Pinacoteca Nazionale. Though more famous works by Sienese masters are found elsewhere, this remains an impressive and representative showcase of the city's great artists. Look out for plenty of Duccio, the charming narrative detail of Simone Martini's *Beato Agostino* altarpiece, and Giovanni di Paolo's *Presentation at the Temple:* Despite two goes at a composition stolen straight from Ambrogio Lorenzetti (in the Uffizi), he still couldn't get the perspective right. Downstairs are the cartoons by Sienese Mannerist Domenico Beccafumi (1486–1551), from which some of the marble panels on the Duomo pavement were created. ⏱ *1 hr. Via San Pietro 29.* ☎ *0577-281161. Admission 4€. Sun–Mon 8:30am–1:30pm, Tues–Sat 8:15am–7:15pm.*

❻ ★ Martini Marisa. Siena's top purveyor of hand-painted Sienese *majolica* (ceramics) uses designs

Bareback Anarchy & Royal Pomp

Twice a year, on July 2 and August 16, Europe's most daring horse race takes place on Siena's Campo. Jockeys representing 10 of the city's 17 districts *(contrade)* fly around the dirt-filled square three times with one aim: winning the banner, **il Palio.** Forget sportsmanship. The single rule is that no jockey can grab another horse's reins. But you can drug an opponent the morning of the race, kidnap him the night before or, as he rides by, "whip him with a leather belt made from the skin of the bull's penis, which leaves the deepest welts and lasting scars," explained a marshal.

All this has taken place in tribute to the Virgin Mary since at least 1310. In the weeks after the race, you'll often find the winning *contrada* out en masse, marching Siena's streets banging drums and singing traditional songs. They may even be sucking child's soothers—in reference to the banner's nickname, *"il Bambino."*

based on the traditional black, white, and burnt sienna motif, based on floor panels in the Duomo. *Via del Capitano 5.* ☎ *0577-288177. AE, MC, V.*

7 ★ Battistero. The 14th-century Baptistery stands on its own little square on top of a steep flight of steps, hiding behind a Gothic facade. Its prize possession is a baptismal font embellished with some of the finest sculpture of the *Quattrocento.* The hexagonal marble font (1411–30) is by Jacopo della Quercia in the Gothic–Renaissance style. Two of the bronze statues around the basin, *Faith* and *Hope,* are by Donatello. Reliefs on the font include Ghiberti's *Baptism of Christ* and *John before Herod* (similar in style to his "Gates of Paradise" in Florence), and *Herod's Feast* by Donatello, all from 1427. Vecchietta frescoed the ceiling and lunettes around 1450. ⏱ *30 min. Piazza San Giovanni (off Piazza del Duomo).* ☎ *0577-283048. www. operaduomo.siena.it. Admission 3€. Mar–Oct daily 9:30am–7:30pm; Nov–Feb daily 10am–5pm.*

8 ★★★ Duomo. The architectural highlight of Siena's golden age is the **Cathedral of Santa Maria Assunta** (its formal name). Beginning in the 12th century, architects set out to create a dramatic facade with colored bands of marble mixing the Romanesque and Italian Gothic styles. Inside, between 1369 and 1547, over 40 Sienese artists, including Francesco di Giorgio and Domenico Beccafumi, created the 56 Biblical and allegorical marble intarsia designs on the floor (only on view mid-Aug to Nov). The artistic highlight is the **Libreria Piccolominea,** added in 1485 by Cardinal Francesco Piccolomini (later Pope Pius III), to house the library of his more famous uncle, Pope Pius II. Frescoes by Umbrian painter Pinturicchio tell the story of Pius II's life, starting in the back right as you walk in. The nearby 13th-century pulpit is by Nicola Pisano (Giovanni's father). ⏱ *45 min. Piazza del Duomo.* ☎ *0577-283048. Admission 3€; 6€ when floor on display. Mar–Oct Mon–Sat 10:30am–7:30pm, Sun 1:30–5:30pm; Nov–Feb Mon–Sat 10:30am–6:30pm, Sun 1:30–5:30pm.*

Siena's 12th-century Duomo is the city's great architectural triumph.

⑨ ★★ Museo dell'Opera Metropolitana. Anyone with a serious interest in Sienese art should make for here: Duccio di Buoninsegna's

1311 *Maestà* is where it all began. Not only did Duccio invent a genre, he influenced the generation that included Simone Martini and the Lorenzettis. The Sienese were so pleased with his giant two-sided altarpiece it was paraded through the streets on its way to the Duomo. In the same room is Pietro Lorenzetti's 1342 *Birth of the Virgin,* which, fortunately for us, he managed to finish before plague finished him. Downstairs are Giovanni Pisano's original sculptures for the Duomo.

The art is housed in a building originally intended to be the right aisle of a massive new cathedral, until the Black Death descended. A climb to the **Facciatone,** from inside the museum, rewards you with dizzying views down into the Campo. ⏱ *1 hr. Piazza del Duomo 8.* ☎ *0577-283048. www.opera duomo.siena.it. Admission 6€. Mar–Oct daily 9:30am–7:30pm; Nov–Feb daily 10am–5pm.*

Siena After Dark

Besides enjoying the spectacle of an evening lounging in the Campo, Sienese line up at **Brivido,** Via dei Pellegrini 1–3 (at Via di Città; ☎ 0577-280058) from March through October for the best homemade gelato in town—it's a virtual tradition on summer nights. That said, the *panpepato* flavored gelato at less conveniently located **Kopa Kabana,** Via de' Rossi 52 (☎ 0577-223744) is up there with the best I've ever tasted. **Enoteca Italiana,** Fortezza Medicea (☎ 0577-228834; www.enoteca-italiana.it) is the only state-sponsored wine bar in Italy, in vaults that were built for Cosimo de' Medici in 1560. Drink by the glass, or buy one of 1,600 bottles on sale. Enoteca i Terzi, Via dei Termini 7 (☎ 0577-44329; www.enoteca iterzi.it) is under the vaulted ceiling of a 12th-century tower, with wines by the glass. The Dublin Post, Piazza Gramsci 20–21 (☎ 0577-289089) is Siena's liveliest Irish pub—with Harp, Kilkenny, Guinness, and a small menu, plus free Wi-Fi. Rock, pop, and traditional Irish music set the mood. You'll find a younger crowd, DJs spinning house, and beer and cocktails til late at neon-lit Gallery, Via Pantaneto 16–22 (no phone).

Travel Tip

The best value way to see Siena's ecclesiastical sights is with the **Opera della Metropolitana** pass. Valid for 3 days, and costing 10€, it gets you into the Duomo, Battistero, Museo dell'Opera, and modest **Oratorio di San Bernardino**. It also allows access to the recently discovered **Cripta**, an overpriced though atmospheric trip through the frescoed (pre-Duccio) chambers of the ancient cathedral under the Duomo. Buy the pass from the Museo dell'Opera.

⑩ ★★ kids **Santa Maria della Scala.** This 14th-century hospital, one of Europe's oldest, is slowly being turned into a museum and cultural complex displaying art and archaeological treasures. Unique is the **Pellegrinaio,** the old Pilgrims' Ward, frescoed with scenes from everyday life in the hospital in the 1440s. Elsewhere seek out a disturbing *Massacre of the Innocents* by Matteo di Giovanni, in the

Casa di Santa Caterina.

Cappella della Madonna; the tiny oratory where St. Catherine used to pray all night; and the labyrinthine basement—a great spot to get lost.

The Papesse, Siena's modern art museum, moved here in 2008 and was rebranded **sms contemporanea.** 🕐 1 hr. Piazza del Duomo 2. ☎ 0577-224811. www.santamaria dellascala.com. Admission 6€. Daily 10:30am–6pm.

⑪ **Casa di Santa Caterina.** Caterina Benincasa (1347–80), 24th child of a Sienese dyer, grew up to become the patron saint of Italy. She took the veil at the age of 16, and experienced what she called a "mystical marriage" to Christ 3 years later. The house where she lived as a Dominican nun still stands today, except it now has a Renaissance loggia and two baroque oratories, the **Oratorio della Cucina** being the most lavishly appointed, with a 16th-century majolica floor. 🕐 20 min. Costa di San Antonio 6 (at Via dei Pittori). ☎ 0577-288175. Free admission. Daily 9am–12:30pm and 3:30–6pm.

The interior of Siena's Duomo.

12 ★ **San Domenico.** This severe-looking church in the monastic Gothic style was founded in 1125 and since the 1300s has been closely linked with St. Catherine, who is said to have had her visions here. Inside you can see a small frescoed portrait by her contemporary, Andrea Vanni (1332–1414), the only known picture by someone who knew her. Slightly grislier, her head is preserved and venerated inside the **Cappella di Santa Caterina.** It's surrounded by Sodoma's frescoed scenes from her life, including her controversial appearance at the *Execution of Niccolò di Toldo.* 🕓 *20 min. Piazza San Domenico. No phone. Free admission. Apr–Oct 7am–1pm and 3–6:30pm; Nov–Mar 9am–1pm and 3–6pm.*

Shopping Tip

Market day in Siena is Wednesday at **La Lizza** from 8:30am to 1:30pm. Everything's for sale—not just fresh fruits, vegetables, and flowers, but shoes, crafts, and leather handbags too. An antique market also takes place at Piazza del Mercato on the third Sunday of every month.

13 **Cortecci.** The city's best designer clothing is sold in this house of fashion, going strong since 1935. You get better prices than in Florence on designer names such as Gucci, Missoni, Givenchy, Ermenegildo Zegna, Salvatore Ferragamo, and Giorgio Armani. *Banchi di Sopra 27.* ☎ *0577-280984. AE, DC, MC, V.*

14 ★★ **Vitra.** Admire modern designs in all shapes and sizes at this funky artisan glassware store. Everything is handmade in Siena. *Via dei Termini 2 (at Piazza Indipendenza).* ☎ *0577-51208. MC, V.*

15 **Sena Vetus.** The staff could be more helpful, but collectors may want to storm the gates anyway to browse the antique furniture and jewelry.

There are always smaller pieces for the bargain hunter. They also handle paintings from the 1700s and 1800s. *Via di Città 53.* ☎ *0577-42395. AE, MC, V.*

The Siena skyline and the surrounding countryside.

Where to **Stay**

The dining room at Certosa di Maggiano

★★ Certosa di Maggiano

PORTA ROMANA   Siena's most luxurious hideaway is in a 14th-century monastery littered with antiques.

Half-board required in summer. No kids under 12. *Strada di Certosa 82.* ☎ *0577-288180. www.certosadi maggiano.com. 17 units. Doubles 238€–590€ w/breakfast. AE, MC, V. Closed Nov–Mar.*

★★ Chiostro del Carmine

CENTRO STORICO   This atmospheric hotel set round a Carmelite cloister manages to combine proximity to the sights with a feeling of detached peace and tranquility. Well-equipped, modern rooms have retained much of the former convent's character. *Via della Diana 4.* ☎ *0577-223885. www.chiostrodelcarmine.com. 20 units. Doubles 89€–189€ w/breakfast. MC, V.*

Chiusarelli CENTRO STORICO

Under 10 minutes' walk from Piazza del Campo, this 1870 building with columns and caryatids has midsized to large neoclassical rooms, many with views (quietest in the rear). *Viale*

Italy's Perfectly Preserved Fortified Village

In his *Commedia,* Dante compared the towers of Monteriggioni to giants. Throughout Tuscany, vendors sell aerial photos of this remarkably well-preserved village on its hill above the Val d'Elsa. All 14 of the town's towers and its ring of walls are still here, more or less, and still looking like that "circle of titans" guarding the lowest level of Dante's *Hell.* In the fading glow of a dying day, it appears a red gold set against the deep amber–green of the surrounding vegetation.

There's just enough room inside the fortress-cum-hamlet for two piazzas along with some medieval stone houses and their gardens. Because Monteriggioni has only two streets, lined with handcraft shops, chances are you won't get lost.

Monteriggioni makes an easy day trip from Siena (it's right by the Firenze–Siena highway, 20km northwest of town). You need allow no more than 1½ hours to see everything.

A luxurious room at Certosa di Maggiano, in a converted 14th-century monastery.

Curtatone 15. ☎ 0577-280562. www.chiusarelli.com. 49 units. Doubles 127€ w/breakfast. AE, DC, MC, V.

Duomo CENTRO STORICO This restored 12th-century *palazzo* is perfectly located, but some rooms lack character (unless you get a cathedral view). Units 61 and 62 have terraces overlooking the Duomo. *Via Stalloreggi 38.* ☎ 0577-289088. www.hotelduomo.it. 20 units. Doubles 105€–150€ w/breakfast. AE, DC, MC, V.

★ **Garden** NORTH SIENA This 18th-century building a mile north of the walls is one of Siena's best moderately priced hotels, with a garden and pool. Rooms in the "Villa" have the most character and space; all have views. *Via Custoza 2.* ☎ 0577-567111. www.gardenhotel.it. 122 units (24 in Villa). Doubles 103€–240€ w/breakfast. AE, DC, MC, V.

★★ **Grand Hotel Continental** CENTRO STORICO This aristocratic hotel on Siena's most fashionable street has 15th-century architecture and frescoes, medium to large rooms with deluxe marble baths, and tasteful period decoration. *Banchi di Sopra 85.* ☎ 0577-56011.

www.royaldemeure.com. 51 units. Doubles 250€–560€ w/breakfast. AE, DC, MC, V.

★★ **Palazzo Ravizza** CENTRO STORICO Siena's coziest *pensione* since the 1920s, this Renaissance *palazzo* has antiques, frescoes, large, high-ceilinged rooms, and even fine dining. *Pian dei Mantellini 34.* ☎ 0577-280462. www.palazzo ravizza.it. 30 units. Doubles 150€–230€ w/breakfast. AE, DC, MC, V.

Piccolo Hotel Etruria CENTRO STORICO Rooms in the main building of this central, immaculate, but basic family-run hotel are largest, with the most character. *Via delle Donzelle 3.* ☎ 0577-288088. www.hoteletruria.com. 13 units. Doubles 86€. AE, MC, V.

★ **Santa Caterina** PORTA ROMANA With Siena's most hospitable owners, this 18th-century villa with midsized rooms and antiques is surrounded by a terraced garden overlooking the hills south. *Via E. S. Piccolomini 7.* ☎ 0577-221105. www.hscsiena.it. 22 units. Doubles 115€–185€ w/breakfast. AE, DC, MC, V.

Where to **Dine**

Al Mangia CENTRO STORICO *TUSCAN/INTERNATIONAL* The best place on the Campo, in 12th-century quarters, makes dishes such as *pici alla Senese* (handmade pasta with fresh tomatoes, tarragon, and cheese) from the finest local ingredients. *Piazza del Campo 43.* ☎ *0577-281121. Entrees 18€–30€. AE, DC, MC, V. Lunch, dinner daily.*

★ **Al Marsili** CENTRO STORICO *SIENESE/ITALIAN* A mass of cross-vaulted ceilings, old bricks, and stones, Siena's most elegant cellar restaurant serves wild boar and goose pâté or guinea hen *alla Medici,* alongside Tuscan classics. This beautiful restaurant stands

Al Mangia's sidewalk tables on Piazza del Campo.

between the Duomo and Via di Città. *Via del Castoro 3.* ☎ *0577-47154. Entrees 14€–18€. AE, DC, MC, V. Lunch, dinner Tues–Sun.*

★★★ **Botteganova** NORTH SIENA *TUSCAN* Michele Sonentino's restaurant is Siena's finest, with light innovations on Tuscan staples and 400 local vintages. Reservations recommended. *Strada Chiantigiana 29.* ☎ *0577-284230.* www.anticatrattoria botteganova.it. *Entrees 22€–24€; tasting menu 37€–45€. AE, DC, MC, V. Lunch, dinner Mon–Sat. Closed Jan and 10 days in Aug.*

★★ **Cane e Gatto** CENTRO STORICO *SIENESE CASALINGA* There's no menu at this intimate, family-run restaurant: You're served five courses of whatever was fresh at market, prepared with love in a typical Sienese style. Wine is extra. *Via Pagliaresi 6.* ☎ *0577-287545. Menu 65€. MC, V. Dinner Fri–Wed.*

★ **Castelvecchio** CENTRO STORICO *TUSCAN/VEGETARIAN* Find vegetarian heaven in this ancient eatery. There are always meat and poultry dishes, but the rich harvest of the Tuscan countryside is given special attention on the short, inventive, daily menu. *Via Castelvecchio 65 (at Via San Pietro).* ☎ *0577-49586. Entrees 11€–15€. MC, V. Lunch, dinner Mon–Sat.*

★ kids **Gallo Nero** CENTRO STORICO *TUSCAN/MEDIEVAL* Authentic medieval dishes like chicken cooked with lemons and stuffed roast pig feature at this atmospheric brick-vault decorated with mock Lorenzetti frescoes. There are gluten-free dishes, too. *Via del Porrione 65–67.* ☎ *0577-284356.*

Traditional Tuscan peasant soup.

Pettinaio 7.
☎ 0577-280042. Entrees 14€–25€. AE, MC, V. Lunch, dinner daily.

★★ **Le Logge** CENTRO STORICO *SIENESE/TUSCAN* This central osteria—which at the end of the 19th century was a pharmacy, dispensing creams and medicines to cure the ill— serves the freshest seasonal cuisine in a refined and old-fashioned atmosphere. The menu changes daily and always overflows with flavor. The veal is the best in town, and the delicate black truffle is used liberally in season. Reservations recommended. *Via del Porrione 33.* ☎ 0577-48013. Entrees 16€–18€. AE, DC, MC, V. Lunch, dinner Mon–Sat.

★★ **L'Osteria** CENTRO STORICO *TUSCAN/SIENESE* This neighborhood osteria halfway downhill to San Francesco is as local as it comes this close to the Campo. The grill is the star: Beef all ways, veal, and *cinta senese,* the finest breed of pig, native to the Chianti. *Via de' Rossi 79–81.* ☎ 0577-287592. Entrees 8.50€–17€. AE, MC, V. Lunch, dinner Mon–Sat.

★ **Papei** CENTRO STORICO *SIENESE* Trust this family-run trattoria for simple yet well-prepared classic Sienese fare such as rabbit in white wine with rosemary and sage or pappardelle in wild boar *ragù. Piazza del Mercato 6.* ☎ 0577-280894. Entrees 8€–11€. AE, MC, V. Lunch, dinner Tues–Sun.

www.gallonero.it. Entrees 9.50€–15€. AE, DC, MC, V. Lunch, dinner daily.

Guido CENTRO STORICO *SIENESE/ GRILL* Modern cuisine—among Siena's best grilled meats (from only pure-bred Chianina cattle) and *antipasti* plates—is served among old beams, arched ceilings, and brick walls. The medieval restaurant sits just off the promenade near Piazza del Campo. *Vicolo Pier*

Volterra

1. Porta all'Arco
2. Spartaco Montagnani
3. Palazzo dei Priori
4. Duomo
5. San Francesco
6. Pinacoteca e Museo Civico
7. Camillo Rossi
8. Teatro Romano
9. Fabula Etrusca
10. Museo Etrusco Guarnacci
11. alab'Arte
12. L'Incontro
13. Qvo Vadis?

Where to Stay
14. Albergo Nazionale
15. La Locanda
16. Park Hotel Le Fonti
17. San Lino
18. Villa Nencini

Where to Eat
19. Antica Osteria dei Poeti
20. Da Beppino
21. Enoteca del Duca
22. Il Sacco Fiorentino
23. Web & Wine

Volterra rises like a fortress, 540m (1,800 ft.) above the rolling agricultural plains of the Valdicecina. The Etruscans who settled here in the 9th century B.C. made their living trading and working what's under your feet: alabaster (for sculpting) and alum (for dyes). The town still has a medieval appearance, with foreboding *palazzi*, cobblestone streets and alleyways, and shops hawking craftwares. Come for the alabaster, the panoramic views, a Mannerist masterpiece, and a major Etruscan museum. START: **Volterra is on the S68 30km (19 miles) west of where it branches off the Florence–Siena raccordo. Trip length: 28km (18 miles) from San Gimignano, 50km (31 miles) from Siena, and 72km (45 miles) from Florence.**

① ★ **Porta all'Arco.** Volterra's remaining ancient gate, all that's left of what were once 7½km (4½ miles) of Etruscan city walls, marks the start of a steep ascent into the Centro Storico. So important is the gate to the town that Partisans defending Volterra in 1944 risked their lives bricking it up in case it became the target of a Nazi assault. ⏱ 5 min.

② ★ **Spartaco Montagnani.** The town's most distinguished alabaster sculptor has been turning out fused bronze statuettes since

The plain facade of Volterra's Duomo belies its lush interior.

1978, most inspired by Etruscan originals. Look for the seal of *Bronzo garantito,* which distinguishes these hand-finished objects from lesser wares. *Via Porta all'Arco 6.* ☎ *0588-86184. AE, MC, V.*

3 ★ **Palazzo dei Priori.** Built between 1208 and 1257, this is the oldest Gothic town hall in Tuscany; Florence's Palazzo Vecchio was modeled after it. The council hall and antechamber are open to the public. On view is a damaged *Annunciation with Four Saints* by Jacopo di Cione from 1383. Opposite, across Piazza dei Priori, is the **Palazzo Pretorio,** with its **Torre del Porcellino,** a tower named for the stone boar that protrudes near the top. ⏱ *20 min. Piazza dei Priori.* ☎ *0588-86050. Admission 1€. Mar–Oct daily 10:30am–5:30pm; off season Sat–Sun 10am–5pm.*

4 ★ **Duomo.** A simple 12th-century facade hides a lush interior with a coffered Renaissance ceiling. Immediately left of the entrance is the **Cappella dell'Addolorata,** with a charming terra cotta *Nativity* embellished with frescoes by Benozzo Gozzoli. More moving still is the carved wooden *Deposition* in the right transept, from 1228.

The octagonal **Baptistery** across the little piazza, from 1283, has an inlaid marble font (1502) by Andrea Sansovino. ⏱ *30 min. Piazza San Giovanni. No phone. Free admission. Mon–Thurs, Sat–Sun 8am–noon and 3–6pm; Fri 8am–noon and 4–6pm.*

5 ★ **San Francesco.** Dating to just a few years after St. Francis's death, this former convent at the western edge of the medieval town rewards the 5-minute downhill trek. The highlight is the **Cappella della Croce,** frescoed in 1410 by Cenni di Francesco. His subject matter, like Piero Della Francesca 40 years later in Arezzo, is *The Legend of the True Cross.* ⏱ *15 min. Piazza San Francesco 3. No phone. Free admission. Mon–Thurs, Sat–Sun 9am–noon and 3–6pm; Fri 9am–noon and 4–6pm. Hours erratic, especially off season.*

6 ★★ **Pinacoteca e Museo Civico.** This combined picture gallery and museum of artifacts is acclaimed for its religious paintings—mostly the work of Tuscan artists from the 14th to the 17th century. Taddeo di Bartolo's *Enthroned Madonna* altarpiece from 1411 is a glory in gold. Room 12 houses the real treasures, including an

Alabaster, or *Pietra Candida*

Volterra is nicknamed "the town of alabaster." Since the days of the Etruscans, locals have shaped objects both practical and artistic from these calcium sulphate deposits. Revived in the late 19th century, the industry has been going strong since, turning out ghostly-white lampshades, sculptures, jewel boxes, and even elegant sinks. To learn more about the craft, visit the town's alabaster museum, the Ecomuseo dell'Alabastro, Piazzetta Minucci (☎ 0588-87580).

astoundingly modern, angst-ridden *Deposition* painted by a young Rosso Fiorentino in 1521, and two large 1491 Luca Signorelli panels, notably an intricate, fantastical *Annunciation*. ⏱ *45 min. Via dei Sarti 1.* ☎ *0588-87580. Admission 8€ (includes Museo Etrusco). Mid-Mar to Oct daily 9am–7pm; off season daily 8:30am–1:45pm.*

7 ★ **Camillo Rossi.** This workshop, founded in 1912, is one of Volterra's best outlets for alabaster *objets. Piazza Pescheria 1.* ☎ *0588-86133.* www.rossialabastri.com. *AE, DC, MC, V.*

8 **kids** **Teatro Romano.** From Volterra's medieval ramparts you can look down on the remains of a 1st-century Roman theater, and later spa baths, among the best preserved in Italy. ⏱ *10 min. Viale Francesco Ferrucci (at Porta Fiorentina).* ☎ *0588-87850. Admission 2€. Mid-Mar to Oct daily 10:30am–5:30pm; off season Sat–Sun 10am–4pm.*

9 ★★ **Fabula Etrusca.** Intricate handmade jewelry cast using ancient

goldsmith techniques and to original Etruscan designs. Pack your credit card. *Via Lungo le Mura del Mandorlo 10.* ☎ *0588–87401.* www. *fabulaetrusca.it. DC, MC, V.*

10 ★★ **Museo Etrusco Guarnacci.** This gem has one of the best (and most poorly displayed) Etruscan

Jewelry based on original Etruscan designs for sale at Fabula Etrusca.

A bit of the Teatro Romano in Volterra.

votive figure of a young boy. Other highlights include the *Urna degli Sposi,* depicting a grumpy looking pair of newlyweds, and a series of reliefs of Homer's *Odyssey.* ⏱ *45 min. Via Minzoni 15.* ☎ *0588-86347. Admission 8€ (includes Pinacoteca). Mid-Mar to Oct daily 9am–7pm; off season daily 8:30am–1:45pm.*

⓫ **alab'Arte.** To see alabaster in various stages of completion, have a poke around Volterra's last open sculptural workshop. You're free to buy anything that takes your fancy. *Via Orti S. Agostino 28.* ☎ *0588-87968. www.alabarte.com. MC, V.*

Volterra's nightlife is on the quiet side. ⓬ **L'Incontro** (Via Matteotti 18; $), our favorite wine bar in the historic center, sells Tuscan vintages by the glass and crazy *gelato* flavors like biscuit or mojito.

⓭ **Qvo Vadis?** (Via Lungo le Mura del Mandorlo 18; ☎ 0588-80033; $) is Irish inspired, with Guinness on tap. It's the buzziest joint in town for the under-30 crowd.

collections in Italy. The 600 cinerary urns, dating from the 6th to the 1st century B.C., are made of alabaster, tufa, and terra cotta. The most celebrated piece is in Room XV: an elongated bronze known as the *Ombra della Sera,* an early-3rd-century B.C.

Crumbling Etruria

Northwest of the city center (3½km), Le Balze is one of Tuscany's more quietly frightening scenes—a bowl-shaped ravine where fast-paced erosion is devouring the edges of Volterra. Aided by periodic earthquakes, it has already exposed and then destroyed much of the Etruscan necropolis at this end of town. Now it threatens the medieval Badia church, abandoned after an 1846 quake brought the precipice to its doorstep. The best spot to appreciate the scale of the erosion is from the minor road out of town towards Montecatini Valdicecina.

Where to Stay

Albergo Nazionale CENTRO STORICO This *palazzo* in the historic center became a hotel in 1890. Though now slightly dated, the location is hard to beat. Ask for a room with a view. *Via dei Marchesi 11.* ☎ *0588-86284. www.hotelnazionale-volterra.com. 38 units. Doubles 78€–85€ w/breakfast. AE, DC, MC, V.*

★★ La Locanda CENTRO STORICO This converted convent is our top choice for a spacious room in the heart of the old town. A couple of doubles have hydromassage baths. *Via Guarnacci 24–28.* ☎ *0588-56048. www.hotel-lalocanda.com. 18 units. Doubles 89€–180€ w/breakfast. AE, MC, V.*

Park Hotel Le Fonti SOUTH VOLTERRA In the hills south of the center, this hotel achieves a delicate balance between modern amenities (two outdoor pools) and an old Tuscan ambience. *Via di Fontecorrenti 8.* ☎ *0588-85219. www.parkhotellefonti.*

com. 67 units. Doubles 90€–165€ w/breakfast. AE, DC, MC, V.

★ San Lino CENTRO STORICO A safe bet inside the medieval walls. It was built as a convent in 1480, and converted to a hotel with modern facilities in 1982. The best rooms are on the second and third floors. *Via S. Lino 26.* ☎ *0588-85250. www.hotelsanlino.com. 44 units. Doubles 85€–105€ w/breakfast. AE, DC, MC, V.*

Villa Nencini WEST VOLTERRA This cozy inn, a steep 10-minute walk downhill from Porta San Francesco, was converted from a 17th-century villa, with panoramic views. Rooms in the older building are antique in style; the newer wing offers larger rooms and wraps around an outdoor pool. *Borgo Santo Stefano 55.* ☎ *0588-86386. www.villanencini.it. 36 units. Doubles 67€–88€ w/breakfast. AE, DC, MC, V.*

Volterra's Piazza dei Priori.

Where **to Dine**

Boar meat is a staple of Tuscany's old Etruscan recipes.

★ **Antica Osteria dei Poeti**
CENTRO STORICO *TUSCAN/VOLTER-RAN*   For Tuscan staples like pappardelle with hare or Volterran cooking, try this traditional dining room right on the main drag. The superb Tuscan wine list has options from 10€ to over 100€ a bottle. *Via Matteotti 54.* ☎ *0588-86029. Entrees 7€–22€. AE, MC, V. Lunch, dinner Fri–Wed.*

Da Beppino CENTRO STORICO
TUSCAN/PIZZA   If the kids won't accept anything but pizza, but you're after something more local, this atmospheric little trattoria bridges the divide successfully. *Via delle Prigioni 13–21.* ☎ *0588-86051. Entrees 7€–13€. AE, MC, V. Lunch & dinner Fri–Wed. Closed Nov 10th–30th and Jan 10th–30th.*

★★ **Enoteca del Duca** CENTRO
STORICO *MODERN TUSCAN*   The town's finest dining is installed in a restored, 16th-century building with high ceilings and terra-cotta floors. Try the *lavagnette* (homemade egg pasta) with celery and Pecorino pesto, or the pigeon breast. *Via di Castello 2.* ☎ *0588-81510. Entrees 12€–28€. AE, DC, MC, V. Lunch, dinner Wed–Mon. Closed Jan 23–Feb 6, 2nd half Nov.*

★ **Il Sacco Fiorentino** CENTRO
STORICO *TUSCAN*   Visit this popular neighborhood tavern not for its decor, but for its tasty menu and market-fresh ingredients, prepared with Tuscan flair. I like to visit in autumn for the game dishes such as pan-fried pigeon with radicchio. *Piazza XX Settembre 18.* ☎ *0588-88537. Entrees 8€–15€. AE, DC, MC, V. Lunch, dinner Thurs–Tues. Closed late June.*

Web & Wine CENTRO STORICO
ITALIAN   Order plates of salami and pasta, sip the best Tuscan vintages like Sassicaia or Tignanello, and surf the Web from your seat on the medieval terrace. *Via Porta all'Arco 13.* ☎ *0588-81531. www. webandwine.com. Entrees 7€–20€. MC, V. Lunch, dinner daily (closed Thurs in winter).* ●

Web & Wine, an Internet cafe cum trattoria.

The
Savvy Traveler

Before You Go

Government Tourist Offices

In the U.S.: 630 Fifth Ave., Suite 1565, New York, NY 10111 ☎ 212/245-5618; 500 N. Michigan Ave., Chicago, IL 60611 ☎ 312/644-0996; and 12400 Wilshire Blvd., Suite 550, Los Angeles, CA 90025 ☎ 310/820-1898.

In Canada: 175 Bloor St. E., South Tower, Suite 907, Toronto, ONT, M4W 3R8 ☎ 416/925-4882; www.italiantourism.com.

In the U.K. & Ireland: 1 Princes St., London, W1B 2AY ☎ 020/7408-1254; www.italiantouristboard.co.uk.

In Australia and New Zealand: Level 4, 46 Market St., Sydney, NSW 2000 ☎ 02/9262-1666; www.italian tourism.com.au.

Entry Requirements

U.S., Canadian, U.K., Irish, Australian, and New Zealand citizens with a valid passport don't need a visa to enter Italy if they don't expect to stay more than 90 days and don't expect to work there. If after entering Italy you find you want to stay more than 90 days, you can apply for a permit for an extra 90 days, which as a rule is granted immediately. Go to the nearest *questura* (police headquarters) or your home country's consulate.

For passport information and applications in the **U.S.,** call ☎ **877/487-2778** or check http://travel.state.gov; in **Canada,** call ☎ **800/567-6868** or check www.passport canada.gc.ca; in the **U.K.,** call ☎ **0300/222-0000** or visit www.ips.gov.uk; in **Ireland,** call ☎ **01/671-1633** or check http://foreignaffairs.gov.ie; in **Australia,** call ☎ **131-232** or visit www.passports.gov.au; and in **New Zealand,** call ☎ **0800/225050** or check www.passports.govt.nz.

Allow plenty of time before your trip to apply for a passport; processing usually takes 3 weeks but can take longer during busy periods (especially spring). When traveling, safeguard your passport and keep a copy of the critical pages with your passport number in a separate place. If you lose your passport, visit the nearest consulate of your native country as soon as possible for a replacement.

The Best Times to Go

April to June and late September to October are the best months to visit Tuscany. However, they are also the most expensive: Hotels are generally on high-season rates, for May, June, and September at least.

From late June through mid-September, when the summer rush season is full blown, Siena and the Tuscan hilltowns can teem with visitors. August is the worst month weather-wise, when it's usually uncomfortably hot and muggy; but it's also a good month to bag a serious deal on a room in Florence. (When you get there, expect theaters, many upscale restaurants, and some nightclubs to be closed, however.) And from August 15 to the end of the month, the entire region goes on vacation, and many family-run restaurants and shops are closed (except at the spas, beaches, and islands—where 70% of the Italians head).

From late October to Easter, many attractions go on shorter winter hours, or occasionally close for renovation. Some hotels and restaurants take a month or two off between November and February, spa and beach destinations such as Viareggio become padlocked ghost towns, and it can get much colder

Previous page: Pine and cypress trees line a Tuscan landscape.

than you'd expect; it might even snow in the hills.

Festivals & Special Events

SPRING. Easter is always a big event in Tuscany, especially in Florence at the **Scoppio del Carro** (Explosion of the Cart), with its Renaissance pyrotechnics on Easter Sunday. An 18th-century cart, pulled by two snowy white oxen loaded with fireworks, arrives at the Piazza del Duomo, where it's ignited.

More cultural, Florence's **Maggio Musicale Fiorentino** (Musical May) features a month's worth of opera, concerts, and dance recitals in *palazzi* and churches around the city; these days it continues through June. ☎ 055-2779350. www.maggiofiorentino.com.

The wacky **Festa del Grillo** (Cricket Festival) takes place in midto late May, the First Sunday after Ascension Day. In Florence's Cascine Park, vendors sell crickets in decorated cages. After a parade along the Arno, participants release the crickets into the grass.

The last weekend in May, Cortona hosts the **Giostro dell'Archidado,** a crossbow competition with participants clad in 14th-century costume. ☎ 0575-630352.

The first Sunday in June (next in Pisa in 2010), the **Regatta of the Ancient Maritime Republics** takes place—a rowing competition among the four medieval maritime republics of Venice, Amalfi, Genoa, and Pisa. manifestazioni.storiche@comune.pisa.it.

Also in Pisa, the **Luminara di San Ranieri** celebrates the city's patron saint by lining the Arno with flickering torches, from dusk on June 16.

SUMMER. During the last Sunday in June, Pisa stages its **Gioco del Ponte** (Game of the Bridge) when teams in Renaissance costumes on opposite banks of the river have a tug-of-war with a 7-ton cart. ☎ 050-910506.

St. John the Baptist's Day, June 24, sees the first in the week-long series of **Calcio Storico Fiorentino.** Florence's Piazza Santa Croce is transformed into a pitch for these ancient, and rough "football" matches.

From mid-June to early August, Fiesole hosts **Estate Fiesolana,** a summertime festival of music, ballet, film, and theater. Most performances take place in the ruined Roman amphitheater. ☎ 055-055. www.estatefiesolana.it.

The biggest event of the Tuscan calendar is the **Palio delle Contrade,** the twice-annual bareback horse race between the 17 districts of Siena. The race occurs around the dirt-packed main square, with parades and partying afterwards. The first is on July 2; the second on August 16. See p 166.

The **Giostra dell'Orso** (Joust of the Bear) takes place in Pistoia on July 25. The match pits mounted knights in medieval garb against targets shaped like bears. www.giostradellorso.it.

In San Gimignano, **Sangimignanese Summer** is a festival of concerts, opera, and film staged in July and August (some outdoors). For a two weeks in either July or August, Siena's Accademia Musicale Chigiana presents the **Settimana Musicale Senese,** one of Italy's best concert and opera programs. ☎ 0577-22091. www.chigiana.it/concerti.htm.

Montepulciano's major festival happens on the last Sunday in August. The town's districts race wine barrels up the length of the Corso to the Duomo, in the **Bravio delle Botti.**

The first Sunday of September in Arezzo, the **Giostra del Saracino** (Saracen's Joust) takes place—a tournament between mounted

Useful Websites

www.yourwaytoflorence.com: Accommodations, shopping, tourism, art, history, wines, even weather forecasts—a city catchall.

www.ilpalio.org: The all-things Palio site has history, race trivia, video of recent Palios, and a list of winners since 1644.

www.pisa-airport.com: Information about Pisa's Galileo Galilei International Airport, Tuscany's international gateway.

www.theflorentine.net: The website of Florence's major English-language magazine.

www.firenzeturismo.it: Comprehensive and functional official site for Florence tourism.

www.sangimignano.com: The best online resource on the town, including hotels, restaurant details, and events.

www.turismo.toscana.it: This official resource is superb for an overview of Tuscany as a whole.

www.trenitalia.it: The state railway website is an essential planning tool for train travel across Tuscany.

www.terresiena.it: Tuscany's best provincial website covers an area from San Gimignano in the north to the Val d'Orcia in the south.

www.greve-in-chianti.com: Planning resource for Chianti wine country, south of Florence.

www.wga.hu: Online art museum with a comprehensive Renaissance collection.

---

knights in 13th-century armor and the effigy of a Saracen warrior. ☎ 0575-377462.

AUTUMN. All Lucca is festooned with candles on the evening of September 13, for the **Luminara di Santa Croce.** A holy procession starts from the cathedral.

The second week of September also sees the **Rassegna del Chianti Classico,** a 3-day wine festival centered around Greve.

In October the opera, concert, and ballet season opens in Florence at the **Teatro Comunale.** ☎ 055-2779350. www.maggiofiorentino.com.

In Montalcino, on the last weekend of October, residents celebrate the **Sagra del Tordo** or "Feast of

the Thrush." Locals in medieval costume stage an archery tournament, parades, and plenty of gastronomy, including BBQ thrush.

WINTER. On December 25, the year's final **Display of the Virgin's Girdle** (the Sacro Cingolo) takes place in Prato. The belt that the Virgin handed to "Doubting" Thomas on her Assumption is revealed inside the Duomo, with Renaissance-styled drummers in attendance. The solemn ceremony is repeated on Easter Day, May 1, August 15 (the Feast of the Assumption), and most importantly September 8, the Virgin's Birthday. ☎ 0574-24112.

Italy's second-largest **Carnevale** is hosted by Viareggio. Events take place throughout February. ☎ 0584-47077. www.viareggio. ilcarnevale.com.

Cellphones (Mobiles)

Italy (like most of the world) is on the GSM (Global System for Mobiles) wireless system. GSM phones function with a removable plastic SIM card, encoded with your phone number and account information. World phones are the only U.S. phones that are compatible.

If necessary, U.S. visitors can rent a world phone before leaving home from **InTouch USA** ☎ 800/ 872-7626 (www.intouchglobal.com), **RoadPost** ☎ 888/622-3393 (www. roadpost.com), or **Cellhire** ☎ 877/ 244-7242 (www.cellhire.com).

U.K. and Irish mobiles all work in Italy; call your service provider before departing to ensure that the international call bar is off, and to check call charges, which can be extremely high. Remember that you are also charged for calls you *receive* on a U.K. mobile used abroad.

The best option, for everyone, is to buy a SIM card when you get to Tuscany (make sure your handset is unlocked first). The major Italian networks are **Vodafone, Wind, TIM,** and **3.** A local rechargeable SIM costs about 5€ and gives you far cheaper local calls (under .10€/min.). Show your passport when buying. You will also find a handset for under 50€, if you don't have one already.

Money

Italy falls somewhere in the middle of pricing in Europe—not as expensive as, say, London or Scandinavia, but not as cheap as Spain or Greece. Tuscany comes just behind Venice in terms of the costliest bit of Italy to travel, but the advice in this book should help guide you to the best options to fit any budget.

It's a good idea to exchange at least some money—just enough to cover airport incidentals and transportation to your hotel—before you leave home, so you can avoid lines at airport ATMs. You can exchange money at your local American Express or Thomas Cook office or your bank (often, though, only at major branches). If you're far away from a bank with currency-exchange services, American Express offers traveler's checks and foreign currency—though with a $15 order fee and additional shipping costs— to U.S. customers at www.american express.com or ☎ **800/807-6233.** In the U.K. call ☎ 01273-696933.

Keep a record of the serial numbers separate from the checks.

Currency

In January 2002, Italy retired the lira and joined most of Western Europe in switching to the **euro.** Coins are issued in denominations of .01€, .02€ .05€, .10€, .20€, and .50€, as well as 1€ and 2€; bills come in denominations of 5€, 10€, 20€, 50€, 100€, 200€, and 500€.

Exchange rates are listed in most international newspapers. To get a transaction as close to this rate as possible, pay with your credit card (though check foreign transaction fees with your card provider before leaving home).

Traveler's checks, while still the safest way to carry money, are going the way of the dinosaur. The evolution of international computerized banking and consolidated ATM networks has led to the triumph of plastic throughout the Italian peninsula—even if cold cash is still the most trusted currency, especially in family joints, where credit cards may not be accepted.

You'll get the best rate locally if you **exchange money** at a bank or use one of its ATMs. The rates at "Cambio/change/wechsel" exchange booths are invariably less favorable but still a good deal better than what you'd get exchanging money at a hotel or shop (a last-resort tactic only).

ATMs

The ability to access your personal bank account through the **Cirrus** (☎ 800/424-7787; www.master card.com) or **PLUS** (☎ 800/843-7587; www.visa.com) network of ATMs (or "cashpoints")—or get a cash advance on an enabled Visa or MasterCard—has grown by leaps and bounds in Italy in recent years. All you need to do is search out a machine that has your network's symbol displayed, pop in your card, and punch in your PIN (make sure it's four digits; six-digit PINs won't work). It'll spit out local currency drawn directly from your home account (and at a more favorable rate than converting traveler's checks or cash). Keep in mind that many banks impose a fee every time a card is used at a different bank's ATM, and that fee will probably be higher for international transactions (up to $5 or more). Banks in Italy do not (at least yet) charge you a second fee to use their ATMs.

An ATM in Italian is a *Bancomat* (though Bancomat is a private company, its name has become the generic word for ATMs). Increased internationalism has been slowly doing away with the old worry that your card's PIN, be it on a bank card or credit card, need be specially enabled to work abroad, but it always pays to check with your issuing bank to be sure. If at the ATM you get a message saying your card isn't valid for international transactions, it's likely the bank just can't

make the phone connection to check it (occasionally this can be a citywide epidemic); try another ATM or another town.

If your card is equipped with the "Chip and PIN" security technology, be prepared to enter your PIN when you use the card to make purchases.

Credit Cards

Visa and MasterCard are almost universally accepted at hotels, restaurants, and shops; some also accept American Express. Diners Club is gaining a little ground, especially in Florence and in more expensive establishments throughout the region. If you arrange with your card issuer to enable the card's cash advance option (and get a PIN as well), you can also use them at ATMs. To use "Chip and PIN" credit cards, you'll need to know your PIN number to make a purchase.

Wire Services

If you find yourself out of money, a wire service can help you tap willing friends and family for funds. Through **MoneyGram** (☎ 800/666-3947 in U.S.; ☎ 0800-8971-8971 in U.K.; www.moneygram.com), you can get money sent around the world in less than 10 minutes. MoneyGram's fees vary based on the local agent the money is wired from and to, but a good estimate from the U.S. is $10 for anything up to $500 and $15 for up to $1000, with a sliding scale for larger sums. From the U.K, sending £100 costs £4.99, with a sliding scale for larger sums. Fees can be a little higher for transferring online with a credit card. A similar service is offered by **Western Union** (☎ 800/325-6000 in U.S.; ☎ 0800-833833 in U.K.), which accepts Visa and MasterCard credit or debit cards. You can arrange for the service over the phone, at a Western Union office, or online at www.westernunion.com. A sliding scale applies to prices, which may differ depending on agent and for online transactions.

For all wire transfer companies, a currency exchange rate also applies. Additionally, your credit card company may charge a fee for the cash advance as well as a higher interest rate.

Getting **There** & Getting **Around**

By Plane

The logical air entry point to Tuscany is Pisa's **Galileo Galilei Airport** (☎ 050-849300; www.pisa-airport.com), 3km (2 miles) south of Pisa and 84km (52 miles) west of Florence. Major airlines such as **Ryanair** (www.ryanair.com) and **British Airways** (www.ba.com) connect Pisa to several European cities, and there are five flights a week with **Delta** (www.delta.com) direct to **New York JFK.** Half-hourly trains whizz from the airport to Pisa Centrale station in 5 minutes. (1.10€); six times a day you can connect direct to Florence (1½ hr., 5.60€) without changing at Pisa Centrale. A faster alternative for anyone heading straight to Florence is the airport shuttle bus operated by **Terravision** (☎ 05-026080; www.terravision.eu). The 70-minute journey runs 13 times a day and costs 10€.

Tuscany's other major airport is **Amerigo Vespucci** (☎ 055-30615; www.aeroporto.firenze.it), in the suburb of Peretola, 5km (3 miles) west of central Florence. It's largely a domestic airport—**Alitalia** (www.alitalia.it) connects regularly with Rome and Milan. **Meridiana–Eurofly** (www.meridiana.it) also flies there direct from London's Gatwick Airport, Madrid, and Barcelona; **Lufthansa** (www.lufthansa.com) connects daily to Munich and Frankfurt. To reach the center take the half-hourly Volainbus service (4.50€) run by **ATAF** (☎ 055-56501; www.ataf.net). It terminates at Santa Maria Novella.

Italy's major intercontinental gateways are Milan's **Malpensa Airport** (☎ 02-74852200; www.sea-aeroportimilano.it), and Rome's **Fiumicino Airport** (☎ 06-65951; www.adr.it). Both are connected by several major airlines to hubs across North America. **Alitalia** (www.alitalia.it) can connect you straight on to Florence, but if you're spending time touring locally before heading to Tuscany, the train is much the best bet. By rail, Florence is under 3 hours from Milan or Venice, under 2 hours from Rome (☎ 892021; www.trenitalia.it). See "By Train," below.

By Train

Every day, around 20 **Eurostar** trains (☎ 08705-186186 in U.K.; ☎ +44 1233/617-575 elsewhere; www.eurostar.com) zip from London St. Pancras to Paris's Gare du Nord via the Channel Tunnel, in 2¼ hours. In Paris, you can transfer to Gare de Lyon station for one of three daily direct TGV trains to Milan (80€–95€ one-way; 7½ hr.), from where you can connect to Pisa (4 hr.) or Florence (2¾ hr.). There is also a daily Euronight (EN) train direct from Paris to Florence (the "Palatino"), with sleeping cars that can be reserved. The night train leaves Paris Bercy just before 7pm and gets into Florence's Campo di Marte around 7:15am. One-way tickets cost from 100€ per person for a (cramped) six-berth couchette, to 180€ for a two-berth sleeper. Paris–Italy trains are operated by **Artesia** (www.artesia.eu). All international trains need seat reservations in advance: Contact **Rail Europe** (www.rail europe.com in U.S.; www.rail europe.co.uk in U.K.).

The main Tuscan rail stations, receiving trains from most parts of Italy, are Florence and Pisa. Siena is an important provincial hub. Most arrivals in Florence are at the Modernist **Stazione Santa Maria Novella,** Piazza della Stazione (☎ 848-888088; ☎ 892021 or www.trenitalia.it for nationwide rail information). Some trains stop at the less convenient **Stazione Campo di Marte,** on the eastern fringe of the center; a 24-hour bus service (#12) links the two terminals. Fast *(ES)* trains arrive from Milan in under 3 hours, costing 36€ for a one-way ticket; and from Rome, in around 1¾ hours, costing the same. Slower trains are cheaper.

In Pisa, trains arrive at **Stazione Pisa Centrale,** Piazza della Stazione (☎ 050-917591), at the southern end of town. Of the major terminals in Tuscany, the best links are between Florence and Pisa, with trains departing every hour, at least. The trip between the two cities takes about an hour, costing 5.60€ for a one-way ticket.

Hourly trains also run direct between Rome and Pisa, taking 3 to 4 hours and costing 17€ to 27.50€ for a one-way ticket, depending on the train.

Trains link Lucca and Pisa half-hourly, taking only 25 minutes and costing 2.40€ for a one-way ticket.

In Siena, trains arrive at **Stazione Siena,** Piazza Rosselli. The station is 15 minutes by frequent bus from the heart of Siena. The most useful link is the hourly service between Florence and Siena, taking 1½ hours and costing 6.10€ for a one-way ticket. (Though a bus between the two cities is even more convenient—see "By Bus," below.)

Journeys between Pisa and Siena require a change at Empoli.

See p 100 for more on visiting Tuscany by rail.

By Bus

A number of regional bus companies provide the best links between rail hubs like Florence, Siena, or Pisa, and the smaller towns of Tuscany. Among the most useful are: **CPT** (Pisa–Volterra link) (☎ **050-505511;** www.cpt.pisa.it); **LFI** (Arezzo) (☎ **0575-39881;** www.lfi.it); **SITA** (Florence–Siena and Chianti link), (☎ **055-214721;** www.sitabus.it); **Tra.In** (Siena and around) (☎ **0577-204111;** www.trainspa.it). Most have downloadable timetables available online.

By Car

For motorists, the main link is the most traveled road in Italy—the **A1** autostrada (Italy's spinal expressway). This route comes in from the north and Milan, moving southeast toward Bologna before cutting abruptly south across the Apennines to Florence, the destination for most drivers heading to Tuscany. If you're already in the south, you can travel the same road north between Rome and Florence.

Skirting the western coast of Italy, including the Versilia Riviera, the **A12** heads down from Genoa. North of Pisa the A12 meets up with **A11,** which cuts east toward Florence. Florence and Siena are also linked by an expressway (the *raccordo*) with no route number; from Florence just follow the green signs for Siena.

For visitors heading to Arezzo and eastern Tuscany, follow the autostrada (A1) as though you're going to Rome, until you reach the exits for Arezzo to the immediate east of the road.

Autostrade are superhighways, denoted by green signs and a number prefaced with an A, like the A1 from Rome to Florence. A few aren't numbered and are simply called *raccordo*, a connecting road between two cities (such as Florence–Siena and Florence–Pisa–Livorno, the "FI–PI–LI"). Autostrade are usually toll roads, though not too expensive. There's a toll calculator at www.autostrade.it: Florence to Lucca, for example, costs 3.60€; Florence to Rome is 13.80€.

Strade Statale are state roads, usually two lanes wide, indicated by blue signs. Their route numbers are prefaced with an SS or an S, as in the S222 from Florence to Siena. On signs, however, these official route numbers are used infrequently. Usually, you'll just see blue signs listing destinations by name with arrows pointing off in the appropriate directions. Even if it's just a few miles down the road, often the town you're looking for won't be mentioned on the sign at the appropriate turnoff. It's impossible to predict which of all the towns that lie along a road will be the ones chosen to list on a particular sign. Sometimes, the sign gives only the first minuscule village that lies past the turnoff; at other times it lists the first major town down that road, and some signs mention only the major city the road eventually leads to, even if it's hundreds of miles away. It pays to study the map and fix in your mind the names of all the possibilities before coming to an intersection.

The **speed limit** on roads in built-up areas around towns and cities is 50kmph (31 mph). On the autostrada it's 110kmph (68 mph), except on weekends when it's upped to 130kmph (81 mph). Italians have an astounding disregard for these limits—perhaps one reason why Italy, statistically-speaking, has Western Europe's most dangerous roads.

Nevertheless, police can ticket you and collect the fine on the spot. At 0.5 mg/l, Italy's official blood alcohol limit is stricter than in the U.S or U.K. The traffic police will throw you in jail if they pull you over and find you inebriated.

If you're from outside the E.U. but driving a private car in Tuscany, before leaving home, apply for an **International Driver's Permit;** in the U.S, from the American Automobile Association (AAA; ☎ **800/222-1134** or 407/444-4300; www.aaa.com). In Canada, the permit is available from the Canadian Automobile Association (CAA; ☎ **613/247-0117;** www.caa.ca). Technically, you need this permit, your actual driver's license, and an Italian translation of the latter (also available from the AAA and CAA) to drive in Italy, though in practice the license itself generally suffices. If you're driving a rented car, a valid driver's license from your home country is usually fine—but check with your rental company.

If someone races up behind you and flashes their lights, that's the signal for you to slow down so they can pass you quickly and safely. Stay in the right lane on highways; the left is only for passing and for cars with large engines and the pedal to the metal. On a two-lane road, the idiot passing someone in the opposing traffic who has swerved into your lane expects you to veer obligingly over into the shoulder so three lanes of traffic can fit—he would do the same for you. Probably.

Benzina (gas or petrol) is even more expensive in Italy than in the rest of Europe. Even a small rental car guzzles between 50€ and 60€ for a full tank.

There are many pull-in filling stations along major roads and on the outskirts of towns, as well as 24-hour rest stops along the autostrada. Almost all stations are closed for *riposo* and on Sundays, but many have a pump fitted with a machine that accepts bills so you can self-service your tank at 3am. Unleaded gas is *senza piombo*. Diesel (which is cheaper) is *gasolio*.

Car Rentals

In Tuscany, all roads lead to Florence, but you won't need a car once you get there: The Centro Storico is best explored on foot, and parking is expensive. Your best tactic is to tour Tuscany by car at the start or end of your trip, picking it up or returning it as you leave or arrive in Florence. You're usually allowed to park in front of your hotel long enough to unload your luggage. You'll then want to proceed to a garage. (Ask the concierge at your hotel to recommend the nearest.)

You'll save money by booking a car before leaving home. The major U.S. rental companies operating in Italy are **Avis** (☎ 800/331-1212; www.avis.com), **Budget** (☎ 800/472-3325; www.budget.com), and **Hertz** (☎ 800/654-3001; www.hertz.com). U.S.-based companies offering European car rental include **Auto Europe** ☎ 800/223-5555; www.autoeurope.com), **Europe by Car** (☎ 800/223-1516; www.ebc travel.com), and **Kemwel Holiday**

Auto (☎ 877/820-0668; www.kemwel.com). In some cases, members of the **American Automobile Association (AAA)** or AARP qualify for discounts.

From the U.K., we recommend **Holiday Autos** (☎ 0871/472-5229; www.holidayautos.co.uk). Its pre-paid vouchers include insurance, which is sky-high in Italy. A reliable local alternative is **Europcar** (☎ 06-96709592, ☎ 877/940-6900 in North America; www.europcar.it).

Both stick shift (manual) and automatic are commonly available at car-rental companies. The former is preferable for negotiating Tuscany's hilly terrain.

We'd also recommend you opt for the **Collision Damage Waiver (CDW),** even though it can be expensive. A bump in Italy isn't that uncommon. You'll pay less for CDW if you purchase it through a third-party insurer such as **Travel Guard** (☎ 800/826-1919 in U.S; www.travelguard.com).

Car-rental agencies also require you to purchase a theft protection policy (it may be included in the price, however). Before buying added insurance, check your own personal auto insurance policy and credit card terms and conditions to see if they already provide cover.

Fast **Facts**

AREA CODES   Italy no longer uses separate city codes. Dial all numbers as written in this book.

BUSINESS HOURS   General hours of operation for **stores, offices,** and **churches** are from 9:30am to noon or 1pm and again from 3 or 3:30pm to 7pm. That early afternoon shutdown is the *riposo,* the Italian *siesta.* Most stores close on Sunday or on Monday (morning only or all day).

Some government services and business offices are open to the public only in the mornings. Traditionally, museums are closed Mondays, but check entries in the relevant chapters for exact hours. The biggest "sights" generally stay open all day, but many close for *riposo* or open only in the morning (9am–2pm is common at smaller sites). Some churches open earlier than 9am, and the largest often stay open all day. **Bank hours** tend to be Monday through Friday from 8:30am to 1:30pm and 2:30 to 3:30pm or 3 to 4pm.

Use the *riposo* as the Italians do—take a long lunch, stroll through a park, travel to the next town, or return to your hotel to recoup your energy. The *riposo* is especially welcome in August.

CRIME See "Safety," below. Also note that it is illegal for you to knowingly buy **counterfeit goods** (and, yes, paying 10€ for a "Rolex" counts as *knowingly*). Tourists have left with large fines among their holiday souvenirs. Feeding the **pigeons** in Lucca is also punishable with a fine.

DRUGSTORES You'll find **green neon crosses** above the entrances to most *farmacie* (pharmacies). You'll also find many *erborista* (herbalist shops), which usually offer more traditional herbal remedies along with pharmaceuticals. Most keep everything behind the counter, so be prepared to point or mime. **Language tip:** Most minor ailments start with the phrase *mal di*, so you can just say "Mahl dee" and point to your head, stomach, throat, or whatever. Pharmacies rotate which will stay open all night and on Sundays, and each store has a poster outside showing the month's rotation.

ELECTRICITY Italy operates on a 220 volts AC (50 cycles) system. You'll need a simple adapter plug and, for non-Europeans, probably a current converter. Get whatever you need before leaving home, as they can be devilish to find in Italy.

U.S. travelers searching for more information can find it from **The Franzus Company** (☎ 800/211-9611; www.franzus.com). You can also pick up the hardware at electronics stores, travel specialty stores, luggage shops, airports, and from

Magellan's (☎ 800/962-4943; www.magellans.com).

EMBASSIES/CONSULATES The **U.S. Embassy** is in Rome at Via Vittorio Veneto 119a (☎ 06-46-741; www.usembassy.it). The **U.S. consulate** in Florence—for passport and consular services but not visas—is at Lungarno Vespucci 38 (☎ 055-266-951; http://florence.usconsulate.gov), open to emergency drop-ins Monday through Friday from 8:30am to 12:30pm. Afternoons 2 to 4:30pm and for non-emergencies, the consulate is open by appointment only; call ahead or book online.

The **U.K. Embassy** is in Rome at Via XX Settembre 80a (☎ 06-4220-0001; www.britishembassy.gov.uk), open Monday through Friday from 9am to 5pm. The **U.K. consulate** in Florence is at Lungarno Corsini 2 (☎ 055-284-133). It's open Monday to Friday 9:30am to 1pm and 2 to 5pm.

Of English-speaking countries, only the U.S. and U.K. have consulates in Florence. Citizens of other countries must go to Rome for help: The **Canadian Consulate** in Rome is at Via Zara 30 (☎ 06-854441; www.canada.it), open Monday through Friday from 8:30am to 12:30pm and 1:30 to 4pm. **Australia**'s Rome consulate is at Via Bosio 5 (☎ 06-852721; www.italy.embassy.gov.au). The consular section is open Monday through Friday from 9am to 5pm. **New Zealand**'s Rome consulate is at Via Clitunno 44 (☎ 06-853-7501; www.nzembassy.com), open Monday through Friday from 8:30am to 12:45pm and 1:45 to 5pm. The embassy for **Ireland** is at Piazza di Campitelli 3, Rome (☎ 06-6979-121; www.ambasciata-irlanda.it), open weekdays 10am to 12:30pm and 3 to 4:30pm.

EMERGENCIES Dial ☎ 113 for any emergency. You can also call ☎ 112 for the *carabinieri* (gendarmerie-style police), ☎ 118 for an ambulance, or ☎ 115 for the fire department. If your car breaks down, dial ☎ 116 for roadside aid from the Automotive Club of Italy.

HOLIDAYS   Offices and shops are closed on the following: January 1; January 6 (Epiphany); Easter Sunday *(Pasqua);* Easter Monday *(Pasquetta);* April 25 (Liberation Day); May 1 (Labor Day); August 15 *(Ferragosto);* November 1 (All Saints' Day); December 8 (Immaculate Conception); December 25 (Christmas Day); December 26 *(Santo Stefano).* Towns and cities also shut on their patron saint's day (for example, June 24, St. John the Baptist, for Florence).

HOSPITALS   The emergency ambulance number is ☎ 118. Hospitals in Italy are partially socialized, and the care is efficient, personalized, and of a high quality. There are also well-run private hospitals. Pharmacy staff tend to be competent healthcare providers, so for less serious problems their advice will do fine. For significant but non-life-threatening ailments, you can walk into most hospitals and get speedy care—with no questions about insurance policies, no forms to fill out, and no fees to pay. **Obviously it's still crucial to carry an appropriate travel health insurance policy.** E.U. citizens should take an **EHIC** card to be certain of free reciprocal health care; forms are available in the U.K. from post offices or at **www.ehic.org.uk.** Most hospitals will be able to find someone who speaks English, but there's also a Florence-based **free medical translator** available at ☎ 055-425-0126.

INTERNET ACCESS   Cybercafes are in healthy supply in cities. In smaller towns you may have a bit of trouble, but increasingly hotels are setting up Internet points. In a pinch, hostels, local libraries, and, sometimes, pubs will have a terminal for access. **Internet Train** (www.internettrain.it) is a franchise-based chain of Internet points across Italy. Charge your pre-payment card at one branch and you can use it again at any of 25 across Tuscany. **Wi-Fi** is less common, but spreading. Antiterror laws in Italy means that all Internet point users must present their passports.

LANGUAGE   Though Italian is the local language around these parts, English is common, especially among under 40s. Anyone in the tourism industry will know the English they need to facilitate transactions. Most Italians are delighted to help you learn a bit of their lingo as you go, and they will certainly appreciate your attempts to converse with them in their native tongue. To help, we've compiled a lists of key phrases and menu terms later in this chapter; see p 203.

LIQUOR LAWS   Driving drunk is illegal, and unwise on Italy's twisty, narrow roads (or anywhere, for that matter). The legal drinking age in Italy is 16. Public drunkenness (aside from people getting noisily tipsy and flush at big dinners) is unusual.

LOST & FOUND   Be sure to tell all of your credit card companies the minute you discover your wallet has been lost or stolen and file a report at the nearest police precinct *(questura).* Your credit card company or insurer may require a police report number or record of the loss. Most credit card companies have an emergency toll-free number to call if your card is lost or stolen; they may be able to wire you a cash advance or deliver an emergency credit card in a day or two.

To report a lost or stolen card, call the following Italian toll-free numbers: **Visa** at ☎ 800-819-014, **MasterCard** at ☎ 800-870-866, or

American Express at ☎ 800-874-333, or for U.S. cardholders collect at ☎ 336-393-1111 from anywhere in the world. As a backup, write down the emergency number that appears on the back of each of your cards (*not* the toll-free or freephone number—you can't dial those from abroad; if one doesn't appear, call the card issuer and ask).

Identity theft and fraud are potential complications of losing your wallet, especially if you've lost your driver's license along with cash and credit cards. Notify the major credit-reporting bureaus immediately; placing a fraud alert on your records may protect you. The three major U.S. credit-reporting agencies are **Equifax** (☎ 888/766-0008; www.equifax.com), **Experian** (☎ 888/397-3742; www.experian.com), and **TransUnion** (☎ 800/680-7289; www.transunion.com). Finally, if you've lost all forms of photo ID, call your airline and explain the situation; they might allow you to board the plane if you have a copy of your passport or birth certificate and a copy of the police report you've filed.

MAIL   The Italian mail system is notoriously slow, and friends back home may not receive your postcards before they see you again in person. Postcards, aerograms, and letters, weighing up to 20g (.7 oz.), cost .65€ to send. Buy stamps from postal offices or wherever you see the black-and-white "T" *(tabacchi)* sign. Ask for *"un francobollo per gli Stati Uniti / per Gran Bretagna,"* and so on.

NEWSPAPERS & MAGAZINES   Visitors will see plenty of familiar mastheads. The *International Herald Tribune* and *USA Today* are available at many newsstands, even in small towns. You can also find the *Wall Street Journal Europe,* and European editions of *Time* and *Newsweek.* U.K. daily and Sunday newspapers are available (a day or two behind) in all decent-sized newsagents. Florence's bi-weekly *The Florentine* is the major English-language publication with listings; Lucca's monthly *Grapevine* does the same. Italian-speakers should go for *La Nazione,* a national daily published in Florence; or *Il Tirreno,* more widespread closer to the coast.

POLICE   For emergencies, call ☎ 113. Italy has several different police forces, but you'll most likely only ever deal with two. The first is the urban *polizia,* whose city headquarters is called the *questura* and can help with lost and stolen property. The most useful branch—for serious crimes—is the *carabinieri* (☎ 112), an order-keeping, crime-fighting civilian police force.

RESTROOMS   Public toilets are going out of fashion, but most bars will let you use their bathrooms without a scowl or forcing you to buy anything. Ask *"Posso usare il bagno?"* (poh-soh oo-zar-eh eel ban-yo). *Donne/signore* are women and *uomini/signori* men. Train stations usually have a bathroom, for a fee. In many of the public toilets that remain, the little old lady with a basket has been replaced by a coin-op turnstile.

SAFETY   Other than the inevitable pickpockets, especially in Florence, random violent crime is practically unheard of in Tuscany. However, the area round Florence's Santa Maria Novella, and the Cascine park, are best avoided at night; ditto around Santo Spirito in the small hours.

You won't find quite as many gangs of **pickpocketing children** as in Rome, but they have started roving the Santa Maria Novella area of Florence. If you see a small group of unkempt children coming at you, often waving cardboard and jabbering in Ital-English, yell *"Va via!"* (go away) or simply "No!," or invoke the *polizia.*

In general, just be smart, especially in crowded spots. Keep your passport, traveler's checks, credit and ATM cards, and photocopies of important documents under your clothes in a money belt or neck pouch. **For women:** Beware of drive-by purse snatchings, by young thieves on mopeds, in Florence. Keep your purse on the wall side of the sidewalk and sling the strap across your chest. If your purse has a flap, keep the clasp facing your body. **For men:** Keep your wallet in a front pocket and perhaps loop a rubber band around it. (The rubber catches on the fabric of your pocket and makes it harder for a thief to slip the wallet out.)

SMOKING   Italy banned smoking inside all bars, restaurants and offices in 2005. Note, however, that smoking on outdoor terraces (including in restaurants) is allowed.

TAXES   There's no sales tax added to the price tag of your purchases, but there is a **value-added tax** (in Italy, IVA) automatically included in just about everything. For major purchases, you can get this refunded (p 62). Occasionally upscale hotels don't include the 13% luxury tax in their quoted prices. Ask when making your reservation.

TELEPHONES & FAX   There are several types of public pay phones: those that take coins only, those that take both coins and phone cards, and those that take only **phone cards** (carta or scheda telefonica). You can buy prepaid phone cards at any tabacchi (tobacconists), most newsstands, and some bars in several denominations. Break off the corner before inserting; a display tracks how much money is left as you talk. Don't forget to take the card with you when you leave! Some public phones also take credit cards.

For **operator-assisted international calls** (in English), dial toll-free

☎ 170. Note, however, that you'll get better rates by calling a home operator for collect calls, as detailed here: To make calling card calls, insert a phone card or coin—it'll be refunded at the end of your call—and dial the local number for your service. For **Americans:** AT&T at ☎ 172-1011, MCI at ☎ 172-1022, or Sprint at ☎ 172-1877. These numbers will raise an American operator for you, and you can use any one of them to place a collect call even if you don't carry that phone company's card. **Canadians** can reach Tata at ☎ 172-1001. **Brits** can call BT at ☎ 172-0044. The **Irish** can get a home operator at ☎ 172-0353. **Australians** can use Optus by calling ☎ 172-1161 or Telstra at ☎ 172-1061; **New Zealanders** can phone home at ☎ 172-1064.

To **dial direct internationally** from Italy, dial ☎ 00, then the country code, the area code, and the number. Country codes are as follows: the United States and Canada 1; United Kingdom 44; Ireland 353; Australia 61; New Zealand 64. Make calls from a public phone if possible because hotels charge inflated rates, but take along plenty of schede to feed the phone. Cheap rate **international calling cards** are also available from tobacconists. Most internet points are equipped for **VOIP** (Voiceover Internet Protocol) calling using services like Skype.

To call free **national telephone information** (in Italian) in Italy, dial ☎ 12. International information for Europe is available at ☎ 176. For international information beyond Europe, dial ☎ 1790.

Your hotel will most likely be able to send or receive **faxes** for you, sometimes at inflated prices, sometimes at cost. Otherwise, most cartolerie (stationery stores), copista or fotocopie (photocopy shops),

Internet cafes, and some *tabacchi* (tobacconists) offer fax services.

TIME ZONE Italy is 6 hours ahead of Eastern Standard Time in the United States, an hour ahead of GMT or BST in the U.K. and Ireland.

TIPPING In **hotels,** a service charge is usually included in your bill. In family-run operations, additional tips are unnecessary and sometimes considered rude. In fancier places with a hired staff, however, you may want to leave a .50€ daily tip for the maid, pay the bellhop or porter 1€ per bag, and a helpful concierge 2€ for his or her troubles. In **restaurants,** 10% to 15% is usually included in the bill, alongside a fixed charge for *"pane e coperto"* (bread and cover)—to be sure, ask *"è incluso il servizio?"* You may want to leave up to an additional 10% for good service, but don't feel obliged. At **bars and cafes,** leave your change up to the next euro or two on the counter for the barman; if you sit at a table, you're being charged extra anyway, so there's no need to feel a duty to leave more than for a barman. **Taxi** drivers expect around 10%.

WATER Although most Italians take mineral water with their meals, tap water is safe everywhere, as are any public drinking fountains you run across. Unsafe sources will be marked *"acqua non potabile."* If tap water comes out cloudy, it's only calcium or other minerals inherent in a water supply that often comes untreated from fresh springs.

A Brief **History**

1100–700 B.C. Villanovan culture thrives in what we now call Tuscany.

800–300 B.C. The Etruscans are the major power in central Italy.

600–510 B.C. The Etruscan Tarquin dynasty rules as kings of Rome.

508 B.C. Lars Porsena, Etruscan king of Clusium (now Chiusi), attacks the young Roman Republic and wins.

295–265 B.C. Rome conquers Etruria and allies with Umbria. The Roman Empire spreads throughout central Italy and Latinizes local culture.

59 B.C. Julius Caesar founds Florentia, and Florence is born.

56 B.C. The First Triumvirate (Caesar, Pompey, and Crassus) meets in Lucca.

A.D. 250 Florence's first Christian martyr, St. Minias, is beheaded in the city.

313 Roman Emperor Constantine the Great, a convert himself, declares religious freedom for Christians.

476 After a long decline, the Roman Empire falls.

570–774 The Lombard duchies rule over much of Tuscany and neighboring Umbria.

774–800s Charlemagne and the Carolingian dynasty picks up where the Lombards left off.

1115 Florence is granted independent status within the Holy Roman Empire (a territory that covered modern-day central Europe).

1125 Florence razes neighbor Fiesole to the ground. Florentine expansion begins.

1155 Frederick I Barbarossa is crowned Holy Roman Emperor and attempts to take control of part of Italy.

1173 Pisa begins its bell tower. Eleven years later, someone notices the tilt.

1215 Florentine families form factions reflecting the conflict between emperor and pope. Those favoring the pope are known as Guelphs, pro-Imperial supporters as Ghibellines.

1250–1600 Intellectual pursuit of knowledge and study of the classical and Arab worlds begins to take precedence over Christian doctrine and superstition: the Humanist era.

1260 Ghibelline Siena defeats Guelph Florence at the Battle of Montaperti. Siena dedicates itself to the Virgin Mary in thanks.

1284 Genoa trounces Pisa's fleet in the naval Battle of Meloria. A long Pisan decline begins.

1300 The Guelph triumph in Florence is secure, but they immediately split into the White and the Black factions.

1302 Dante is exiled from Florence on trumped-up charges. He never returns, and is buried in Ravenna in 1321.

1303–77 The pope moves from Rome to Avignon. St. Catherine of Siena is instrumental in returning the papacy to Italy.

1304–10 Florentine Giotto frescoes the Arena Chapel, in Padua. Western painting would never be the same.

1308–21 Dante writes the *Divine Comedy*, which sets the Tuscan dialect as the precursor of modern Italian.

1310 Siena runs its first Palio on record.

1348 The Black Death rips through Italy, killing more than half the population. Siena loses more than two-thirds of its citizens.

1355 Siena's government of the Nine (the *"Nove"*) falls, ending almost a century of stability.

1361 Florence conquers Volterra.

1378–1417 The Western Schism: Avignon, Rome, *and* Pisa each appoint a pope, and the competing pontiffs get busy excommunicating one another.

1384 Florence conquers Arezzo.

1401 Lorenzo Ghiberti wins the competition to cast the baptistery doors in Florence. May the Renaissance begin!

1406 Florence conquers Pisa.

1434–64 Cosimo "il Vecchio" consolidates Medici power over Florence.

1435 Leon Battista Alberti publishes *De Pictura*, the seminal work of Renaissance art theory, largely on optics and perspective.

1439 The Council of Florence: Eastern and Western churches briefly reconcile their ancient differences.

1458 The coronation, in Rome, of Sienese Pope Pius II is re-created outside the Palazzo Pubblico for the benefit of citizens of Siena.

1469–92 The rule of Lorenzo de' Medici "the Magnificent" in Florence, under whose patronage the arts flourish.

1475 Michelangelo Buonarotti is born in Caprese, near Arezzo.

1494 Puritanical Dominican Fra' Girolamo Savonarola helps drive the Medici from Florence and takes control of the city.

1495 The "Bonfire of the Vanities": At Savonarola's urging, Florentines carry material goods seen as decadent—including paintings by Botticelli, Lorenzo di Credi, and others—to Piazza della Signoria and burn them.

1498 At the pope's urging, Florentines carry Savonarola to Piazza della Signoria and set *him* on fire.

1498–1512 The Florentine Republic is free from the Medici.

1501–04 Michelangelo carves *David,* "*Il Gigante."*

1505 For a few months, Leonardo da Vinci, Michelangelo, and Raphael all live and work in Florence at the same time.

1527 Emperor Charles V sacks Rome. Medici Pope Clement VII escapes to Orvieto, where by papal bull he refuses to annul Henry VIII's marriage to Catherine of Aragon and helps give rise to the Anglican Church.

1530 The Medici firmly take back power in Florence.

1550 Vasari publishes *The Lives of the Artists,* effectively the first art history book.

1555–57 Florence conquers Siena. The Sienese Republic makes a last stand at Montalcino.

1569 Cosimo I de' Medici is the first Grand Duke of Tuscany.

1581 The Uffizi opens as a painting gallery.

1633 Despite being championed by the Medici, Galileo is forced by the Church to recant his idea that Earth revolves around the Sun.

1737 Gian Gastone, last of the Medici Grand Dukes, dies.

1796–1806 Napoléon sweeps through Tuscany, eventually declaring himself king of Italy.

1805 Napoléon gives Lucca to his sister Elisa Baciocchi as a duchy.

1814–15 Napoléon is exiled on Elba, which he rules as governor.

1824 Lorraine Grand Duke Leopold II starts draining the marshes of the Maremma. The reclamation is complete in 1950 with the defeat of malaria.

1848–60 The *Risorgimento* movement struggles for a unified Italy.

1860 Tuscany joins the new Kingdom of Italy.

1865–70 Florence serves as Italy's capital.

1921 The Italian Communist Party is founded, in Livorno, and goes on to play a major part in postwar democratic politics.

1922 Mussolini becomes the Fascist dictator of Italy.

1940–45 World War II. Fascist Italy initially participates as an Axis power, before descending into civil war between Fascists and Partisans.

1944 Nazi troops withdraw from Florence, blowing up the Arno bridges. Supposedly on Hitler's direct order, the Ponte Vecchio is spared.

1946 Italy becomes a republic.

1948 Italy's regions are created: Tuscany and Umbria finally get an official dividing line between them.

1966 The Arno flood in Florence. Up to 6m (20 ft.) of water and mud destroys or damages countless works of art. Over 100 people die.

1985 Italy's worst winter on record; the frost hits grapevines heavily and comes close to destroying all the olive trees in Tuscany.

1988 Pedestrian zones go into effect in major cities, making historic centers traffic-free (almost).

1993 On May 27, a car bomb rips through the west wing of the

Uffizi, killing five people and damaging many paintings. Italy's Christian Democratic government, in power since the end of World War II, dissolves in a flurry of scandal. In a chain reaction, far left and right also splinter; more than 16 major parties vie for power in various improbable coalitions.

1997 In Assisi, in neighboring Umbria, a series of earthquakes hit, and part of the basilica's ceiling collapses, destroying frescoes and damaging Giotto's *Life of St. Francis.*

1999 Tuscany rejoices when local filmmaker Roberto Benigni, after victory at Cannes, gathers three Oscars for his Holocaust fable *La Vita è Bella (Life Is Beautiful).*

2001 The first cases of BSE (mad cow disease) in Italy are confirmed.

Beef consumption plummets 70%, and the government considers banning such culinary institutions as the *bistecca alla fiorentina.* The year ends on a high note when the Leaning Tower of Pisa reopens to the public, after more than a decade of desperate measures to keep it from collapsing. (Don't worry—it still leans.)

2002 Florence's football team, Fiorentina, known as *La Viola,* goes out of business. But her return to the highest echelons of European competition will take just 6 years.

2008 The city of Florence makes the first moves toward issuing a formal pardon for Dante, exiled 700 years previously. For the third time since the Millennium, Bruco wins Siena's Palio.

Art & Architecture

Architecture

Ambulatory Continuation of the side aisles to make a walkway around the chancel space behind the main altar of a church.

Apse The semicircular or polygonal space behind the main altar of a church.

Arcade A series of arches supported by columns, piers, or pilasters.

Architrave The long vertical element lying directly across the tops of a series of columns (the lowest part of an entablature); or, the molding around a door or window.

Badia Abbey.

Baldacchino A stone canopy over a church altar.

Basilica A form of architecture first used for public halls and law courts in ancient Roman cities. Early Christians adopted the form—a long rectangular room, divided into a central nave with side aisles but no transept—to build their first large churches. A "basilica" is now sometimes used to denote an important church without a bishop's seat.

Bay The space between two columns or piers.

Bifore Divided vertically into two sections.

Blind Arcade An arcade of pilasters (the arches are all filled in), a defining architectural feature of the Romanesque style.

Caldarium The hot tub or steam room of a Roman bath.

Campanile A bell tower, usually of a church but also of public buildings; it's often detached or flush against the church rather than sprouting directly from it.

Cantoria Small church singing gallery, usually set into the wall above the congregation's heads.

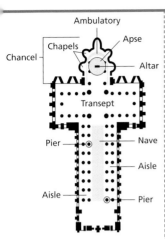

Church Floor Plan

Capital The top of a column. The classical "orders" (types) are Doric (plain), Ionic (with scrolls, called volutes, at the corners), and Corinthian (leafy). There's also Tuscan (even simpler than Doric; the column is never fluted or grooved, and usually has no base) and Composite (Corinthian superimposed with Ionic). In many Paleochristian and Romanesque churches, the capital is carved with primitive animal and human heads or simple biblical scenes.

Cappella Italian for chapel.

Caryatid A column carved to resemble a woman (see also *telamon*).

Cattedrale Cathedral (also Duomo).

Cavea The semicircle of seats in a classical theater.

Cella The innermost, most sacred room of a Roman pagan temple.

Chancel Space around the high altar of a church, generally reserved for the clergy and the choir.

Chiesa Italian for church.

Chiostro Italian for cloister.

Ciborium (1) Another word for *baldacchino* (above); (2) Box or tabernacle containing the Host (the symbolic body and blood of Christ taken during communion).

Cloister A roofed walkway open on one side and supported by columns; usually used in the plural because often four of them faced one another to make interior open-air courtyards, centered around small gardens, found in monasteries and convents.

Collegiata A collegiate church, having a chapter of canons and a dean or provost to rule over it but lacking the bishop's seat that would make it a cathedral.

Colonnaded Lined with columns.

Cornice Protruding section, usually along the very top of a wall, a facade, or an entablature; a pediment is usually framed by a lower cornice and two sloping ones.

Cortile Courtyard.

Crenellated Topped by a regular series of teethlike protrusions and crevices; these battlements often ring medieval buildings or fortresses to aid in defense.

Crypt An underground burial vault; in churches, usually found below the altar end and in Italy often the remnant of an older version of the church.

Cupola Dome.

Cyclopian Adjective describing an unmortared wall built of enormous stones by an unknown, central Italian, pre-Etruscan people. The sheer size led the ancients to think they were built by the Cyclopses.

Duomo Cathedral (from *domus*, "house of God"), often used to refer to the main church in town even if it doesn't have a *cathedra*, or bishop's seat—the prerequisite for a cathedral.

Entablature Section riding above a colonnade, made up of the architrave (bottom), frieze (middle), and cornice (top).

Forum The main square in a Roman town; a public space used for assemblies, courts, and speeches and on which important temples and civic buildings were located.

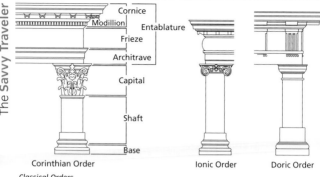

Corinthian Order   Ionic Order   Doric Order

Classical Orders

Frieze A decorative horizontal band or series of panels, usually carved in relief and at the center of an entablature.

Frigidarium Room for cold baths in a Roman bath.

Greek Cross Building ground plan in the shape of a cross whose arms are of equal length.

Latin Cross Building ground plan in the shape of a Crucifix-style cross, where one arm is longer than the other three (this is the nave).

Liberty Italian version of Art Nouveau or Art Deco, popular in the late 19th and early 20th centuries.

Loggia Roofed porch, balcony, or gallery.

Lozenge A decorative, regularly sided diamond (square on its corners), made of either marble inlay or a sunken depression, often centered in the arcs of a blind arcade on Romanesque architecture.

Lunette Semicircular wall space created by various ceiling vaultings or above a door or window; often it's decorated with a painting, mosaic, or relief.

Matroneum In some Paleochristian and early Romanesque churches, the gallery (often on the second floor) reserved for women, who were kept separate from the men during mass.

Narthex Interior vestibule of a church.

Nave The longest section of a church, usually leading from the front door to the altar, where the worshipers sit; often divided into aisles.

Palazzo Traditionally a palace or other important building; in contemporary Italian it refers to any large structure, including office buildings (and has become the common way to refer to a city block, no matter how many separate structures form it).

Paleochristian Early Christian, used generally to describe the era from the 5th to the early 11th century.

Pediment A wide gable at the top of a facade or above a doorway.

Piano Nobile The primary floor of a palace where the family would live, usually the second (American) but sometimes the third floor. It tends to have higher ceilings and larger rooms and be more lavishly decorated than the rest of the *palazzo*. The ground floor was usually for storage or shops and the attic for servants.

Pier A rectangular vertical support (like a column).

Pietra forte A dark gray, ocher-tinged limestone mined near Florence. Harder than its cousin *pietra serena* (below), it was used more sparingly in Florentine architecture.

Pietra serena A soft, light-gray limestone mined in the Florentine hills around Fiesole and one of the major building blocks of Florence's architecture—for both the ease with which it could be worked and its color, used to accent door jambs and window frames in houses and columns and chapels in churches.

Pieve A parish church; in the countryside, often primarily a baptismal site.

Pilaster Often called pilaster strip, it's a column, either rounded or squared off, set into a wall rather than separate from it.

Porta Italian for door or city gate.

Portico A porch.

Refectory The dining room of a convent or monastery—which, from the Renaissance on, was often painted with a *Last Supper* to aid religious contemplation at the dinner table.

Sacristy The room in a church that houses (or housed) the sacred vestments and vessels.

Sanctuary Technically the holiest part of a church, the term is used to refer to the area just around or behind the high altar.

Spandrel Triangular wall space created when two arches in an arcade curve away from each other (or from the end wall).

Spoglio Architectural recycling; the practice of using pieces of an older building to help raise a new one. (Roman temples were popular mines for both marble and columns to build early churches.)

Sporti Overhanging second story of a medieval or Renaissance building supported by wooden or stone brackets.

Stele A headstone.

Stemma Coat of arms.

Stucco Plaster composed of sand, powdered marble, water, and lime; often molded into decorative relief, formed into statuary, or applied in a thin layer to the exterior of a building.

Telamon A column sculpted to look like a man (also see caryatid).

Tepidarium The room for a warm bath in a Roman bath.

Terme Roman baths, usually divided into the calidarium, tepidarium, and frigidarium.

Torre Italian for tower.

Transept The lateral cross-arm of a cruciform church, perpendicular to the nave.

Travertine A whitish or honey-colored form of porous volcanic tufa mined near Tivoli. The stone from which ancient Rome was built.

Tribune The raised platform from which an orator speaks; used to describe the raised section of some churches around and behind the altar from which Mass is performed.

Two-light Of a window, divided vertically into two sections (see also *bifore*). A three-light window is divided vertically into three sections.

Tympanum The triangular or semicircular space between the cornices of a pediment or between the lintel above a door and the arch above it.

Painting, Sculpture & Ceramics

Aerial perspective The tendency of objects to blur toward the background color as they approach the horizon, a phenomenon mastered by Tuscan painters by the mid-1400s.

Altarpiece A painting placed on or hung above the altar, often made from poplar wood and consisting of two or more panels. After 1310, all churches were required to have one.

Ambone Italian for pulpit.

Amphora A two-handled jar with a tapered neck used by the ancients to keep wine, oil, and other liquids.

Arriccio The first, rough layer of plaster laid down when applying fresco to a wall. On this layer, the artist makes the rough *sinopia* sketches.

Bottega The workshop of an artist. (On museum signs, the word means the work was created or carried out by apprentices or assistants in the stated master's workshop.)

Bozzetto A small model for a larger sculpture (or sketch for a painting); in the later Renaissance and Baroque eras, it also came to mean the tiny statuettes turned out for their own sake to satisfy the growing demand among the rich for table art.

Bucchero Etruscan black earthenware pottery.

Canopic vase Etruscan funerary vase housing the entrails of the deceased.

Cartoon In Italian *cartone*, literally "big paper," the full-size preparatory sketch made for a fresco or mosaic.

Chiaroscuro Using patches of light and dark colors in painting to model figures and create the illusion of three dimensions. (Caravaggio was a master at also using the technique to create mood and tension.)

Cinerary urn Vase or other vessel containing the ashes of the deceased; Etruscan ones were often carved with a relief on the front and, on the lid, a half-reclining figure representing the deceased at a banquet.

Contrapposto A twisted pose in a figure, first used by the ancients and revived by Michelangelo; a hallmark of the Mannerist school.

Diptych A painting with two sections or panels.

Ex voto A small plaque, statue, painting, or other memento left by a supplicant, signifying either his or her gratitude to a saint or the Madonna, or imploring the saint's help in some matter.

Fresco The multistep art of creating a painting on fresh plaster (*fresco* means "fresh").

Gesso Calcium sulphate, or gypsum, applied in up to 7 layers to treat a wooden panel before painting.

Graffiti Incised decorative designs, made by painting the surface in two thin layers (one light, the other dark), then scratching away the top layer to leave the designs in contrast. Called *"sgraffito"* in Italian.

Grotesques Carved or painted faces, animals, and designs, often deliberately exaggerated or ugly; used to decorate surfaces and composite sculptures (such as fountains) and to illuminate manuscripts.

Illuminated Describing a manuscript or book, usually a choir book or bible, that has been decorated with colorful designs, miniatures, figures, scenes, and fancy letters, often produced by anonymous monks.

Intarsia Inlaid wood, marble, precious stones, or metal.

International Gothic Highly decorative style of painting with its roots in the art of Simone Martini. Leading Florentine exponents were Fra' Angelico and Gentile da Fabriano.

Majolica Tin-glazed earthenware pottery usually elaborately painted; a process pioneered and mastered in Italy in the 14th to 17th century.

Pala Altarpiece.

Pietra dura The art of inlaying semiprecious stones to form patterns and pictures; often called "Florentine mosaic" and increasingly popular from the late 15th century.

Pinacoteca Painting gallery.

Polyptych A panel painting having more than one section that's hinged so it can be folded up. Two-paneled ones are called diptychs (see above), three-paneled ones triptychs (see below). Any more panels use the general term.

Porphyry Any igneous rock with visible shards of crystals suspended in a matrix of fine particles.

Predella Small panel or series of panels below the main part of an altarpiece, often used to tell a story of Christ's Passion or a saint's life comic-strip style.

Putti Cherubs (sing. *putto*); chubby naked toddler boys sculpted or painted, often with wings.

Sacra conversazione Type of painting in which saints are arranged with the Madonna in a unified space, rather than relegated to wings, as in a polyptych (see above).

Sarcophagus   A stone coffin or casket.

Schiacciato   Literally, "flattened." A sculpture form pioneered by Donatello; figures are carved in extremely low relief so that from straight on they give the illusion of three-dimensionality and great depth, but from the side are oddly squashed.

Sfumato   A painting technique, popularized by Leonardo da Vinci, as important as perspective in achieving the illusion of great depth. The artist cloaks objects (landscape features like hills, or facial features) in a filmy haziness;

the farther away the object, the blurrier it appears, and the more realistic the distance seems.

Sinpoia   Underpainting or sketch made in red-brown pigment, the first drawing made on a wall to be frescoed.

Stoup   A holy-water basin.

Tempera   Type of paint in which pigments are bound with egg yolk; used for almost all paintings before oil took over around 1500.

Tondo   A round painting or sculpture.

Trecento   The 14th century (in Italian, literally "300s"), often used to describe that era of art dominated by the styles of Giotto and the International Gothic.

Triptych   A painting with three sections or panels.

Useful Terms & Phrases

Tuscan, being the local lingo of Dante, is considered the purest form of Italian. (In Siena they will tell you that, actually, it's Sienese dialect that's perfect.) That means travel in Tuscany will help you learn the most word-perfect Italian there is. Here are some key phrases to get you started.

Molto Italiano: A Basic Italian Vocabulary

ENGLISH	ITALIAN	PRONUNCIATION
Thank you	Grazie	graht-tzee-yey
Please	Per favore	PEHR fah-VOHR-eh
Yes	Si	see
No	No	noh
Good morning or Good day	Buongiorno	bwohn-DJOR-noh
Good evening	Buona sera	BWOHN-ah SAY-rah
Good night	Buona notte	BWOHN-ah NOHT-tay
How are you?	Come sta?	KOH-may STAH?
Very well	Molto bene	MOHL-toh BEHN-ney
Goodbye	Arrivederci	ahr-ree-vah-DEHR-chee
Excuse me (to get attention)	Scusi	SKOO-zee
Excuse me (to get past someone on the bus)	Permesso	pehr-MEHS-soh

The Savvy Traveler

ENGLISH	ITALIAN	PRONUNCIATION
Where is . . . ?	Dovè . . . ?	doh-VEH?
the station	la stazione	lah stat-tzee-OH-neh
a hotel	un albergo	oon ahl-BEHR-goh
a restaurant	un ristorante	oon reest-ohr-AHNT-e
the bathroom	il bagno	eel BAHN-nyoh
To the right	A destra	ah DEHY-stra
To the left	A sinistra	ah see-NEES-tra
Straight ahead	Avanti (or sempre diritto)	ahv-vahn-tee (SEHM-pray dee-REET-toh)
I would like	Vorrei	voh-RAY
Some (of)	Un po (di)	oon poh dee
This/that	Questo/quello	QWAY-sto/QWELL-oh
A glass of	Un bicchiere di	oon bee-key-AIR-ay-dee
(mineral) water	acqua (minerale)	AH-kwah (min-air-AHL-lay)
carbonated	gassata (or con gas)	gahs-SAH-tah (kohn gahs)
uncarbonated	senza gas	SEN-zah gahs
red wine	vino rosso	VEE-no ROH-soh
white wine	vino bianco	VEE-no bee-AHN-koh
How much is it?	Quanto costa?	KWAN-toh COH-sta?
It's too much.	È troppo.	ay TRO-poh
The check, please.	Il conto, per favore.	eel kon-toh PEHR fah-VOHR-eh
Can I see . . . ?	Posso vedere . . . ?	POH-soh veh-DARE-eh?
the church	la chiesa	la key-AY-zah
the fresco	l'affresco	lahf-FRES-coh
When?	Quando?	KWAN-doh
Is it open?	È aperto?	ay ah-PAIR-toe
Is it closed?	È chiuso?	ay key-YOU-zoh
Yesterday	Ieri	ee-YEHR-ree
Today	Oggi	OH-jee
Tomorrow	Domani	doh-MAH-nee
Breakfast	Prima colazione	PREE-mah coh-laht-tzee-OHN-ay
Lunch	Pranzo	PRAHN-zoh
Dinner	Cena	CHAY-nah
What time is it?	Che ore sono?	kay OR-ay SOH-noh
Monday	Lunedì	loo-nay-DEE
Tuesday	Martedì	mart-ay-DEE
Wednesday	Mercoledì	mehr-cohl-ay-DEE
Thursday	Giovedì	joh-vay-DEE
Friday	Venerdì	ven-nehr-DEE
Saturday	Sabato	SAH-bah-toh
Sunday	Domenica	doh-MEHN-nee-kah

Numbers

1	uno	(OO-noh)
2	due	(DOO-ay)
3	tre	(tray)
4	quattro	(KWAH-troh)
5	cinque	(CHEEN-kway)
6	sei	(say)
7	sette	(SET-tay)
8	otto	(OH-toh)
9	nove	(NOH-vay)
10	dieci	(dee-AY-chee)
11	undici	(OON-dee-chee)
20	venti	(VEHN-tee)
21	ventuno	(vehn-TOON-oh)
22	venti due	(VEHN-tee DOO-ay)
30	trenta	(TRAYN-tah)
40	quaranta	(kwah-RAHN-tah)
50	cinquanta	(cheen-KWAN-tah)
60	sessanta	(sehs-SAHN-tah)
70	settanta	(seht-TAHN-tah)
80	ottanta	(oht-TAHN-tah)
90	novanta	(noh-VAHNT-tah)
100	cento	(CHEN-toh)
1,000	mille	(MEE-lay)
10,000	dieci milla	(dee-AY-chee MEE-lah)

Italian Menu & Food Terms

Acciughe or Alici Anchovies.

Acquacotta "Cooked water," a watery vegetable soup thickened with egg and poured over stale bread.

Affettato misto Mix of various salami, prosciutto, and other cured meats; served as an appetizer.

Agnello Lamb.

Agnolotti Semicircular ravioli (often stuffed with meat and/or cheese).

Anatra Duck.

Anguilla Eel.

Antipasti Appetizers.

Aragosta Lobster.

Arista di maiale Roast pork loin, usually served in slices, flavored with rosemary, garlic, and cloves.

Baccalà (alla livornese) Dried salted codfish (cooked in olive oil, white wine, garlic, and tomatoes).

Bistecca alla fiorentina Florentine-style steak, made with Chianina beef, grilled over wood coals, and then brushed with olive oil and sprinkled with pepper and salt.

Bocconcini Small veal chunks sautéed in white wine, butter, and herbs. (Also the word for ball-shaped portions of any food, especially mozzarella.)

Braciola Loin pork chop.

Branzino Sea bass.

Bresaola   Air-dried, thinly sliced beef filet, dressed with olive oil, lemon, and pepper—usually an appetizer.

Bruschetta   A slab of bread grilled and then rubbed with garlic, drizzled with olive oil, and sprinkled with salt; often served *al pomodoro* (with tomatoes).

Bucatini   Fat, hollow spaghetti. Classically served *all'amatriciana* (with a spicy hot tomato sauce studded with pancetta [bacon]).

Cacciucco   Seafood soup-stew of Livrono in a spicy tomato base poured over stale bread.

Cacio or Caciotto   Southern Tuscan name for pecorino cheese.

Cannellini   White beans, the Tuscan's primary vegetable.

Cannelloni   Pasta tubes filled with meat and baked in a sauce (cream or tomato). The cheese version is usually called manicotti (though either name may be used for either stuffing).

Cantuccio   Twice-baked hard almond cookies, vaguely crescent-shaped and best made in Prato (where they're known as *biscotti di Prato*).

Capocollo   Aged sausage made mainly from pork necks.

Caprese   A salad of sliced mozzarella and tomatoes lightly dressed with olive oil, salt, and pepper.

Capretto   Kid goat.

Caprino   Soft goat's-milk cheese.

Carciofi   Artichokes.

Carpaccio   Thin slices of raw cured beef, pounded flat and often served topped with arugola (rocket) and parmesan cheese shavings.

Casalinga   Home cooking.

Cavolo   Cabbage.

Ceci   Chickpeas (garbanzo beans).

Cervelli   Brains, often served *fritti* (fried).

Cervo   Venison.

Cibrèo   Stew of chicken livers, cockscombs, and eggs.

Cinghiale   Wild boar.

Cipolla   Onion.

Coniglio   Rabbit.

Cozze   Mussels.

Crespelle alla fiorentina   Thin pancakes wrapped around ricotta and spinach, covered with tomatoes and cheese, and baked in a casserole.

Crostini   Small rounds of bread toasted and covered with various pâtés, most commonly a tasty liver paste.

Dentice   Dentex; a fish similar to perch.

Fagioli   Beans, almost always white cannellini beans.

Faraona   Guinea hen.

Farro   Emmer or spelt, a barley-like grain (often in soups).

Fave   Broad (fava) beans.

Fegato   Liver.

Focaccia   Like pizza dough with nothing on it, this bready snack is laden with olive oil, baked in sheets, sprinkled with coarse salt, and eaten in slices plain or split to stuff as a sandwich. In Florence, it's also popularly called *schiacciato*.

Formaggio   Cheese.

Frittata   Thick omelet stuffed with meats, cheese, and vegetables; often eaten between slices of bread as a sandwich.

Fritto misto   A deep-fried mix of meats, often paired with fried artichokes, or seafood.

Frutti di mare   A selection of shellfish, often boosted with a couple of shrimp and some squid.

Funghi   Mushrooms.

Fusilli   Spiral-shaped pasta; usually long like a telephone cord, not the short macaroni style.

Gamberi (gamberetti)   Prawns (shrimp).

Gelato   Dense version of ice cream (*produzione propria* means homemade).

Gnocchi   Pasta dumplings usually made from potato.

Granchio   Crab.

Granita   Flavored ice; *limone* (lemon) is the classic.

Involtini   Thinly sliced beef or veal rolled with veggies (often celery or artichokes) and simmered in its own juices.

Lampreda   Lamprey (an eel-like fish).

Lenticchie   Lentil beans; Italy's best come from Castellúccio, in Umbria.

Lepre   Wild hare.

Lombatina di vitello   Loin of veal.

Maiale   Pork.

Manzo   Beef.

Mascarpone   Technically a cheese but more like heavy cream, already slightly sweet and sweetened more to use in desserts like tiramisù.

Melanzana   Eggplant (aubergine).

Merluzzo   Cod.

Minestrone   A little-bit-of-everything vegetable soup, usually flavored with chunks of cured ham.

Mortadella   A very thick mild pork sausage; the original bologna (because the best comes from Bologna).

Mozzarella   A nonfermented cheese, made from the fresh milk of a buffalo (but increasingly these days from a cow), boiled and then kneaded into a rounded ball; served as fresh as possible.

Oca   Goose.

Orata   Sea bream.

Orecchiette   Small, thick pasta disks (literally, "little ears").

Osso buco   Beef or veal knuckle braised in wine, butter, garlic, lemon, and rosemary; the marrow is a delicacy.

Ostriche   Oysters.

Paglio e fieno   Literally, "hay and straw," yellow (egg) and green (spinach) tagliatelle mixed and served with sauce.

Pancetta   Salt-cured pork belly, rolled into a cylinder and sliced—the Italian bacon.

Panforte   Any of a number of huge barlike candies vaguely akin to fruitcake; a dense, flat honey-sweetened mass of nuts, candied fruits, and spices.

Panino   A sandwich.

Panna   Cream (either whipped and sweetened for ice cream or pie; or heavy and unsweetened when included in pasta sauce).

Panzanella   A cold summery salad made of stale bread soaked in water and vinegar mixed with cubed tomatoes, onion, fresh basil, and olive oil.

Pappa al Pomodoro   A bready tomato-pap soup.

Pappardelle alle lepre   Wide, rough pasta in hare sauce.

Parmigiano   Parmesan, a hard salty cheese usually grated over pastas and soups but also eaten alone as *grana*.

Pecorino   A rich sheep's-milk cheese; in Tuscany it's eaten fresh and soft, or *stagionato* (aged, sometimes with truffle or chilli).

Penne strascicate   Hollow pasta quills in a creamy ragù (meat-and-tomato sauce).

Peperonata   Stewed peppers and onions under oil; usually served cold.

Peperoncini   Hot chilli peppers.

Peperoni   Green, yellow, or red sweet peppers.

Peposo   Beef stew with peppercorns.

Pesce al cartoccio   Fish baked in a parchment envelope.

Pesce spada   Swordfish.

Piccione   Pigeon.

Pici or Pinci   A homemade pasta made with just flour, water, and olive oil, rolled in the hands to produce lumpy, thick, chewy spaghetti to which sauce clings. This local name is used around Siena and to its south.

Piselli   Peas.

Pizza   Comes in two varieties: *rustica* or *al taglio* (by the slice) and *al forno* in a pizzeria (large, round pizzas for dinner with a thin, crispy crust). Specific varieties include *margherita* (plain pizza of tomatoes, mozzarella, and basil), *napoletana* (tomatoes, oregano, mozzarella, and anchovies), *capricciosa* (a naughty combination of prosciutto, artichokes, olives, and sometimes egg or anchovies), and *quattro stagioni* (four seasons of fresh vegetables, sometimes also with ham).

Polenta   Cornmeal mush, ranging from soupy to a dense cakelike version related to cornbread; often mixed with mushrooms and other seasonal fillings, served plain alongside game or sometimes sliced and fried.

Pollo   Chicken; *alla cacciatore* is huntsman style, with tomatoes and mushrooms cooked in wine; *alla diavola* is spicy hot grilled chicken; *al mattone* is cooked under a hot brick.

Polpette   Small veal meatballs.

Polpo   Octopus.

Pomodoro   Tomato (plural *pomodori*).

Porcini   Large, wild bolete mushrooms, what the French call *cèpes*.

Porri   Leeks.

Ribollita   A thick, almost stewlike vegetable soup made with black cabbage, olive oil, celery, carrots, and whatever else *Mamma* has left over, all poured over thick slabs of peasant bread.

Ricotta   A soft, fluffy, bland cheese made from the watery whey (not curds, as most cheese) and often used to stuff pastas. *Ricotta salata* is a salted, hardened version for nibbling.

Risotto   Rice, often arborio, served sticky.

Rombo   Turbot fish.

Salsa verde   Green sauce, made from capers, anchovies, lemon juice and/or vinegar, and parsley.

Salsicce   Sausage.

Saltimbocca   Veal scallop topped with a sage leaf and a slice of prosciutto and simmered in white wine.

Salvia   Sage.

Sarde   Sardines.

Scaloppine   Thin slices of meat, usually veal.

Scamorza   An air-dried (sometimes smoked) cheese similar to mozzarella; often sliced and grilled or melted over ham in a casserole, giving it a thin crust and gooey interior.

Schiacciata   See "Focaccia."

Scottiglia   Stew of veal, chicken, various game, and tomatoes cooked in white wine.

Semifreddo   A cousin to *gelato* (ice cream), it's a way of taking nonfrozen desserts (tiramisù, zuppa inglese) and freezing and moussing them.

Seppia   Cuttlefish (halfway between a squid and small octopus); its ink is used for flavoring and coloring in some pasta and risotto dishes.

Sogliola   Sole.

Spezzatino   Beef or veal stew, often with tomatoes.

Spiedino   A shish kebab (skewered bits of meat, onions, and slices of tomato or peppers grilled).

Spigola   A fish similar to sea bass or grouper.

Stracciatella   Egg-drop soup topped with grated cheese; also a flavor of ice cream (vanilla with chocolate ripple).

Stracotto   Overcooked beef, wrapped in bacon and braised with onion and tomato for hours until it's so tender it dissolves in your mouth.

Strozzapreti   Ricotta-and-spinach dumplings, usually served in tomato sauce; literally "priest chokers." Also called *strangolaprete*.

Stufato   Pot roast, usually in wine, broth, and veggies.

Tagliatelle   Flat pasta.

Tartufo   (1) Truffles; (2) An ice cream ball made with a core of fudge, a layer of vanilla, a coating of chocolate, and a dusting of cocoa; order it *affogato* (drowning), and they'll pour brandy over it.

Tonno   Tuna.

Torta   A pie. *Alla nonna* is Grandma's style and usually is a creamy lemony pie; *alle mele* is an apple tart; *al limone* is lemon; *alle fragole* is strawberry; *ai frutti di bosco* is with berries.

Torta al testo   A flat, unleavened bread baked on the hearthstone and often split to be filled with sausage, spinach, or other goodies.

Tortellini   Rings or half-moons of pasta stuffed with ricotta and spinach or chopped meat (chicken and veal). Sometimes also called *tortelli* and *tortelloni*.

Trippa   Tripe (cow's stomach lining). Served *alla fiorentina* means casseroled with tomatoes and onions, topped with grated parmesan cheese.

Trota   Trout.

Vermicelli   Very thin spaghetti.

Vitello   Veal. A *vitellone* is an older calf about to enter cowhood. *Vitello tonnato* is thinly sliced veal served cold and spread with tuna mayonnaise.

Vongole   Clams.

Zabaglione/zabaione   A custard made of whipped egg yolks, sugar, and Marsala wine.

Zampone   Pig's feet, usually stewed for hours.

Zuccotto   A tall liqueur-soaked sponge cake, stuffed with whipped cream, ice cream, chocolate, and candied fruits.

Recommended **Books**

GENERAL & HISTORY   *Florence, Biography of a City* (1993) is popular historian Christopher Hibbert's overview on the city of the Renaissance, written in accessible prose. Hibbert is also author of *The House of Medici: Its Rise and Fall,* a group biography of Florence's most famous rulers.

Frances Stonor Saunders' *Hawkwood: Diabolical Englishman* is more than just the story of the English mercenary's brutal Tuscan campaigns; it's also the most comprehensive account of medieval life and power politics in pre-Renaissance Tuscany.

The Stones of Florence contains Mary McCarthy's often

scathing, but usually fond, views on contemporary Florence (written in the early 1950s). It's also an indispensable art- and architecture-historical companion.

The only favorable sequel to McCarthy's classic is **The City of Florence** by Yale professor R. W. B. Lewis.

Recently, a few literary histories set in Florence have enjoyed wild success. Ross King's slim tome **Brunelleschi's Dome** tells the fascinating story behind the building of Florence's Duomo. Dava Sobel's **Galileo's Daughter** uses the scant documents available to re-create the relationship between the great Pisan scientist and one of his illegitimate daughters, and his fight against the blasphemy charges, which nearly got him killed.

More recent history is covered by Iris Origo in *War in Val d'Orcia,* her personal diary of life on a Tuscan farm (and the front line) in 1943 and 1944.

ART & ARCHITECTURE The first work of art history ever written was penned in 1550 (with a later, expanded edition published in 1568) by a Tuscan artist. Giorgio Vasari's **Lives of the Artists, Vols. I and II** is a collection of biographies of the great artists from Cimabue to Vasari's 16th-century contemporaries.

For a more modern art-history take, the indispensable but expensive tome/doorstop is Frederick Hartt's **History of Italian Renaissance Art.** An easier, more colorful introduction, complete with illustrations, is Michael Levey's **Early Renaissance** and his **High Renaissance.**

Michelangelo, a Biography by George Bull is a scholarly, well-written take on the artist's life. For a livelier look, try Irving Stone's **The Agony and the Ecstasy.** Written as a work of historical fiction, it takes some liberties with the established record, but it's a good read.

LITERATURE & FICTION No survey of Tuscan literature can start anywhere but with Dante Alghieri, the 14th-century poet whose **Divine Comedy,** also published separately as **Inferno, Purgatorio,** and **Paradiso,** was Italy's first great epic poem since antiquity and the first major work to be written in the local vernacular (in this case, Florentine) instead of Latin. Allen Mandelbaum's edition of **Inferno** has the Italian and English side by side.

The next generation of Tuscan writers produced Giovanni Boccaccio, whose **Decameron,** a story of 100 tales told by young nobles fleeing the Black Death, is Italy's *Canterbury Tales.*

Tuscany also came up with the third great medieval Italian writer, Francesco Petrarca (Petrarch), whose **Selections from the Canzoniere and Other Works** (2008), in a brand new translation, gives you a taste for lyrical poetry.

Even more real-world practical was Niccolò Machiavelli, whose handbook for the successful Renaissance leader, **The Prince** (2008), won him fame and infamy simultaneously.

If you don't have time for all of the above, pick up **The Italian Renaissance Reader,** edited by Julia Conaway Bondanella and Mark Musa, with selections from Boccaccio's *Decameron,* Petrarch's *Canzoniere,* Leonardo da Vinci's notebooks, Benvenuto Cellini's *Autobiography,* Machiavelli's *The Prince,* Michelangelo's sonnets, and others.

E. M. Forster's **A Room with a View,** half of which takes place in Florence, and **Where Angels Fear to Tread,** set in San Gimignano, are perfect tales of uptight middle-class British Edwardian society and how it clashes with the brutal honesty and seductive magic of Italy.

For kids, the Tuscan classic is *Pinocchio,* by Carlo Collodi.

Index

See also Accommodations and Restaurant indexes, below.